Up on a Hill and Thereabouts

Up on a Hill and Thereabouts

An Adirondack Childhood

GLORIA STUBING RIST

excelsior editions

State University of New York Press
Albany, New York

Cover photo from collection of the author

Published by State University of New York Press, Albany

Excelsior Editions is an imprint of State University of New York Press

For information, contact State University of New York Press, Albany, NY
www.sunypress.edu

Production by Diane Ganeles
Marketing by Anne M. Valentine

Library of Congress Cataloging-in-Publication Data

Stubing Rist, Gloria.
   Up on a hill and thereabouts : an Adirondack childhood / Gloria Stubing Rist.
        pages cm
   Summary: "Childhood recollections of life in the Adirondack Mountains during the Great Depression"—Provided by publisher.
   ISBN 978-1-4384-4890-9 (pbk. : alk. paper)
   1. Rist, Gloria Stubing—Childhood and youth. 2. Depressions—1929—New York (State)—Chilson. 3. Depressions—1929—New York (State)—Adirondack Mountains Region. 4. Country life—New York (State)—Chilson. 5. Country life—New York (State)—Adirondack Mountains Region. 6. Chilson (N.Y.)— Social life and customs. 7. Adirondack Mountains Region (N.Y.)—Social life and customs. 8. Chilson (N.Y.)—Biography. 9. Adirondack Mountains Region (N.Y.)—Biography. I. Title.

   F129.C5245R57 2013
   974.7'5042092—dc23   2013000132

10 9 8 7 6 5 4 3 2 1

To my kids, Roxy, Vern and Ernie;
my grandkids, Mike, Brandon and Byron;
my great-grandkids, Austin, Bella and Willow;
and my cousin Nancy Marnell.

~

The author and her family wish to thank Rob Brill
for initially bringing *Up on a Hill and Thereabouts*
to SUNY Press's attention, and for his
enthusiastic and professional support in the
subsequent preparation of the manuscript.

Contents

Preface

In the early days of the 1930s, life for kids tucked away in the quiet woodlands of the Adirondack Mountains in a little hamlet known as Chilson was rich with nature and filled with human characters.

The following stories are recollections of one woman who, beginning more than eighty years ago, spent her childhood on the hillsides and in the woods of the eastern edge of the Adirondacks.

This is a child's-eye view of days long gone, of a place and of people who are forever in her heart, so that the memories are fresh.

Nicknames

Mim — My mother (Mary)
Bubby — My brother (Harland)
Yada — Me (Gloria)
Cowboy — Harold Hayford
Bob — My stepfather (Robert Ford)

Some of the other names in this book are not the actual names of the people. These names are fictitious.

—GSR

Heading for the Mountains

My first memories are of living with my great-grandfather and great-grandmother Stone in their home in the Bronx. I have some memories of what happened there, but that's another bunch of stories to tell. The stories I am going to write are about Chilson, as that's where I lived from ages five to sixteen. My childhood was very different from yours. It was a different way of life, long gone. I just thought you might like to know about how it was then, back in the Great Depression of the 1930s.

It's enough to say that Mim, my mother, couldn't stand living with my father any longer, and one morning, Mim told me she was going to Chilson to live and was taking Bubby, my brother, with her. She said I was going to stay with my grandmother and my father until she came back for me in six weeks. She said she couldn't take both of us, so she was taking Bub as he was the youngest. I was five years old. She also said that she wanted me to stay and finish my school year—first grade.

The next day, when I came home from school, Mim and Bub were gone. She hadn't said goodbye. I knew it was because she didn't want me to cry. The next six weeks were the most lonesome, awful time of my life. No one gave me the letters Mim sent. I thought she had forgotten me. I knew my grandmother and my father didn't want me, but they were not going to let Mim have me, just for spite. I knew because I heard them talking about it one night when they thought I was upstairs. I heard my father say, "I told Mary on the phone today that she cannot have Gloria." Was I ever a scared, lonely, unhappy little girl.

A couple of days later, in the afternoon, Mim walked in. She and Uncle Tobe had come after me. What a wonderful feeling of joy! Mim was back, and I was safe again.

She said, "Come on," and we went up to the third floor to the spooky room where I slept. We threw what few things I had into an old suitcase.

My grandmother followed. She threw one of the tantrums she always threw when she wasn't getting her own way. She raved and screamed and told Mim she couldn't take me. Mim said I was going, and we went down the stairs.

Just as we started out the front door, my father walked in. He blocked the doorway and said, "Forget it, you're not taking Gloria anywhere."

Mim put down the suitcase and pulled a gun out of her pocket. She said, "Yada, take your suitcase and go get in the car." Then she said, "Ernest, I mean business." She pointed the gun right at him. My father turned white and stepped away from the door.

I ran out to where Uncle Tobe was, blissfully ignorant, waiting in the car. He put my suitcase, and me, in the backseat. I didn't tell him what was going on inside the house. I don't know what he would have done if he knew.

Finally, Mim came out of the house with her hand in her pocket. The gun was out of sight, but she had it in her hand in case my father followed her. Nothing moved from the house. Mim got in the car and we took off. I don't think Mim ever told Uncle Tobe what she had done.

It's a long way from Crestwood to Chilson. As we rolled along, it got dark, and I lay down on the backseat. I slept some, but woke up often. My head hurt and I felt sicker and sicker.

When early morning came, we were still going. I watched the sun come up over the beautiful mountains.

Mim started singing, *"When it's springtime in the mountains, I'll be coming back to you. Little sweetheart of the mountains, with your bonnie eyes so blue."* Mim could never sing. She couldn't carry a note, but it was the most beautiful singing I ever heard.

It was one of the happiest moments of my life, rolling along in that car—going to Chilson and farther and farther away from Crestwood. The only thing was, I kept feeling sicker and sicker.

So I lay back down on the seat, and the next thing I knew, Mim said, "Here we are," and there we were at Aunt Dean's house in Stoney Lonesome, almost to Chilson.

We walked in and Bubby was there, along with a bunch of cousins I met for the first time. It was great. I kept sneezing a lot, so Mim looked me over good. She said, "My God, she's got the measles."

They rushed me upstairs, but it was too late. I had peppered Bub and my cousins good. Of course, they wouldn't break out with the measles for ten days or so.

In the meantime, sick as I felt, I knew I was in the mountains where I belonged. Nothing else mattered.

Moving on from Stoney Lonesome

The first thing of importance, as I understood it, was to find a place to live. Aunt Dean's little house was just not big enough for two families. Mim had been born and raised in Chilson, so that was the natural spot to look for a place for us to live. We couldn't afford even an old house, but if we could just get some land . . .

Mim, finally, talked Aunt Frances into selling her a plot of land that she owned in Chilson. It was two acres and it cost $39. I don't know where Mim got the money, but she did, and we owned land at last.

Over to Chilson we went to check it out. The land was right at the top of Chilson Hill. Down in the valley, we could see a long sliver of Lake Champlain shining in the sun. The lot had a low hill on one side of it, but the rest of it was a big flat field with a brook running on the back side. But best of all, our land was all covered with beautiful wildflowers, and some of the biggest maple trees I'd ever seen. I knew we were home.

Someone gave Mim an old leaky tent. We pitched that below the side hill, and we had a place to sleep. We had only a few old blankets, but it was the first of June, and the ground wasn't too cold for sleeping.

Somewhere we found an old kerosene cook stove. This was set up on the other side of the lot in case it blew up. Only one burner worked and that was a sickly green when lit (it should have been a clear blue). That stove was definitely trying to tell us something. But we made oatmeal on it, and Mim could brew her black tea, so we were in great shape.

However, summer wasn't going to last forever. Mim thought if she could put up a roadside stand by fall, she'd have made enough to build "something for us to live in"—her words. I didn't bother my head about it as I could go barefoot, make mud pies, and Mim was there. Bub and I never worried about anything when Mim was there.

Our home was on a dirt road, but it was the main road between Ticonderoga and Schroon Lake. The state road was going to be built right through there, and that should bring some business—after all, the men who would be working on the road had to buy cigarettes and coffee somewhere.

The Wrights, our neighbors on the farm next to us, had an old shed that was falling down way over back in their field. Years before, it had been used to store corn for their animals to eat in the winter. Mim asked if she could buy the old shed. They said they wouldn't sell it, but she could have it if she finished tearing it down and carrying it away. It did have a lot of good boards on it. So early one morning, Mim took her hammer and started tearing it down. As each board came down, Bub and I would carry it up through the field and over to our "lot." Mim helped with the carrying too, after she got the shed all torn down. It took us three weeks working steady to do it, but we were pretty proud when all the boards were in a big pile on our land.

Mim started building. She put up a building about fifteen by sixteen feet. It wasn't quite square, and you could see through the cracks between the boards of the walls. She didn't have anything for a roof, so we had to continue to stay in the tent because of rain.

Mim took one big board and got some black paint from Grandpa Granger. Mim wrote "Top of the Hill" on the board and nailed it up on the top board of our building, next to where the roof was supposed to be, but wasn't. In front of the door opening, which had no door, she set an old card table donated by Uncle Tobe. Mim put a carton of Wings cigarettes that she got from Lord knows where on the card table with a couple of mugs and spoons. She had a pot of coffee brewing on the sickly green flame of the kerosene stove. That was it. We were in business! We were waiting for the men to go through working on the road.

Yada(me), Mim and Bubby on our "plot of land."

But nobody came. That week the state had canceled the road-work for a while.

Mim didn't say anything to us kids, but young as I was, I realized we were in big trouble. There we were, a woman and two little kids, no money, no food, nobody to help, and winter was coming. Mim never once considered going to Ti to sign up for "Relief." What a horrible thing that would have been—pride would not allow it. The New Deal was never going to get us!

So that Monday morning, Mim put the coffee on and went down to the brook to get some more water. She told me to watch "the store." I couldn't believe it, but a car drove up and stopped. A man got out and looked around. He said he'd take a pack of gum, but I didn't have any gum. He said, okay then, he'd take a cup of coffee. I panicked. Mim had told me never to go near our stove that could blow up at any minute. What should I do? But just then, Mim walked in and I told her the man wanted a cup of cof-fee. Mim smiled and hurried around getting the coffee. She looked so pretty. The man said to get a cup of coffee for herself, too. They

6

sat down and started talking. He said his name was Cowboy. I stayed out back of the building, but I could hear them. Cowboy said he'd be back the next morning to help finish our building.

And believe it or not, the next morning he was there. He brought tar paper for our roof and an old window. After he got the roof on, he sawed through one of the walls of the building and set in the window. He didn't have any door, but he said he'd get us one. We hung the tent over the door opening for the time being. Then we all went over to Aunt Dean's for supper. Uncle Summer had caught a lot of bullheads, and no one had any way to keep them in the summer heat—none of us had any electricity, let alone refrigeration. So Aunt Dean had invited us over to help eat up the bullheads. Aunt Dean liked Cowboy right away, and I could see that Cowboy and Mim liked each other a lot.

That's how Cowboy came into our lives, staying for about five years. I don't know why Mim didn't marry him, maybe because she wasn't divorced from my father, and we had no money, and everything just drifted along. But he was awfully good to us kids, the nearest to a real father I ever had.

Anyway, early in the winter, Cowboy went down to Putnam to work, building a store. He was lucky to get it as work was scarcer than hen's teeth. He came home weekends. Once he brought a small wood-burning cook stove to heat our building, which had become our home. He put tar paper on the insides of the walls to keep the cold out. He built a wood floor, which was much better than our dirt floor. He brought food and wood for the stove. We couldn't use the stove because we didn't have a stovepipe, but, finally, Grandpa Granger let us borrow the stovepipe from his maple sugar shed until spring, so we had some heat and warm food. Mim and I lugged water from the brook and heated it on the stove. She washed Cowboy's clothes and ours on a scrub board. We hung the clothes near the ceiling to dry. It made it damp in the house, but the clothes would freeze solid outdoors.

Cowboy did all he could for us. Mim started making "homebrew" and sold it, which helped. Bub and I went to school on the bus. Bub and I were both in first grade; Mim thought it best because I hadn't finished the first grade in Crestwood before she came and got me. We were warm at school from 9 a.m. to 3:30 p.m. We tried to go to the toilet there, too, as we had none at home. We didn't get enough boards to build an outdoor privy until the next summer. Meanwhile, it was pretty chilly squatting out back in the snow with the north wind whistling up in under you.

One night Cowboy was away working, and we had an unexpected, awful, storm. The snow sifted in around the tar paper, and the wind was very drafty across the room. About midnight, we woke to hear *Whoosh—break*—one side of the house pulled loose and slowly keeled right over on the ground. Mim pulled on her boots and rushed out and tried to lift up the wall, which had remained in one piece. Bubby and I helped too. We took some rope and tied it in place. We propped all the boards we could find against the outside of the wall to help hold it up.

Mim was worried. She said the snow was going to drift in and cover us. I said, "Don't worry, Mim. The wind is blowing from the other direction. The snow won't get through. Not much, anyway." She started laughing. She hugged me and said, "Chip off the old block."

We grabbed blankets and all the coats and lay down together in the middle of the floor as far from the walls as possible. Maybe another wall would fall, and maybe this time on top of us. But as the storm raged on, the walls held.

It was bitter cold, and we lay there shivering, wishing for morning to come. At least tomorrow would be another day toward spring, and Cowboy was due home, too.

In the meantime, we curled up closer together and waited for daylight, one frozen hour after another.

Nellie and My Birthday Cake

Mim, Bub and I went to Marion's birthday party. She was one of my schoolmates. I was fascinated with the birthday cake, but mostly with the balloons. We each got one. I couldn't get over the colors. I got a yellow one. I wanted a red one (my favorite color), but I couldn't ask for it. That would be impolite. You took what you got. The party was fun and when we went home, I was walking down the road, proudly floating my yellow balloon over my head on its string, when it popped. It fell to the ground, just a little piece of flat yellow rubber.

I was devastated and started bawling and blatting. You could hear me a half-mile away. People walking away from the party in the other direction stopped, turned around and looked back. Mim was embarrassed. She said, "For God's sake, Yada, stop that!" I squalled on. In exasperation, Mim said, "Look, you can have a party on your birthday, and we'll have balloons." I choked out, "Can I have a red one?" Mim said, "Yes, just shut up!" I wiped my nose and eyes on my dress and had to be satisfied with what Mim said.

That Christmas, Mim, Bub and I went down to Crestwood in Uncle Tobe's old car that we borrowed to visit my grandparents Stubing and Dad. The visit was a disaster. I don't know why we went, but Dad had sent the money for gas to come down. I guess, as we didn't have any money for Christmas at home, Mim thought it would be better than nothing. I'd rather have the memory of nothing.

Anyway, Mim was mad at Grandma Stubing because she made Bub and me eat our Christmas dinner in the kitchen.

Grandma had put up the ironing board across the doorway so that we couldn't get from the kitchen into the dining room, but our cousin Ronald Smith, our same age, ate in style with the grownups. Mim jumped over the ironing board and ate with Bub and me. I couldn't believe Mim could jump that high, but she was mad. As soon as we ate, Mim shooed us out the back door and into our car. We'd only gotten there that morning, and our suitcase was still on the backseat. We never even said goodbye, just tore out of there. Mim said, "We'll never go there again. To heck with 'em." I was sure glad to hear her say that.

We were happily rolling along toward Chilson. It was snowing and a little slippery, but we were singing and moving along okay. We got up near Red Hook when Mim suddenly said, "Hang on, kids," and started blowing the horn like crazy. Bub and I were in the backseat. I glanced out the front windshield and saw a car coming right at us, fast, on our side of the road. There was a big crash, then silence, with the smell of antifreeze in the air. We sat there for what seemed like ages. Then people came around. I got Bub out of the backseat. His knee was cut, and I wrapped my scarf around it. We stood by the front door of the car, by Mim. She was dazed and kept saying, "Please help me out." Bub and I couldn't free her. Finally, an ambulance came, and they got her out. We were taken to Red Hook Hospital. I heard our driver say, "The four people in the other car weren't hurt, but they were stone drunk, wouldn't you know it?"

The doctor at the hospital looked over Bub and me. He checked our cuts and bruises and said we'd be okay. He said Mim might have internal injuries, that she mustn't walk, and she was to stay in a wheelchair.

Bub and I pushed Mim out in the hall, and she called Cowboy at his mother's home in Hague. That's where he went for Christmas while we were gone. We were lucky Cowboy answered. If it had been his mother, she might not have told him we were calling. She didn't think Cowboy should "go steady" with a woman who had two kids.

Cowboy said, "Stay where you are. I'll be right there," and he was there in three hours or so, record time.

They wanted Mim to stay in the hospital, but she signed herself out. Cowboy only had $20 to pay the hospital bill, and we had to get out of there before the bill rose. Cowboy carried Mim to the car, and we headed back to Chilson.

We got Mim to Dr. Cummings, and he took an X-ray. He said Mim had to have a kidney removed. It was crushed and bleeding. That's why she was in pain.

Mim was stubborn. She said she couldn't have the operation right then because she had no one to take care of us kids. The truth was, she didn't have any money. The doctor said to go home, stay very quiet, and it was just possible the kidney might heal by itself. He also said if the pain got any worse, or if she had a fever, to get herself down there, pronto. Mim didn't get any better through January, February or into March. Cowboy was working all kinds of odd jobs, and they were saving every cent possible for Mim's operation. Finally, in the later part of March, Mim could stand the pain no longer. She had to go into Ticonderoga Hospital.

So Bubby was shipped off to stay with Gram and Grandpa Granger, and Uncle Amacy and Aunt Alice took me. Mim had her operation and was coming along okay. I was pretty lonesome, but Aunt Alice was good to me, and I was getting enough to eat.

Then spring was bursting out all over, and the brook opened. The water looked so beautiful, cold and inviting that I kneeled over and took a big drink out of it. Although it looked clean, the water had to be full of germs, as in a couple of days I got awfully sick. Aunt Alice took one look at me and slapped me into bed. I guess I was delirious a lot and vomiting and had diarrhea continuously. I don't remember. Aunt Alice took good care of me.

Came the morning when I woke up clearheaded, feeling better, only weak. Aunt Alice said Mim was home, and I'd be going back the next day. Sure enough, I was bundled up, and Uncle Amacy drove me to our "sleeping house." They had done all they could for me, and I'm sure they were glad to see me go. I don't blame them. I wasn't their responsibility.

Uncle Amacy carried me in and set me down inside the door. Mim was in bed. Uncle Amacy said, "Well, I'm glad you're all

Our sleeping house that Mim built.

feeling better," and he took off. Mim looked sad, and she said, "Come on, Yada," and I crawled into bed with her. It was cold in the house. We had no fire, and Mim didn't tell me, but no food. Cowboy didn't have any money left, so he had to go to work down Putnam way. He'd be back in about ten days. In the meantime, Mim had told him Aunt Dean was going to bring food and help out. That was a lie, but Mim didn't want Cowboy to worry. He had to go. Aunt Dean didn't have anything, either, so she couldn't have helped us if she wanted to.

Henry D. stopped in. He wanted to borrow a tire wrench from Cowboy. He didn't know Cowboy wasn't there. Henry told us Nellie, his wife, had slipped walking up Mud Hill. She fell down and hit her head. No one knew how long she lay there until Oley came along with his manure spreader. Oley lifted her into the back of his spreader and brought her home. Mim asked how she was, and Henry said she was fine. He said she told him her head ached and she felt dizzy, but he said there was nothing wrong with her, she just wanted attention. Then he said, "So long," and left.

As dusk set in, Mim and I settled down to wait. For what, I don't know. We knew we'd have no supper. We'd worry about breakfast the next day. Mim hugged me tight, and we talked about Bubby. We missed him but were glad he was at Grandma Granger's. At least he was safe and not hungry. Then we went to sleep.

The next morning was my birthday. I didn't say anything to Mim. I knew there'd be no party, no cake. Cake? Just give us a slice of bread.

Mim couldn't get up or walk very well, so I took a glass canning jar, opened the door, and scooped snow into the jar from the pile outside. I put the cover on the jar and put it down near our feet in the bed. The warmth would melt the snow and we'd have a little water to drink.

I knew I should go to the Osciers or Wrights to see if someone would drive me over to Grandma Granger's to get help. They would've done something maybe, but Mim said, "No, we'll wait a little while longer." Wait for what? But young as I was, I agreed with her. We would be ashamed to let anyone know how bad off we were. Our pride never went away, no matter what.

An hour or so later, I happened to look out the window and saw Nellie coming over the road. She was carrying a long iron pan used to boil down maple syrup. The pan was about two and a half feet by three feet. She had tied a feed bag towel over the top of it.

Mim and I watched her walking along. Sometimes she staggered or meandered around in the road. Once or twice she stopped to rest. What could she be doing, and where was she going? She came up to our door and walked in.

She looked so white and tired, but her face was beaming. "Happy birthday, dear Yada, happy birthday to you," she sang, and Mim joined in: "Happy birthday, dear Yada, happy birthday to you!" Nellie whipped the cover off the pan, and there was the most delicious, and biggest, birthday cake I had ever seen. It had boiled maple sugar frosting on it, my favorite, and "Yada" was written on it, traced out in butternut meats.

Nellie hadn't forgotten my birthday. She knew we had nothing, and she couldn't offer us food—our pride, you know. So she had made a cake big enough to feed us for a long time—and remember, she didn't have much in the way of extra food, either.

Mim was worried about her. Nellie told us her head ached, and sometimes she couldn't see for a few minutes at a time, and she was dizzy. Mim tried to get her to lie down with us and rest, or at least promise to go right home and go to bed. Nellie said, "No." She had to go home and get supper. Henry would be mad if it wasn't on time.

Nellie gave me a hug and started for the door. Suddenly she stopped, turned around, and said, "Yada, always be a good girl. If you don't, I'll know it and come back and fix your wagon." What did she mean? I looked at Mim and she shook her head, as if to say, "Don't say anything." Nellie waved and walked out the door.

We watched Nellie stagger some as she walked over the road. She stopped once or twice and held her head, but she made it to her house and went in the door.

We were worried about her, but we were so hungry we lit into that cake. We ate big pieces washed down with the water from our canning jar. It was the first time we weren't hungry for a couple of days. It kept us going and lasted until Cowboy came home with some money a week later.

A few days after that, Clayton Wright came in and told us that Nellie was getting supper, and when she bent down to check on the biscuits in the oven, she fell over and was dead before she hit the floor.

Nellie must have known she wasn't going to make it. Hadn't she told me to always be a good girl or she'd come back and fix my wagon?

Of course, Mim and I couldn't go to the funeral, so we had our own little service for Nellie. Mim recited the 21st Psalm, and I said the Lord's Prayer. Then we had a few minutes of silence. We each had our own loving thoughts about Nellie as we tucked her, forever, away in our hearts.

The Peeking Game

The first school Bub and I went to in Chilson was halfway down Chilson Hill on the back road. It was an old log cabin with long desks and benches to sit on. Mim took us down and left us there. There was a young man teacher—I can't even remember his name—and he never spoke to me all day. He held his classes, and I never moved from my desk for anything. This went on for three days.

Finally, I went home the last day and told Mim I wasn't going back there. I was terribly afraid, and I didn't know why. I'm sure the teacher was very nice. I was just so shy, and he probably realized what was going on with me, and he was waiting until I got over being scared.

I was crying so hard that Mim knew that school wasn't for us, so the next morning, she took us up to the two-room schoolhouse in "Upper Chilson." Mim had gone to school there herself.

The sun was shining as we went across the doorstep of the school, and I looked up at Mrs. Forth's smiling face. She was motherly-looking and kind-looking. I felt this warm, safe feeling wash over me, and I knew this was the place for me, my school.

Our side of the school (our room) went from grades one to four, the other side ("the big kids") went from grades five to eight. Mr. Forth, Mrs. Forth's husband, taught the big kids.

Bub and I were happy. Bubby was the cutest little thing, and everyone made a fuss over him. No one paid much attention to me, which suited me just fine. I could, in my own time, study everybody and everything, and get settled in.

Our old two-room schoolhouse and our new one-room schoolhouse.

Things went quietly along for a month or so. Then I noticed some of the older boys, when we were outdoors during the noon hour, would point at Marie, Betty, Ruth, me or one of the older girls from their side of the school. As the boys pointed, they would whisper to one another and laugh behind their hands.

Pearl, a girl from the "big side," was sort of protective of me. She looked out for me, probably because Mim and her mother had gone to school together, and her mother told her to be nice to me.

Anyway, one noon hour I asked her what the boys were laughing at. She made me promise not to tell, which I did, then she told me. She said the boys watched, through their window, any girl who went by going out back to the girls' privy. Immediately, one of the boys would raise his hand to go to the boys' privy (they took turns). The boy would then hurry out back, over behind his privy, come up behind the girls' privy, and peek up underneath. He had a ringside seat to the view up under the toilet seat holes. They called it "the peeking game." Pearl told me that when I went to the privy, to make sure to scooch down under their window when I went by, and they wouldn't see me, then no boy would come out to peek on me.

Pearl told me boys had been doing this for years, and she said it was about time we put an end to it. But what could we do?

We had our code of honor—no one ever snitched on another kid in school—but the only way we could get even was to tell Mrs. Forth what was going on.

Maggie was a tattletale. No one ever told her anything. But we buttered her up and told her when she got done going to the toilet, get up fast and look down through the toilet hole at once. We told her she'd see something strange and interesting.

Maggie couldn't wait. The first chance she got, she was off to the privy. Of course, the boys saw her. Maggie did as we told her, and what did she see but Pete's grinning face peeking up at her from the underside of the building.

Gloria (Yada) and Harland (Bubby) Stubing.

We heard this god-awful screaming all the way in from the toilet. Maggie rushed up to Mrs. Forth and told her about Pete. It took Mrs. Forth a few minutes to calm Maggie down and get the story straight.

Then Mrs. Forth went over with righteous indignation to see Mr. Forth. In a few minutes, we saw Mr. Forth going out back to the woodshed with about ten boys. He was carrying his rubber hose. We knew he would line the boys up and give them all hard smacks on the rears. Mrs. Forth and Maggie looked very smug. What they didn't know was what we kids knew about Mr. Forth. He always gave a couple of whacks on the seat, and then told the boys to holler loud and hard. Then he would hit the side of the shed with the rubber hose, and everyone would think the boys would be getting a hard beating. Of course, they never did.

We were glad about that, but at least the boys knew we were wise to them, and they'd lay off their peeking for a while.

The school "higher-ups" found out about the boys, and they were incensed. Mim laughed about that. She said when the men (the "higher-ups") were in school, they all played "the peeking game," but now it was a different story.

After a while, we got two new schools. One was for grades one to four, where the old school used to be; and the other, for grades five to eight, was in the middle of Chilson Hill. We then had inside toilets.

Of course, with indoor toilets, there is absolutely no way to peek up under them. We girls were sure happy about that, and the boys had to reluctantly let the peeking game become just a wishful memory.

Suppertime

It was one of those days. Bubby and I hadn't had any breakfast, and we didn't have any lunch. We didn't ask Mim for either meal because we knew there wasn't any food in the house. The night before, Mim had boiled three small potatoes. She gave Bubby 1 1/2 potatoes, and me 1 1/2. Mim didn't have any. She said she wasn't hungry.

This day we played around down back in the field, and Mim was banging up more boards to make a bigger dance floor on the end of "Top of the Hill."

Bub and I heard Ti Pulp Mill's horn blow, and we knew it was 5 p.m. When we got back to our sleeping house, Mim wasn't there. We went in "Top of the Hill," but she wasn't there, either. Her hammer was there where she had been working, but no Mim. Bub and I were awfully hungry.

Good smells were coming across the field from the Wrights. Their supper was in the oven. I took Bubby's hand, and we drifted that way. We got to the kitchen door and looked in. Mrs. Wright loved Bubby. He was an awfully cute little boy. She picked him up and carried him into the kitchen. I stayed at the kitchen door.

Mrs. Wright said to Bubby, "Do you want a sugar tit?" (A sugar tit is a piece of bread with a little sugar sprinkled on it.) Bubby nodded his head yes. She made him one, even put butter on it. Then she sat in her big rocking chair with him on her lap and rocked him while he ate his sugar tit. She got up, made him another, and then rocked him some more, singing to him. All the while, I stood in the doorway, drooling. I knew I wasn't going to be invited in. I was ashamed because I knew I should go, but I couldn't. Hunger makes you do strange things, and I stayed, standing in the doorway.

Suddenly, Bubby, little as he was, sat up on Mrs. Wright's lap and said, "Yada's hungry too." Up until then, Mrs. Wright had ignored me. She grabbed a piece of bread and thrust it at me. I said, "No thanks," and could have bitten my tongue off the minute I said it. It was my stubborn pride, something I've had all my life, many times to my regret.

I said, "Come on, Bubby," and he climbed off Mrs. Wright's lap, and we went over the road, home.

Mim in front of "Top of the Hill," which she built, with cheese cloth for windows.

We got a drink of water from the rain barrel by the door of our sleeping house and went in. Mim still was nowhere around. Bubby crawled up on the bed and went to sleep. I was happy, at least, that his little tummy had something in it.

I walked outdoors. I thought my empty stomach was going right through my backbone. I remembered that a few days ago, down back of the brook, I'd seen some thimbleberries growing. Maybe they'd be ripe now. They were. I gobbled them up. I went up the brook over in back of Covell's barn. The Covells had finished milking, and they'd placed their barn cat's dish of milk by the door. I don't know why Kit-Kat hadn't drunk the milk yet, probably he was hunting. That dish of milk was spanking clean. Everything about the Covells was spanking clean. I picked up the dish, and drank one half of the milk. I left the rest for Kit-Kat, which was only fair. Then I walked back down along the brook over to the Wrights' barn.

The Wrights had a small room attached to the barn where they kept their milk cold in water-filled open vats. They kept cream there, and cheese too. Small pieces of cheese, too small for anything else, they put to dry on the windowsill to use for grated cheese. There was some there, and two small pieces had dropped to the ground. Birds or mice used to brush pieces off. I knew because I kept track. Any cheese on the ground didn't belong to anyone, or so I led myself to believe. I grabbed up those two pieces of cheese and chewed them down.

It was getting dark. I went to check on Bubby. He was sound asleep. I still didn't know where Mim was. She was nowhere around.

I climbed up on the bed, put my arm over Bubby, and went to sleep too. We had had our "supper."

Tomorrow we'd start over. Up on the hill I knew where another patch of thimbleberries was. They would be our breakfast. Worry about lunch and supper when the time came, and Mim would probably be back by then.

For a Little While, My Friend

It was a bright May morning in 1932. A new girl had come to school. Her name was Betty Hadley, and like me, she was seven years old. We were buddies from the moment our eyes met. All morning, we grinned shyly at one another across the room.

A classmate, Marie, and I always ate our lunch together out beside the school on a big flat rock. The rock was our castle and we considered it our personal property. That day, as we walked toward our rock, Betty was just naturally there, skipping along beside us.

Every day for one happy month, Marie, Betty and I played together during our noon hours. Marie was always with us, but she was on the outside looking in. For in Betty I had found a soul mate. She had an imagination to match my own. We played hopscotch, hide-and-seek and squat tag, but the best games were ones we invented. Sometimes we told wild stories always beginning with "When I grow up . . ." Other times, we just sat and giggled, we were so happy to be together. Betty's eyes would sparkle, and the dimples would dance in and out of her cheeks. How I loved her!

Once, we found a pack of Wings. We spent a couple of noon hours "lightin' up, puffing up a storm" in back of our rock. We didn't especially like smoking, but we had to try it.

We planned for our summer together. We were going to stay overnight and go strawberrying and swimming at Roster Pond. Some Saturday night we were going into town to see a cowboy movie, and we planned to go to the Sunday school picnic together. It was such a good feeling to have such a good friend. I knew we were best friends forever.

Then, that terrible Wednesday morning, the school bus from Lower Chilson Hill didn't arrive. Marie was home with the measles, so I waited alone by the school steps for Betty. The bell rang, and I had to go inside. I didn't think too much about it. Chilson Hill is steep, and sometimes the old bus "heated up." Then the bus driver had to stop and wait a while for it to "cool off."

We were just seated at our desks when Mr. Forth came in from his side of the two-room schoolhouse. He looked sick. He whispered something to Mrs. Forth and then she looked sick. They walked out into the hall, and the low drone of excited voices reached our ears.

Mrs. Forth came back into the room. She said that there had been an accident, that Betty Hadley was dead. Cars didn't have to stop for school buses in those days. Betty had run around the bus right in front of Robbie Hayford's car. He was passing, fast. That was that. Betty was dead. Death had never touched me before, to someone my own age. Death was always something for older people.

Some kids started to cry, some to whisper to each other, and a few raised their hands for permission to ask questions. Everyone was doing something, everyone except me. I just sat there, stunned. A tight band settled around and squeezed my chest. Betty, my friend, was dead.

The rest of the week passed. Noon hours I just sat, numb and alone, on our rock beside the school.

We were to go see Betty Saturday morning. Finally, the time came. Mim scrubbed my face and ears, and I put on my good clothes. My eyes felt scratchy, and the band around my chest was tighter. I couldn't eat any breakfast. For once, Mim didn't insist. She tried to be cheerful. She said it was a beautiful day and that the sky was bright and blue. I wanted to scream, "I don't care. Don't you know that I'm dead too?" But I didn't. I knew she was only trying to help me now. No one could understand. The pain pressed in around me more than ever. I was all alone.

Mim hugged me goodbye as the bus arrived. I dragged myself aboard. Mrs. Forth and my classmates were there. No one spoke as we went down Chilson Hill.

The bus stopped on the bank above Betty's house. My head began to feel loose and wobbly. As I went down the bus steps, I felt like crying, but, to my surprise, I let out a great loud giggle.

Mrs. Forth grabbed me by the shoulder. She shook me until my head was spinning and my shoulder felt as if it were falling off. When she let go of me, I staggered down the path with the rest of the kids. No one said a word.

Then, right in front of us was the little white house, and we were going in the front door. In the door leading to an empty room, empty except for a small white coffin set on two white sawhorses, was Betty's mother, sitting at the head of the coffin. Mr. Hadley wasn't there. I wasn't surprised, because he had run off with another woman a couple of weeks before this happened.

One by one, the kids went by me. Finally it was my turn to walk across the room to stand in front of that little white coffin. I couldn't escape. Someone shoved me forward. Then I was there. The smell of carnations was thick in my nose. I tried not to breathe.

My eyes finally focused, and I was looking at a lovely fragile doll. Everything was white except Betty's beautiful black hair. Her dress, her shoes, her stockings, her face, the flowers in her clasped hands were all white.

There was no expression on her face, just stillness. No dimples danced, and the big brown eyes were closed. It was Betty, all right, and yet she wasn't there. I found myself trying to say, "Please, Betty, come back," but I only stood there, paralyzed, with my shoulder hurting and my head still dizzy from the shaking I had received. It was forever before someone nudged me forward. I forced myself to walk the few feet until I stood in front of Mrs. Hadley.

She was very still. She was a tall raw-boned woman with Betty's beautiful abundant hair. Her eyes were downcast. She seemed to be studying the tightly clenched hands in her lap. My tongue felt swollen, and my mouth was completely dry. I managed to whisper, "I'm sorry."

Her head moved slightly in acknowledgment. I moved on and somehow made it out the door.

We walked slowly back up the path to the bus. I looked up at the sky and thought, "Mim was right. It is a beautiful blue! And Betty is there!"

Then the awful tight band around my chest let go. My love for Betty felt as strong, but the terrible pain was gone. I felt light and free, for at that moment, I knew—"It's only goodbye for a little while, Betty, my so-alive friend."

Uncle Arthur's Tree

I was only two when Uncle Arthur died. Bubby was only a couple of months old, so Mim couldn't go home to Chilson for the funeral. We were living in the Bronx at the time with Great-grandpa and Grandma Stone. I feel like I can remember the sadness and Mimmie crying, but it can't be. I was too young.

Aunt Nettie called Mim from Chilson, and so she found out that Uncle Arthur was awful sick. He was only fifteen. He was Grandpa and Grandma Granger's only son out of the five children they had. He was their pride and joy. The doctor came from Ticonderoga, but he couldn't do anything. He said Arthur had spinal meningitis. Antibiotics were completely unknown at the time.

Uncle Arthur got worse and worse. At first he had bad headaches. He couldn't swallow or eat. He wasted away to only skin and bones. They wrapped him up in cool wet sheets, but they could never get his temperature below 104 degrees. He couldn't stand up. He lost his hearing and his sight.

Grandpa carried Uncle Arthur around in his arms like a baby for hours at a time. It seemed to ease his pain. Uncle Arthur loved Grandpa so much that it quieted him when Grandpa held him close. And that's where he died, in Grandpa's arms.

They drained all the blood from Uncle Arthur's body, and Grandpa poured the blood around the little apple tree that Uncle Arthur had planted under the "haunted room's" (the room where Uncle Arthur died) window. Uncle Arthur's tree grew and thrived. In a few years, it was way up to the second story of the house. Each fall it had some of the biggest, reddest apples I ever saw.

In the back of the clothesline under the haunted room's window was Uncle Arthur's tree.

They were gorgeous. But no one ever ate those apples. They fell off the tree, rotted where they landed and went back into the ground.

One day when I was about five years old, Mim and I were standing by Uncle Arthur's tree. She started talking about him. She said she missed him a lot. She said he was such a happy kid and was always playing jokes on people. She wished I could have known him. And listening to her talk about him made me want to know him too, so I asked Mim how I could do this. She said that she didn't know, but after I pestered her a few times, she said to go sit under Uncle Arthur's tree and wait. If he was anywhere, he'd be there.

So quite a few times over the next couple of years, I did go sit under Uncle Arthur's tree and wait. One spring day, sitting there half asleep, the apple blossoms were showering down around me. They tickled my face, and I had to brush them off. I thought I heard him laugh. Later that summer, while dozing

Aunt Leona, Grandma Granger, Aunt Dot, Grandpa Granger, Uncle Arthur.

there, a little caterpillar crawled up on my hand. I hurriedly brushed it away. He laughed again. I heard him, really! And then that fall, under the tree, I got plunked on the head with one of those big red apples. This time he couldn't suppress a snicker. Another time in the winter, as I was walking by his tree, the cold, cold air snapped a branch like a pistol shot. I jumped and hollered. I distinctly heard him chuckle. I heard him, really! So though I never saw Uncle Arthur, he was there. I know it in my heart. I wish I could have hugged him.

Outside

Another sweet spring morning. I hopped out of bed and into my sunsuit. I ate some cereal without any milk. We were out, so what? Then I went and sat on the doorstep. It was before the new tar road had gone in. Some birds were chirping, and the sun felt so good on my shoulders.

I watched a silver airplane droning along down in the valley, moving slowly above Lake Champlain. I wondered briefly about it. It wasn't the mail plane. That always went over every day about noon. Then it was silent, except for a few flies that buzzed around my legs. Kitty came out and curled up beside me.

It was so quiet and warm in the sun. I was dozing when suddenly I noticed a thin, wiry little man trudging up over Chilson Hill. I watched him come along the flat, moving toward me. I watched him all the way. His feet slowly pushed discouragedly, one in front of the other. He started glaring at me as he trudged along. I knew he was mad, but I couldn't stop staring at him.

When he got in front of me, without stopping, he said, "You don't know nothing about outside. You sit here in your shithouses by the side of the road." He kept on glaring over his shoulder at me as he pushed along the road. Then he was gone.

For one moment something glimmered in my mind—What was "outside"?—but only for a moment. I grabbed an old basin and skipped down to the swamp to see if there were any frogs' eggs yet.

Bigness

One day, Cowboy brought a great big yellow dog home. He said Bubby could name him. The dog was three times as big as Bubby, so he named him "Bigness." Bigness liked me okay, but Bubby was his love. He and Bubby belonged together. They were the typical "boy and his dog" story.

Bubby would run and jump up on the kitchen table, and Bigness would pretend he was "out to get" Bubby. Bigness would jump and growl and fight, pulling on Bubby's foot, which he had grabbed in his mouth. Bigness's eyes would glaze over, and you would think he was raving mad-furious, but he was only playing. He loved Bubby so much.

The Wrights had two mean ugly dogs, a big black police dog named Granger and a big yellow one called Sandy. They used to catch Bigness over on their side of the fence, and they would jump on him and beat him up. Bigness would come yelping home, and we'd have to patch up his wounds. Bigness never fought back. He seemed to know that "over the fence" was their territory. The Wrights' dogs never came over on our property. They just ignored us as though they wouldn't lower themselves to such an extent.

How the Wrights gloated about this! They were proud of their dogs and laughed at Bigness. This galled Mim and us kids, but there was nothing we could do about it. Then, one day in late November, we had our revenge. The Wrights were putting manure on their cornfield just over the fence from our house. Granger and Sandy were walking along the fence right behind the manure wagon. For some reason, probably because they didn't want to walk in the manure, the dogs came under the fence and walked on our side.

No one paid any attention. We kids were playing around when, suddenly, a yellow streak came out from under our porch and lit into both of those dogs! Bigness slashed and bit gashes on both their sides. They both howled and got back under the fence as best they could with Bigness snapping at them all the way. Granted, in the attack, Bigness had surprise on his side, but he had beaten both of the Wrights' dogs, fair and square.

Mim, Bub and I were so proud. The Wrights didn't say anything, but we knew they were seething.

A couple of nights later, Bigness didn't come in when we called. The next morning we didn't want to go to school because Bigness still wasn't home. Mim said to go, and that she'd find him. When we got home from school, we rushed in the house. Bigness wasn't there, and neither was Mim. A note on the table said, "Kids, stay here. I'm out looking for Bigness."

Bubby and I made ourselves a couple of sugar tits and sat down to wait. Pretty soon someone was kicking on our door to get in.

It was Mim, and she was carrying Bigness. She said she found him on the path over back of Ed Latrell's, and that he'd been shot.

Mim told me to put an old blanket on the floor. It was really cold in the house as we had no heat. Cowboy was working down near Hague on a road job. Mim was hoping that when he came back, he'd get us some wood so we could have a fire in the old cook stove—at least heat up the kitchen.

Mim put Bigness down on the blanket, and we put an old coat over him. Bigness was very still and didn't even stir when Bubby said his name and petted him. Bigness had a small hole in the top of his head. It had been bleeding. Mim covered it with a piece of cloth.

We brought our mattresses out of the bedroom and made our beds around Bigness on the floor. If we all stayed in one room, it would be warmer.

After what seemed like ages, Bigness staggered up on his feet, lapped a little water from the dish Mim held out for him,

Bigness and Cowboy with a glass of Mim's home brew in front of "Top of the Hill."

and he gave a little lick on Bubby's hand. Then he lay back down, and I covered him up.

We were in seventh heaven! Bigness was okay. He was going to get better. We piled into our beds around him and went to sleep. In the morning, Bubby woke up first. He reached out to Bigness, and then he screamed. Bigness was stone cold dead.

Bubby put one leg and arm under Bigness and one leg and arm over Bigness, and pulled him close. He cried like I never heard anyone cry. He howled and moaned and bawled. I crawled over and put my arms around them, and I howled and moaned and bawled as hard as Bubby. Mim's face was so stricken. She put her arms around the three of us, and she sobbed and sobbed and sobbed.

Right then, I made a promise in my heart. Someone was going to be sorry for what they had done to Bigness and my little brother.

Voodooing Carly

Carly Harris had killed Bigness. I finally knew it for sure. I kept asking the neighborhood kids about it, and finally Sny Covell told me. Carly had done it. Sny said that the Wrights were so mad that Bigness had taken on both their dogs, Granger and Sandy, and beat them good, that they hired Carly to kill Bigness. Carly wouldn't do it for 50 cents, so they offered him a buck, and that was too much for Carly. Greed got the best of him, so he shot Bigness.

Now I knew for sure I was going to get Carly for that, but how? I found a book about voodoo. It was called "Strange Customs of Jamaica," or something like that. I didn't understand everything it said, but I knew you could put a spell on someone by making a doll and sticking pins in it. That's what I did. I took an old feed bag, cut out an old piece of cloth, and sewed them together. Then I stuffed the doll with cotton. I stuck twigs in the body for arms and legs. Then I stuck two straight pins in it and chanted, "Voodoo, voodoo, do your stuff on Carly." I put the doll way back in the corner of my dresser, under my underwear, and waited. Nothing happened.

When I went by Carly's old shack up on a little knoll back from the road, I saw him sometimes, chopping wood or working around his yard. His five or six chickens walked around scratching as usual, and his old scrawny cat still lay on his doorstep. I remembered how terribly hard Bubby had cried when Bigness died and how awful I felt. So I stuck the pins a little farther into the doll and mumbled some more about Carly. This went on for nearly a week, and as nothing was happening, I sort of forgot about it.

Then one morning, Aunt Ethel and I were rolling along in her little Ford coupe coming back from Lonson's store. Aunt Ethel always let me ride in the rumble seat when she went down to the store if I was around. We were going by Carly's place, and I wasn't paying much attention when Aunt Ethel said, "Did you see that?" I said, "See what?" Aunt Ethel said, "I don't know, but we're going back to find out." So she turned the car around, and back we went, driving slowly by Carly's place. He was out in the yard walking around. His red hair was sticking up in the air and he had no clothes on. He was so thin and his skin was lily-white, except his hands and face, which were dark from the sun. He wasn't doing anything, just walking around from one end of his yard to the other.

I scootched down low in the rumble seat and shut my eyes and then just squinted out of them. I couldn't believe what I was seeing. Aunt Ethel said, "My God," and we went a little farther and then turned around in the road and crawled back by Carly's place again. He was so busy walking back and forth across his yard that he didn't seem to see us. Aunt Ethel drove to the end of the path leading up to his house, and then she stopped. Carly was still walking around. I had never seen a naked man before, so I stood straight up in the rumble seat, opened my eyes, and took a good look. It was worse than I thought.

Well, forget that, 'cause suddenly Carly let out a scream, grabbed his axe off the woodpile, snatched up one of his chickens, and cut its head off in midair. Aunt Ethel was frozen at the wheel of the car. Her mouth was hanging open, and her eyes were riveted on Carly. I don't know what possessed me, but suddenly I screamed out, "Voodoo, voodoo!" Carly stopped dead still with the axe up in the air in one hand and the headless chicken in the other. Chicken blood was all over him. He just stood there staring at us. Aunt Ethel said, "My God, Yada, what'd you do that for?" Then she tried to start the engine. It just went *whir-whir-whir.* By this time, Carly was starting very slowly down his path toward us. He had dropped the chicken, but I noticed he still had his axe in his hand. Aunt Ethel said, "Oh my God!"

again and kept stamping on the car's starter pedal. All we heard was the *whir-whir-whir* of the car's starter. Finally the old car shook and bucked as the engine fired, and we started to slowly rattle down the road. I peeked over the back of the rumble seat. Carly had gotten down to where we had been, and he was waving his axe and hollering at us as we went around Dead Man's Bend.

We went home and told Mimmie what we had seen. She sent me running over to the neighbors to call Ticonderoga and have them send the troopers right up. They got there real fast. Mim jumped in their car to go show them where Carly lived. They left Aunt Ethel and me standing in the dust by the side of the road. We were both pretty miffed because, after all, we had discovered all this. So we jumped in Aunt Ethel's car and rushed back over to Carly's. The troopers were up in his yard trying to wrap a sheet around him. It looked like a sheet, but I know now it was a straitjacket. Carly was screaming and kicking and fighting. Mim was standing in the middle of the path, hollering, "You stop that, Carly Harris, you stop that!"

Aunt Ethel and I went by slowly in order to turn around. There were a couple of cows in the road, and we couldn't get by them, so it took us a little longer to turn around. By the time we got back to Carly's, the troopers had him in the car, and they were all heading down the road toward Ticonderoga. So Aunt Ethel and I kept going. We stopped at the spring for a drink of cold water and then went home. The excitement for the day was over. However, I decided after that performance that I'd never voodoo anyone again.

O'Prince, Grandpa and Me

Grandpa and O'Prince were more than a master and his horse. They were close friends. From the time I was three years old, Grandpa took me with him when he could. He held me up on O'Prince's back until I learned to hold on to the harness and not fall off.

O'Prince was gentle to me, but Grandpa was his love. O'Prince tolerated me because I was Grandpa's tagalong. He accepted that I'd be a nuisance hanging on his back or petting him. I wasn't all bad for O'Prince, though. I'd always slip him my lunchtime apple. If Grandpa saw me, he'd grin his big sunny smile. Then he'd share his apple with me.

In the spring, we plowed the gardens for vegetables and corn. The chickens always grabbed up the worms that the plow turned up. But when I wanted some worms for fishing, I'd go right down between O'Prince's legs and under his belly, and beat the hens to the worms. The hens would cluck and scold, but they didn't dare go under O'Prince like I did.

One day, O'Prince had had it with me crawling around his legs, and he just let go. I got all splattered and wet. Grandpa grabbed me up and took me over to the brook and washed me off. I was so mad, but Grandpa just smiled his big sunny smile all through the performance.

Also that spring, O'Prince drew the sleigh that we used to carry the maple sap from the trees to the sugar house. Grandpa always gave me pieces of maple sugar that I'd share with O'Prince. He loved that, and he'd slaver all over my hand as he chewed up the sugar. Sometimes he'd nibble at my cheek or nudge my shoulder if he didn't think I was giving him enough sugar fast enough. That made me giggle, and I'd holler, "You stop that, O'Prince!" Grandpa would stop work, look at us, and smile his smile. I was the happiest little girl in the world.

In early summer, men would cut and peel poplars over in the woods. O'Prince would always be used to skid the trees over the logging road to the main road. There, a truck would pick them up and take them to the Ticonderoga mill. I'd go with Grandpa and ride O'Prince to guide him, or so I thought. O'Prince would have trotted down the logging road anyway.

Once in a while, the men would cut down a poplar for me to peel. They'd let me work a while, and then Grandpa would say he needed me to guide O'Prince.

When we got back, my poplar would be peeled and ready to go. The men would all be busy working, and I'd say that I couldn't figure out how the tree got finished. The men would be grinning, and Grandpa would flash his big sunny smile. We'd start hauling my poplar to the main road, but not before one of the men would give me a penny for helping them.

O'Prince, Grandpa and me.

When we got home, we'd bed O'Prince down for the night and go in the house. Grandpa would tell Grandma how I'd helped him peel poplar. Gram was always happy to hear what a good worker I was, and Grandpa's smile would be going full blast. How very important I felt!

On winter mornings, around six o'clock, when it had snowed the night before, Grandpa would hitch O'Prince to the wooden plow. If I heard him, I'd wave out the little window by my bed, and Grandpa would wave and smile back. Then I would snuggle down in bed and listen to the runners of the snowplow squeal, squeal, squeal on the road. The runners did that when it was especially cold. It didn't matter that in an hour and a half I'd be running down that road to the main road to catch the bus for school. At 6 a.m., squeal, squeal, squeal-time, I was the warmest, safest little girl ever.

Grandpa, O'Prince and the old wooden plow cleared some of the back dirt roads around Chilson for years.

Things went happily along. Then, one day in late summer, Grandma told me to go pick up my room. It was a mess. She was right. I never straightened it up if I didn't have to. I was just turning to go up the stairs when Grandpa came into the kitchen.

Grandma said, "Poddy, what's the matter?" I looked at Grandpa, and he was white as a sheet. He said, "That damned cow has gored O'Prince!" Grandpa grabbed his rifle off the wall and hurried out.

Grandma looked stricken, but she said, "Now go clean up your room like I told you." I left the kitchen, but instead of going up the stairs, I scurried out the side door and along the grape arbor until I reached the end. I sunk to the ground among the grape leaves and peeked out. I had a good view of the barn and the field where the cows and horses were grazing. The cow was to the left, eating grass. Dolly horse was back near the barn. O'Prince was nibbling hay up near the fence. He looked fine to me. Then I noticed there was a rope or something hanging out his side almost to the ground. When I realized it was some of his insides, I felt sick.

Grandpa had now reached the field. He walked over to old Bos Cow and he just put the gun to her forehead and pulled the trigger. She dropped at his feet. Once a cow had gored a person or animal, you would never trust it again. He never looked at her, but just walked slowly over to O'Prince. I knew what was going to happen. I wanted to run back into the house and crawl under my bed, but I couldn't move. I put my hand in my mouth and bit down hard. I wanted to scream, "Don't! Don't," but I didn't. I knew Grandpa would do what was right. I could not interfere.

Grandpa walked up to O'Prince and patted his shoulder. Suddenly Grandpa, who was always so straight and tall, slumped against O'Prince's shoulder. I heard him sob a few times as he held O'Prince tight.

Then Grandpa quickly put the rifle to O'Prince's head and pulled the trigger. O'Prince sunk slowly to the ground.

By then, Tweedle Armstrong had heard the first shot from down the hill on his farm. He came running to see what was wrong. Tweedle put his arms around Grandpa's shoulder, and they walked back to the barn.

They hitched Dolly to the stone boat and pulled up beside O'Prince. Between them, they rolled O'Prince onto the stone boat and started back to the pasture. They had shovels. I knew they were going to bury O'Prince back where he loved the pasture best, back on the sunny side of the hill.

As Grandpa and Tweedle disappeared around the barn, I jumped up and ran in the house by the side door. I pussyfooted up to my room and really lit into cleaning it up. Tears were running down my cheeks, but if Grandma came up to check on me, I knew she wouldn't stand for any nonsense. With Grandma, no matter what happened, you did your duty!

When I was done, I went in the haunted room and slumped down on the low windowsill. I looked out at Uncle Arthur's tree. It was cold as usual and very quiet in the room. I wished whatever it was that haunted the room would take me away so I wouldn't hurt anymore. Nothing happened.

Then Grandpa called me for supper. I wiped my eyes and went down. Supper was very quiet that night. Nobody said much. Grandpa looked at me, and I saw in his eyes that we would never talk about O'Prince. I understood it was because of the terrible hurt that he felt. I knew the love that was there.

From then on, I still went with Grandpa sometimes. Dolly took O'Prince's place. We got the work done and had some good times, but it was not the same. To me, Grandpa's smile was never quite as sunny ever again.

Rhode Island Reds

Grandma Granger was very proud of her Rhode Island Red hens. Sometimes she'd let me feed them their corn, and I loved doing that. They laid eggs regularly.

The only thing was, even though those hens were her pride and joy, every other Sunday or so, she had no qualms about going out and grabbing one of those hens, whacking off its head on the chopping block, and dropping the hen's body onto the ground where it would flop around until the nerves in it stopped moving.

Gloria (me) feeding Grandma Granger's Rhode Island Red hens.

Now, I knew this was going to happen. Every farm woman did this when she wanted to have chicken for Sunday dinner, but when Gram did it, it horrified me, and I would stand there speechless.

However, I never said a word or interfered because I knew the delicious chicken and dumpling dinner Gram would serve us that evening.

My Miracle

There were two different groups of kids in Chilson. There were the "down Chilson" group and the "upper Chilson" group. The group you belonged to depended on where you lived and who you played with the most. We were really all good friends, but we did have a few contests going between our groups. One of the contests every spring was to see which group could get swimming in the creek the earliest. Come March 1, we all watched the creek carefully for the ice to melt.

The "upper" group always beat us "downies." They lived nearer the creek and could watch it more closely. We decided to beat them one year. Instead of waiting for the ice to be gone, we went in the water earlier—while the ice was breaking up in pieces.

The day was chilly, but we took off our outer clothes and rushed into the water. The rule was that you only had to get up to your waist in the water, and then you could get right out. We all got in and out fast, except for Bubby. He stayed in longer, pushing the chunks of ice around. Finally, after I hollered at him enough, he got out of the water. We were a frozen bunch of kids, but we had won the contest for that year.

The next morning, Bubby was coughing a little bit, but he said he felt okay. He had a new BB gun that Mim had bought him down in Pearl's Department Store. Mim had bought it reluctantly, but Bubby teased so hard that she finally gave in. No one thought much about kids running around with BB guns in those days. Lots of boys had them.

Anyway, it was a nice day, so Mim said he could go out for a while. Bub put his jacket on and disappeared out the door.

About twenty minutes later, Jenny Moore pulled up in her car. She looked shaken, and she handed Mim a BB shot. She said Bubby had been standing on the bank by the road when she went by. Bub shot through her back window, and the BB shot landed on the front seat beside her. We looked at her back window, and sure enough, there was a little round hole through it. Mim appeased Jenny the best she could.

When Jenny had gone, Mim settled down to wait for Bubby. When he came in looking very nonchalant, Mim shook him good and broke his BB gun over her knee. Mim scolded Bub good, and I stayed out of sight behind the kitchen stove. Anyone would have been included in her wrath at that moment. We had supper, and Mim made Bubby go right to bed as part of his punishment. He coughed a lot during the night.

The next morning, Bubby didn't want to get up, and Mim felt his head. It was terribly hot. Mim picked him up, wrapped him in a blanket and rocked him in our rickety old rocking chair. Bubby seemed awfully groggy, and Mim was really scared. She sent me scurrying over to Oscier's to call for Dr. Cummings to come up from Ticonderoga.

Dr. Cummings got there about two hours later. Mim had been trying to get Bubby to drink a little water without any success. Dr. Cummings put his stethoscope to Bubby's chest and he looked worried. Bubby had pneumonia. We put him right to bed and put mustard plasters on his chest to break up the congestion. Remember, there were no antibiotics back then. Dr. Cummings said in ten to twelve days, Bubby would "pass the crisis" and then we'd know. You either got better from pneumonia or you didn't. It was truly in God's hands.

Mary Angus, who had come over from Scotland to marry Frankie Stowell, was the only nurse in Chilson. She heard about Bubby and came right over. Mim was desperate and told Mary she couldn't pay her. Mary said it didn't matter and rolled up her sleeves. She made up our big bed with new white sheets. She said the sheets had been in her trousseau. Mim protested, but Mary said it was the best use she could ever have for those sheets.

Mim and Mary hardly left Bubby's side for a good two weeks. Night and day they sat on each side of the bed. They caught

44

naps sitting in their chairs and resting their heads on the side of Bubby's bed. They tried to feed him and get water into him, and they rubbed his hands and feet and kept him as warm as they could with a hot water bottle at his feet. We didn't have any heat in our house. Bub didn't respond too much.

It fell to me to make the mustard plasters. Mary showed me how to do it. You put two tablespoons of hot powdered mustard in some flour, mixed it with water to make a paste, then scooped it out into an old piece of cloth and wrapped it together. I'd carry it into the bedroom, and Mary would take it. She'd rub some lard on Bubby's chest so the mustard wouldn't burn his skin, and then she'd lay the mustard plaster on his chest. It was supposed to break up congestion in his lungs. When the plaster dried out, I'd make another one. I also kept the bowl by the bed filled with snow. They'd wring cloths out in that and lay them on Bub's head to try and keep his fever down. That was all you could do, just wait for the crisis to pass.

The waiting was what I couldn't stand. It was still three or four days before the crisis would come, and I couldn't stand not knowing what was going to happen. So I started praying to God, "Please, God, give me a sign that Bubby will live." My whole mind was numb to everything but that prayer. I said it over and over again.

A couple of nights later, we had a freezing rainstorm. The next morning, everything was covered with a sheet of clear ice. We had no water in the pail, and we needed a new mustard plaster, so Mim told me to go down to the brook and get some water. The path to the brook was a clear sheet of ice. Slipping and sliding, I made it to the brook, filled my pail, and started back. It was a dark, gloomy day, but every once in a while, the sun would come out from behind the clouds for a few seconds. Nothing mattered to me. All I did was keep on praying, "Please, God, give me a sign that Bubby will get better, please, God," etc., etc., etc.

I slipped and the pail swooshed down the path ahead of me, but it didn't spill. I got up on my hands and knees, still praying, "Please, God, give me a sign that Bubby will get better." I raised my head and looked up at the trees ahead of me.

Just then, the sun came out, and where two icy branches came together, they formed a perfect cross. The sun sparkled and glistened and glimmered on the cross. That cross shone with a brightness that is forever burned into my mind. For a minute I stared at it, and then the sun went back in under the clouds, and it was gone. But I knew God had given me the sign that I had been praying for. Bubby was going to get better.

I went in and told Mim. She started to cry. Bubby was so sick. She said to keep praying Bubby would get better. I said, "Okay," but really I only kept saying, "Thank you, God" over and over because I knew He had shown me that Bubby would be better.

The next morning, Dr. Cummings came up from Ticonderoga. He told Mim the crisis was at hand and made Mim stay in the kitchen with me. I never saw Mim—ever the optimist—so down and broken. I kept telling her, "Bubby is going to be okay. God gave me a sign. He showed me so." But Mim only hugged me close and cried.

Then Dr. Cummings came out of the bedroom. He was crying and smiling at the same time. He said that Bubby had started perspiring and that his fever had broken. Bubby had passed the crisis. He was sleeping peacefully, and although it would take a long time, he was going to get better.

Mim was so happy and relieved and surprised, but I was not surprised at all. For God had answered my prayers and given me a sign that Bubby would get better. It's the only miracle that ever happened to me.

The Blind Man

During those years, quite a few people went through Chilson, always trudging down the road, moving on to somewhere else. There was no work or much of a future anywhere. I'll never forget the blind man.

Mim and Bubby had gone to Ticonderoga with Aunt Dean to buy some food. There wasn't enough room in the car for me, so I had to stay home. After they had gone, feeling sorry for myself, I went outside to look for something to do. The road was empty, and all the neighbors' houses along the road looked empty. I felt alone in an empty world.

I skipped around the side of the house to see if my rabbit was okay in his cage. Yup! So I skipped right back, and there he was on our porch. A man, sitting on our porch! He sat with his hand holding a cane that was resting across his big fat belly. His round face was red, like it was sunburned. He had a big nose, and his eyes looked funny. He kept darting his head in short jerks in all directions as though he didn't want to miss seeing anything. His head turned right toward me, but the expression on his face didn't change. Then I realized he was darting his head around so that his ears wouldn't miss one small sound. He was blind. Finally, he called out, "Is somebody there?" I answered that there was. He said, "Give me a drink of water."

I went to the barrel of water by the back door and brought the dipper back full of water. He felt for it, took it, and drank some. The rest he threw against the side of the house, then threw the dipper after it. I watched him from the edge of the porch. I would have offered him something to eat, but we didn't have anything. Meanwhile, he just sat, and sat, and sat.

47

We had an old record player on the porch beside his chair. I went over and wound it up. The minute the music blared out, he grabbed my arm. I never felt such strength in a person before or since. "Shut that off, you goddamn brat!" I obliged him, quickly. His hand loosened slightly, and I jerked away. I got off that porch real fast.

Again, he just sat, and sat, and sat, until the sun went down. Thank goodness, Mim was due home any minute. Then he got up, tapped his way off the porch with his cane, and started over the road. I ran around the house and up on the knoll out back so I could see what he'd do. I watched him tap, tap, tap his way across the flats and then tap, tap, tap around the bend out of sight. I never saw or heard of him again.

Christmas Came Early

It was the second week of December, and it was snowing. True, there were only a few flakes falling, but it was enough to make me rush to get my Shooting Star sled out of the back shed. I wanted to check it to be sure it was ready for sliding.

I pulled Shooting Star out, and my heart sank into my shoes. One of the sled's runners had somehow snapped right in two. Now you could put new boards on a sled, put on new rope, pound in nails, and chicken-wire the steering handle on if it came loose, but there was no way a broken runner on a sled could be fixed. It meant we would use the boards on the sled for kindling wood and throw the rest away.

Mim said she was sorry, but I'd have to ride with Bubby on his sled. There was no money to get me a new sled. I didn't want to ride with Bubby, and besides, I knew once we were out of sight of Mimmie, he wouldn't let me ride with him anyway.

I moped around the house and sighed big sighs while repeating over and over that I didn't know how I'd get through winter without a sled, but no one paid any attention.

We had a couple of snowstorms, and the snow was packed down slick and smooth on Chilson Hill Road. Bubby was sliding with the kids, and I was pouting around the house. To get some relief from my mutterings and long face, Mim sent me over to Wrights to get a pail of water.

Clarence had just come in from sliding. He saw me and said, "Hey, Yada, yesterday I saw the mailman stop at your house and carry a sled inside." I answered that he must be seeing things as there was no sled there. Clarence said he knew what he saw, but I didn't have to believe him.

Rushing home, I told Mim what Clarence said. She said he must be blind. She couldn't recall seeing any sled. I slumped down in a corner and started to cry. Cowboy was there and, being an old softy, said, "Mary, let's give it to her." Mim said, "But it's for Christmas." But Cowboy was already climbing up in the loft and handing down a new Shooting Star sled. It was beautiful, and it was for me! It was the nicest surprise I've ever had. Christmas came early!

Now that I had my sled, I had to work the handle to get it ready for steering. The Shooting Stars were always tight, and you had to loosen them up. The runners were always painted red, and the paint had to be removed from under them or the sled would hardly move. I spent all the time I could the next couple of days walking the sled around and rubbing the paint off. Finally, after a lot of elbow grease, the runners were shiny clear steel, and Shooting Star was ready for the trial run.

The next day was Saturday, and I could slide all day. I went to bed hardly able to wait for morning to come. The snow was packed hard and smooth on the road. Chilson Hill was ready!

After breakfast, Bub and I were off. Bubby beat me all hollow down to the top of Arthur Hill. Some other kids were there getting ready to go down the hill. They saw me come in a distant second to Bubby. There were some snickers and remarks about my new sled not being as fast as Bubby's old one, but I pretended I didn't hear them.

Cleon Rafferty's house was there, and we went in to get him. His father said to me, "I see you have a new sled." "Yeah," I told him, "but it doesn't go very fast yet." He said, "Bring it in. I'll speed her up for you."

He rubbed some wax on the runners back and forth, back and forth. I asked him what kind of wax it was. He said to never mind, but it would do the trick.

We went outside to run down the hill, which was at least three quarters of a mile long. Cleon was one kid in a big family. We were poor, but they were poorer. Cleon hadn't even put on his coat to go sliding as he had no sled. I called to him to come

50

on, he could slide with me. He wasn't too enthused about it, but after I hollered a couple more times at him, he came out putting on his coat.

The kids were taking off to race down the hill. I "belly-whopped" onto Shooting Star. Cleon gave us a big running start, pushing the sled with his hands. Then he jumped on the back of the sled on his knees. He hunched up with his head down on my back and hung on the sides of the sled with his hands.

I was intent on beating the kids who had uttered the derogatory words about my new Shooting Star.

Well, Shooting Star took off. I never went so fast on a sled before. I was screaming, "Get out of the way, get out of the way!" And we passed every sled on the road.

Suddenly, we were at the last grade before Arthur Hill's big curve. I panicked. We were going so fast that I knew I could never steer around that sharp last curve. I saw up ahead where the old wooden plow that had been used to plow the road had dug way down to the dirt at the side of the road. It had left a long stretch of dirt there.

I twitched the sled over into the dirt. It went a couple of feet, then stopped dead. Cleon shot over my head, and I ended up spinning around in the dirt on my behind.

Other sleds whizzed by going too fast to stop and help. Then, Willy Sears came along on his old clunker of a sled. Not going very fast, he managed to stop. He helped me up. "Where's Cleon? Where's Cleon?"

We glanced quickly around, and in a big fluffy snowbank, all we could see were the bottoms of two boots sticking out. We said together, "Oh, my God, he's dead!" Then we saw one of the feet twitch a little, and we rushed over and dug and pulled Cleon out.

Cleon was so mad that he wouldn't have noticed if he was hurt, which, luckily, he wasn't. He was hopping up and down and hollering, "You tried to kill me! You tried to kill me!"

All the way up the hill, Cleon kept telling the kids, "She tried to kill me! She tried to kill me!" He glared at me all the way. There was no sense in me trying to say I didn't do it.

After he calmed down, Cleon and I became good friends again. I tried to get him to ride with me again, but he wouldn't. He nicknamed me the "Chilson Hiller Thrill Killer."

Shooting Star and I flew over Chilson Hill for the next few years. I never had another wreck, but no one would ever ride with me. In our sliding group, being the "Chilson Hiller Thrill Killer" took care of that.

Keeping Christmas

Mim, Bub and I always kept Christmas. The first couple of years (after our rotten Christmas in Crestwood) we kept it by ourselves. As Top of the Hill got bigger, and we had more room to entertain guests, our Christmases got more expansive.

Each year, Mim raised a turkey along with our roosters. We never were friendly with the turkey because we knew its head was going to be whacked off for Christmas. You didn't eat a friend. I helped Mim make molasses cake and mince pies. Cowboy always got a deer in the fall, and we made mincemeat from venison. We had plenty of wild apples for pies and tarts.

We made dressing from dried homemade bread and wild mushrooms that Grandpa Granger gave us. He was the only one Mim would trust to know which mushrooms to pick and not poison anyone. We put in hazelnuts from up on the ledge and wild leeks. Then we added some eggs into the mixture and stuffed it into the turkey. You haven't lived if you've never tasted that dressing. Mim made six-inch-high homemade rolls served hot and fudge filled with butternuts and gingerbread cookies.

Early Christmas morning, Cowboy would kill the turkey and pluck it. Then he would head for Hague to spend the day with his mother and father. He really wanted to stay with us, but he said his mother would kill him if he didn't show up.

Bub and I peeled potatoes and squash and set the big long table in the Top of the Hill dance hall. Cowboy had put long boards over his sawhorses for us. With Christmas paper over them, it made a festive table.

We invited anyone and everyone who had no place to go for Christmas, and believe me, there were many lonely people around.

Tillie, Chilson's "roam-about," came. It would be her one good meal of the week. Dodger Wright came. He lived in a beat-up log cabin down in the swale. By Lightnin' Cross came. He lived alone with Tinker, his cat. And Injun Jack, who did odd jobs and slept in a barn, was there. Oliver Barnet came. He lived in a little shack by the side of the road. It was rumored little girls weren't safe around him, but we never saw anything out of the way with him. And Russ Hart was there. He was supposed to work for Mim, but I never saw him do anything but sit around and pare his fingernails. And Finn Litchfield would take a day off from working in the woods. He would bring his brother Elmer, if

Russe Hart.

Elmer was sober (very rarely). Finn would get someone to help him with Elmer as he was too fat to walk alone. And Ernest, my good friend Ernest, would skip in just before dinner, all smiles and happy as ever. Because Ernest never drank, the men would give him dimes and quarters to get presents for Mim, Bub and me. When Ernest got the money all together, he'd go down to Ticonderoga and get bedroom slippers for Mim, a little doll for me and a small iron truck for Bubby. How important he was when he sneaked those things under the tree for us! He thought we didn't see him. Ha!

And Charlie Fox came. He wouldn't eat our food, though. He said, "It's tainted with salt, and God knows what else." He said it was getting so you couldn't find anything grown in good old cow manure anymore. He always brought his own dinner of smoked venison, wild cranberry sauce and sourdough biscuits, and he always brought so much that everyone could have all they wanted of Charlie's goodies. No one loved his fare more than me.

And each year, two or three more people would come. However, there was one rule that had to be followed. No one was allowed in drunk. Mim had let that be known and, unbelievably, the men were all for it. No matter how drunk they were the night before, come 11 a.m. Christmas morning (the time to come to "Mim and the kids' house"), they were all washed up, shaved and cold sober, or they didn't show. They always showed.

After our feast, every year a different guest told the story of Jesus's birth. Everyone had a different version of all that had happened that night, but every story ended up the same—brotherly love and peace on earth. We sang hymns. Ernest twanged along on his Jew's harp. We were a motley crew, but never a more sincere bunch kept Christmas.

On the tree, which was mostly decorated with popcorn strings and clumps of wintergreen berries, we had placed the presents for our guests. Each person got a nice big white handkerchief that Bub and I had wrapped for them. That was all we could get enough money together for, but each year the handkerchiefs were greeted with much fuss, and "you shouldn't have done its" by the men.

55

One Christmas, Eddie Duval came drunk as a coot. His family was always kicking him out because he wouldn't work. He just laid around. The minute he came in the door, a couple of the guys picked him up and set him out on the doorstep. Then he got a crying jag on and sat there, blubbering. Mim couldn't stand it, so she loaded up a plate, and I took it out to him. I also took him his present. He was completely dejected because he couldn't come in, but that was out of the question. The next Christmas, guess who was the first one knocking on our door, and sober as a peacock? Eddie Duval.

Every Christmas night, at about 8 p.m., the men would get ready to leave and would thank us profoundly for a nice Christmas. They would walk out like a bunch of church deacons. By 9 p.m., all but Ernest and Charlie Fox would be drunk up at Elmer's house. By 1 a.m., they would have left Elmer's and were sleeping by the side of the road, or in a handy barn, too drunk to walk the mile or so to their places.

But it didn't matter to them. They had kept Christmas with Mim, Bub and me.

The Day I Had Charge

Clayton spun the old Dodge into the yard on two wheels. He jumped out and hollered, "Yada, where's Mim?" Mim had gone to Ti to see the doctor and had taken Bubby with her. She had left me in charge. I had nothing really to do but feed the chickens and stay home until she got back. Clayton said, "The liquor inspector is coming. He's 'boiled up' (his car overheated and it needed water) down by Oliver Barnet's place, so you only have about 30 minutes or so before he's here. Go, get out of here!" And away he went in a cloud of dust to warn the other people on up the road.

For a minute I panicked, but Mim had left me in charge, hadn't she? There was nothing in the house, thank goodness. The gin had all been bottled and put out on the line yesterday. The line was a row of bushes about five hundred feet long that extended from the back of our house down to the state line, in back of our acre. The line was mostly chokecherry trees, pussy willows and poplars. This junk bush had grown up along the rusty old wire fence that separated Wright's land from ours. It looked impregnable, but in certain spots, if you got down on your hands and knees, you could crawl under the brush. In these spots, there were dug-out hollows in the earth. These hollows were always covered with leaves, but you could spot them along the fence, if you knew what you were looking for. In each spot, there were two or three clear glass pint bottles filled with gin, which had been cut with water. Now this gin wasn't bathtub stuff. Only the lowest members of the bootleg class sold that. This was right out of Canada, which is another story for another day. Mim's stuff was hard liquor, the possession of which made the government very mad in those days. The inspector had caught wind of something, and he was heading our way.

I knew there were twenty bottles hidden along the line. I knew because I had counted them around dusk the night before for something to do. Mim didn't know that I knew anything about gin, but mothers are the last to know what their kids know. I probably knew as much about her business as she did. Without changing the expression on my face, I never missed a thing that went on in our family. But if you act innocent and never let on, no one ever suspects.

Anyway, I knew it was up to me. Starting in back of the house, I gathered those bottles, three or four at a time, and ran like mad, placing them just over the back fence onto state land. I knew that even if the inspector found them, as long as they were on state land, he couldn't prove it was our liquor. When I had all the bottles gathered up, I scrambled around and covered them with anything handy—leaves, flat stones, pig mud, and sticks. I made it look as natural as possible in the short time I had.

Then I ran back up the path over to the right side of the knoll where the homebrew was kept. It was in a twenty-gallon crock in a hole in the ground. It was really starting to work—lots of froth was on top of it, and big puffed-up raisins were dunking up and down, ready to pop. I was going to try somehow to empty it or break it, but it was too late. I could hear the liquor inspector's car chugging up the last part of the hill. I only had time to run around the other side of the house. I wiped my sweaty face on the bottom of my dress, and was innocently feeding my rabbit when the inspector and sheriff pulled into the yard.

The inspector called, "Little girl, where's your mother?" I said she was very sick and had gone to Ti to see Dr. Cummings. The inspector looked sort of crestfallen and turned to the trooper for verification. Mim and the trooper were good friends. He knew that Mim had been sick lately, so he said that I was probably telling the truth. I knew that the trooper was one of Mim's best customers. I knew he liked the quality of Mim's stuff and that she only charged fifty cents a pint. And I knew that the trooper didn't want to be there, but it was his job. The law is the law.

I said, "Can I help you, sir?" I decided not to know that the inspector was an inspector. He said, "Ahh, ahh . . ." He was looking at me, and I looked right back at him with big round eyes. How could he tell me that my sick mother was suspected of bootlegging? He probably had a kid my age at home, so he just said, "We want to take a little walk." I grabbed my old skip rope, and out back of the house we went. He poked around the back door for a while, then we walked along, but the inspector poked every little way under the bushes. I skipped rope along between each poke. Then I would wait politely while the inspector dug around. There was a loose leaf here, and a broken twig there that didn't look quite natural, but I didn't have much time to straighten things up when I removed the gin. But no matter, there was nothing anywhere to prove anything.

Me, Clayton, Bubby. Clayton let me know the "liquor inspector" was coming.

We got down to the back fence, and the inspector stood staring over it. I could see the spot where the bottles were. It looked fairly good for the time I had to fix it up. I skipped back and forth up the path a few feet, then back down to the fence again while I waited for the inspector to make up his mind. If he found the liquor now, I would act like I never saw it before in my life. Finally, the inspector decided there was no liquor around and went back up the path.

Oh, no! The smell of yeast was strong in the air, and out of the corner of my eye I could see foam, potato peelings, and fat exploded raisins seeping out from under the bushes on the knoll. I hadn't had time to stir it up, and now the homebrew was over the side of the crock, running away.

The inspector stopped. He sniffed the air and looked toward the knoll. He said, "What's that?" I said, "Sauerkraut." His mouth flew open and he said, as if he couldn't believe his ears, "What?" I said, "We're making sauerkraut." He knew, but don't ever tell me G-men don't have hearts. He just said, "Oh," and then, "Come on" to the trooper. As they drove out of the yard, the inspector waved and called back, "Goodbye, Little Sauerkraut." Sure, he knew, but they were in a hurry trying to catch Canadian goods that day.

I could hear their car chug-chugging down Chilson Hill for a long time after they disappeared from view. But I waited to hear through the grapevine that they were really gone for good. At last, Clayton rattled up in his old Dodge. He yelled out, "It's okay, Yada. I met them going across Ti flats. They're gone!" As he rolled on, I was already hustling down the line to my cache of liquor. I worked like a beaver putting every bottle back under the bushes where I had found them. I rushed over to the homebrew and stirred it up, picking up all the fruit and peelings on the ground.

I was feeding the chickens when Mim and Bub drove up in our beat-up Ford. Mim hugged me and asked, "Is everything okay? Did anything happen while we were gone?" I nonchalantly said, "No. What are we going to have for supper?"

After all, there are things you don't tell sick mothers.

Making the Run

One morning Mim was getting ready for work. Cowboy was getting ready to go pick up "the stock" over the border. Bub and I were ready to leave for school when Clarence Wright came in. He said there was no school because the bus had broken down. What to do? Mim had to go to work. Aunt Ann was depending on her to open up the restaurant over in Schroon that morning. So Cowboy said he'd stay with us kids and pick up "the stock" the next day. Mim said okay and very trustingly left for work. She wouldn't get home until very late in the evening.

Then Cowboy remembered the next day was Saturday and everything was closed up over the weekend in Canada. No pickup of stock anywhere. Cowboy was pacing in the kitchen, frustrated and stewing.

Bubby said, "Take us with you." Cowboy said, "Oh, I can't do that." He had never been caught "making the run," but a couple of his friends had and ended up in jail. Bubby started jumping up and down and hollering, "Take us! Take us! Take us!" over and over. I knew we shouldn't go. I knew Mim would be mad. I was scared to go, but I couldn't stay alone. Cowboy wouldn't let me. And so we took off.

The trip into Canada was uneventful. The big old car purred along. We went by the main road up through Rouses Point. When the guards at the border asked Cowboy where we were going, he said we were going to visit a friend of his and that we were his kids. Bubby looked surprised. I was ready to clobber him if he said anything, but he didn't. The guards looked us over good and looked in the trunk. But they were careless. I think two kids in the car threw them off. Thank God they didn't look underneath the car or we'd probably still be in jail. It was all built up with slides underneath to shove in cases of liquor and then bolt them in. Nothing showed outside the car. A very clever job. Cowboy was a carpenter by trade, and he knew how to build things. Finally, we were allowed to pass over the border and we were off.

I don't know where we went, somewhere this side of Montreal. There was a big old barn. Its door opened up, we drove in, and the door closed behind us. Two gruff-looking men asked Cowboy how much he wanted. He said four cases. He gave them money, and they shoved the cases up under the car and bolted them down. The men opened the barn door and looked carefully all around. Then one said, "Okay, get the hell out of here."

Cowboy backed the old car out and the barn door was slammed behind us. I knew we were now "hot," and we were on our own.

Cowboy went down the road a piece and then cut quickly off on a dirt road. I knew it was not straight over the border this time. The guards checked cars better when they were coming back to the United States from Canada. If they were going to find liquor, it would be coming from Canada, not going there. We were sitting ducks.

Suddenly, I stopped being afraid. Suddenly, I was excited that we had to get through the "special bootlegging" troopers somehow. We whirled off onto another dirt road. Cowboy knew every trail, cow path and road between Chilson and Canada.

I don't know where we came back over the border. I think it was when we went down through a field and onto a cow path. Cowboy started blowing the horn, and by the time we got down to this old farm, a farmer had pulled out a section of his barbed wire fence. We sailed through. Cowboy threw a dollar bill out the window. The farmer waved and hustled around putting his fence back in place. We turned left on the old dirt road in front of the farm and gunned it down right to another dirt road.

That's where we met the troopers. They were parked back behind a tree. Cowboy said, "Oh my God!" and gunned the old car faster. He hollered, "Hang on, kids!" and we shot off. He cut a sharp left and roared on. The troopers were a ways behind, but we could hear them coming with their sirens screaming.

Suddenly I hollered, "Stop, Cowboy, the bridge is out!" He was so intent on steering that he hadn't looked far enough ahead to notice. We screeched to a halt on the edge of the road about twenty feet above the creek that had the broken-out bridge over it.

Cowboy backed up quickly. We couldn't go back up the road because the troopers were coming fast! Cowboy hollered again, "Hang on, kids!" and he turned along the creek and through a field. We went over big stones and between big boulders. How we made it, I don't know. The troopers fired one wild shot at us and turned around. They would cut us off down at the corners. We had to go through there. Cowboy knew what they were doing. There was nothing to do but get there before they did. The old car sputtered once when we came out of that field onto the dirt road. Cowboy said, "Damn!" and slammed the gas to the floor. The landscape was going by the windows like a blur. Bubby was yelling and having a great time.

Finally there were the corners! We beat the troopers there by a car's length and roared through. They were firing their pistols out the windows at us. One bullet came through the back

Mim, Bigness, and Cowboy's car, used for making the run.

63

window. Bubby loved that—the noise and the shattering glass. I just hung on the seat strap and thought, "This is it. I'll never see Sarie (my cat) again!"

We weren't fifty feet through the intersection when Cowboy started grinning. As long as the troopers were behind us, he knew they'd never get us now. We were tearing down the road, off onto this side logging road, then over some trail. The troopers were still sirening along behind us, but their noise was getting fainter and fainter back.

Nobody could outrun Cowboy. I was so proud of him! We ended up over back of Hague but no more troopers were around. We went down the main road right through Ticonderoga and up Chilson Hill, home. Before Mim got home, Cowboy had unloaded the car and had hidden the stock. Bub and I never said a word to her. Cowboy didn't have to tell us not to tell. He knew we wouldn't.

We made an occasional run with Cowboy after that when Mim was away working. But to my sorrow, we never again met any troopers to outrun.

Never Let the Left Hand Know

Eddie Latrell and his mother lived over the flats and around the corner from us. They lived in the woods by the side of the road in a building that Eddie built out of old rough boards. He had scrounged the boards from anyone he could.

In the front part of the building, Eddie had a store. He had painted a sign and nailed it up on his roof. It said, "Latrell's Emporium." It really set the old shack off nicely.

Now, Latrell's Emporium wasn't your usual store as Eddie never had any money to order supplies from Ticonderoga. But he had a great imagination, and you never knew what he'd have for sale.

Eddie sold worms for fishing bait and ginseng and wild horseradish. The horseradish would sear your teeth right off, but everyone ate it with their boiled potatoes.

The ladies gave him any leftover hard candy from parties. He kept it on his counter and sold it, one cent for five pieces. He sold slingshots and whistles that he had whittled. He sold big delicious puff balls that he gathered in the woods and some he grew in a little spot out back of his house.

Eddie's mother knitted socks and mittens when she could get some yarn and when her rheumatism wasn't so bad that she couldn't use her hands to knit. Her beautiful work was always hanging on a rack in the emporium. No one ever bought any as they made their own, but the socks and the mittens looked nice hanging there.

I used to sell Cloverine Salve, and Mrs. Latrell was one of my best customers. She used to warm up old cloths, put the salve on

Eddie Latrell in front of his Emporium.

them, and wrap the cloths around her middle. She said the warm salve helped her "rheumatiz" all over. She always told me to get the ten cents per can from Eddie. He never had any money, so he'd always credit the ten cents on my account in the store toward hard penny candy.

Mim always told me to give Mrs. Latrell the salve even though she didn't have any money, and Mim would pay for it. Mrs. Latrell used about one can of salve a month. When I had to send in my money to the Cloverine Company from my salve sales each month, Mim always found the ten cents for Mrs. Latrell's salve. It wasn't easy, but Mim was always helping people that way. When I drew on my account at the emporium, which was quite often, going home with a stick of hard candy in my mouth was the height of living.

Mrs. Latrell was a nice old lady but had one habit I couldn't figure out. Every time Eddie went by her, she'd whack him with her cane. He just ignored her. One day my curiosity got the better of me (being a nosy kid, I could stand just so much), and I asked her why she whacked Eddie every chance she got. She said, "I have to keep him on his toes."

Keep him on his toes? Eddie was a cripple. He was all disfigured from his hips down. One leg was shorter than the other, and he walked with a crutch. I didn't think he even knew if he had toes, much less cared. But I figured Mrs. Latrell was much, much older than me and therefore smarter. If she said Eddie had to be kept on his toes, fine with me.

Eddie could do anything, even though he was crippled. He was just a lot slower doing it. I gathered hickory nuts and I picked a lot of dandelion greens with Eddie. He made dandelion wine that he sold to the "no backbone slickers" as he called them. They were men who didn't dare drink Mim's homebrew or any of her Canadian stuff as their wives would smell it on their breath. However, "Danger Danny," as they called Eddie's potent wine, left no smell after drinking it. So the "no backbone slickers" stopped in the emporium quite often to get some Danger Danny and get a glow on.

Eddie had his selling arrangements down to a science. He had the ladies, wives of the slickers, come in the forenoon for puff balls or wild horseradish. He told them that he could only keep it fresh till noon—no ice, you know. Eddie had the men trained to come buy Danger Danny in the late afternoon. That kept the two warring forces apart.

In the afternoon, the old bachelors would gather at the emporium; the ladies didn't approve of their happy-go-lucky ways. They played craps and horseshoes and had spitting tobacco contests to see who could spit the farthest.

Eddie was awfully good to me, and he knew I never told about anything I saw at the emporium. So it was a busy part of my social life for a few years, until Yodeling Pin stopped in our house one morning. He told Mim that the emporium had burned down during the night, and Eddie and Mrs. Latrell had burned up in it.

No one knew what could have happened as it was summer and they didn't have their old wood stove going. But Sleazy Jake, who was lying across the road from the emporium, drunk, said he woke up just in time to see Mrs. Latrell through the window take one of her swipes at Eddie with her cane. She hit the kerosene lamp on the table instead. It exploded, with kerosene flying all over. Flames burst out everywhere. Sleazy was too drunk to get up to help, and Mrs. Latrell and Eddie couldn't move fast enough to get through the flames and out the door.

It sounded possible, but Sleazy was so rum-dumb all the time no one could really believe him. Anyway, Mrs. Latrell and Eddie were gone. After the trooper and everyone left, I went over and looked where the emporium had been. All that was left were ashes and an acrid smell and a big sadness in my heart.

I stood there thinking about that yesterday afternoon before Eddie died. It had been time for me to go home for supper, but I lingered on watching Eddie checking to make sure his Danger Danny was well-hidden. He kept it under the floor with a rug nailed over the trapdoor. He didn't want any of the ladies to spot it if they stopped in to buy a puff ball in the morning.

Eddie grinned when he saw me watching him. As I turned to leave, he said, "Remember, Yada, never let your left hand know what your right hand's doing." I've never forgotten his advice, which I have used more than once.

No one really knows what happened that night in the early 1930s. Some said Eddie had been murdered in a drunken brawl at his place, but it was never proven.

Mim told me to believe the first account of what happened. She said I wouldn't feel so bad that way. It was better to believe Eddie died in an accident than that someone we knew might have killed him.

Sauce on the Ceiling

One February day, a package arrived in our mailbox addressed to Bub and me from our father in New York. We opened it and there was the biggest jar of Schrafft's chocolate fudge sauce that we had ever seen. Mim said Dad must have been having lunch in Schrafft's, happened to think we might be hungry, and sent it to us. Bub and I couldn't wait to dig into that fudge sauce, but Mim said, "No, we'll keep it for something special."

Bub and I knew we'd sneak and sample it first chance we got as we watched Mim put the jar of chocolate fudge sauce on the kitchen shelf.

She looked at us, and she always knew what we were thinking, so she got Cowboy's ladder off his truck. She climbed up on the ladder and put the jar of Schrafft's chocolate fudge sauce way up on a two-by-four that stuck out from the ceiling. She climbed down and said, "Now it's safe till we want it."

No matter where you were in the kitchen, you could see that big fat jar of Schrafft's chocolate fudge sauce way up out of reach in no man's land. The more Bub and I looked at it, the more we wanted it. Bub stood on my shoulders, but alas, we still couldn't reach it.

We had no ladder as Cowboy had put it back in his truck and gone away to work with it. We thought of asking Clayton or Carl, kids who were much taller than us, to get the jar down, but we knew they'd take it and be gone with it. We'd be lucky to get a taste, so we couldn't ask them.

Bubby got a long stick and poked the jar, but it was too heavy, and the stick too weak to push the jar off the two-by-four. Good thing because the jar would have fallen to the floor

69

and broken. We knew it, but we would have lapped the sauce off the floor, that's how frustrated we were. Bub tried to lasso the jar of chocolate fudge sauce with his lariat rope. (He was into being a cowboy at that time. Tom Mix was his hero.) He did get the rope half over the jar a couple of times, but it just slid right off when he tried to pull the jar.

I put a chair up on the table, climbed up, and tried to reach the jar, but even standing on my tiptoes, I couldn't reach that jar of chocolate fudge sauce. I fell on the floor, and it's a wonder I didn't break my neck.

We were getting desperate, but no matter what we did, the big jar of chocolate fudge sauce still stood way up at the ceiling out of our reach.

One night, we whispered to Cowboy to get it for us. We said we'd only take a bite and put the jar right back. Cowboy said, "No way, kids. I like living too much."

We tried stomping on the floor to jar the chocolate fudge sauce off the two-by-four. We went out and hit the side of the house to try and shake it off the two-by-four. Nothing worked.

Finally we gave up. There was no way we could get that chocolate fudge sauce until Mim gave it to us, and we finally admitted this to each other. But every day, we continued to look up at it and drool over that jar of Schrafft's chocolate fudge sauce.

One afternoon, we came in from school. For a change, the house was warm, and a nice big supper was bubbling and stewing on the stove. Everything was slicked up, and there were even doilies on the old rocking chair. Mim was bustling around and everything was happy and light. I got the old empty feeling in my gut. When Mim did this, it meant she was going to disappear for a while.

Sure enough, the next day when we got home from school, the house was cold and deserted. The breakfast dishes were piled in the sink. The doilies had slipped off the old rocking chair onto the floor, and Mim was nowhere to be found. We knew we were on our own again for a few days until Mim got back, but we knew she loved us. For there, in the middle of the kitchen table, was the big jar of Schrafft's chocolate fudge sauce right where we could reach it.

My First Symphony

It was getting near time for school to start. Bub and I didn't have any shoes. We didn't need them in the summertime as we went barefoot, but for school, you had to have shoes, and Mim had saved up one dollar to get them.

We got a ride down to Ticonderoga on the mail stage. We got off in front of Pearl's Department Store. Mim told Mrs. Pearl what we wanted. Mrs. Pearl measured our bare feet and then started pulling out boxes. Mim looked at the shoes and kept saying she didn't like them or that they "wouldn't hold up." Mim was really skimming the prices on the side of the boxes; $1.50 for this pair, or $2 for that pair. No wonder they wouldn't do!

Mrs. Pearl pulled out a dilapidated box with $.50 written on the side. Inside was a pair of patent leather shoes, black and shiny, my dream come true. I tried to put them on, but no dice, my sprawled-out bare feet wouldn't fit.

Mim grabbed Bubby and tried them on him. He might have squawked when he saw them, but he was so busy ogling the BB guns hanging on the wall that he never even looked at them. They fit him, and Mim said we'd take them. Now we had to find some for me.

There was a little table with some beat-up shoes thrown on it. Mrs. Pearl said, "Come look over here." She pulled a scuffed-up-looking pair of Buster Browns out of the pile—sturdy, but horrible to a little girl dreaming of sparkling dancing shoes. Mim said, "Try them on." I didn't protest because I saw the price sticker on the sole of one shoe—$.75. I figured we couldn't buy them anyway. They fit me. Then to my horror, Mrs. Pearl said,

"I was just about to mark them down. They're now fifty cents."
Mim grabbed them. My dreams of beautiful dancing shoes went
up in smoke.

We left Ticonderoga and started walking up Chilson Hill. We
lucked out because along came Yodeling Pin Oscier in his old
touring car. He stopped, picked us up, and gave us a ride home.
We only "boiled up" twice before we got there.

Bubby wanted to show off our shoes. I didn't, but for Mim's
sake, I pretended I did. I knew she had done the best she could
to get us shoes.

In the afternoon, we went over to the Wrights and bragged
about our shoes to Clarence. He wasn't too impressed. He said
he already had his shoes for school, and he showed them to us.
They were heavy work boots. My shoes didn't seem quite as bad
when I looked at them. We went home and had our supper of
cornmeal mush and wild raspberries.

It was getting close to dusk, but we still had time to get
home before dark, if we hurried, as we wanted to go to the Covells so they could admire our shoes.

The Covells had gone somewhere. Bub and I waited on their
stoop a few minutes. Then we decided we might as well go
home. We started back over the road. On the right side was a
small sand pit that belonged to the "state road people." They
drew sand out of there as they needed it for road repairs. There
was an uneasy silence hanging over the pit, like something was
about to happen. I don't know what possessed Bub and me, but
we took hold of each other's hands and walked into the sand pit.
There were two or three inches of water on the ground in the
pit, and it got deeper as we walked in farther. The water came
up over our shoes, and then up over our ankles, but we didn't
notice or care. There was something holding the air very still, I
don't know what, but Bub and I stood there holding hands and
waiting.

Then very softly and slowly, toads started to twill and croak
and bellow. The voices of toads swelled and echoed through the
sand pit. There must have been thousands of them gathered
there.

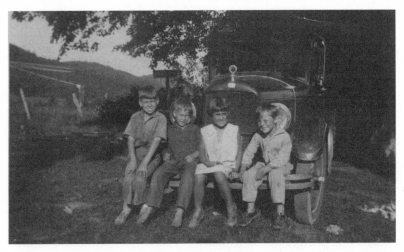

Clarence, Francis, me in my Buster Browns, and Bub in his patent leathers.

The different voices went from very high-pitched to very low. All together, it was deafening, eerie, as the sound swelled louder and louder around us. We couldn't move for five minutes, just stood there mesmerized. The toads' voices were blended into a song that was weird, wild and beautiful. Then it stopped abruptly—pure silence.

Bub and I tiptoed out of there and went home. We left our sad water-soaked shoes by the back door and went in.

Mim didn't scold us when she saw our shoes the next morning. She straightened them out the best she could. She said there was nothing she could do. We would have to wear them. Some of Bubby's black patent leather had peeled off. My Buster Browns pinched my feet from then on, and the soles were never quite flat again.

It didn't matter. The "Symphony of the Toads" had been worth it.

Old Beets

Lolly and Herm (Old Beets) lived back in the woods in Pink Paradise. I don't know whose land they were on, but they squatted there on the half-acre they had cleared in the middle of the forest.

Old Beets scratched out a garden plot on which he had little success growing vegetables, except beets. So he grew many beets in long rows. He said beets contained a lot of iron, and you had to get your iron. He centered all his meals around beets. All the food Lolly and Old Beets ate was cooked with beets in it, or in the red-colored water the beets had been cooked in.

Lolly went along with him on this. When I got a chance, being a very nosy kid, I asked her about it. She told me, "Oh, it keeps him shut up and don't hurt nobody. It ain't no big deal." All the time she'd be buttering up a slice of pink homemade bread with pink homemade butter on it and handing it to me. Lolly made sense to my way of thinking, and Pink Paradise was one of my favorite places in Chilson's 1930s world.

Old Beets would come out to Lonson's store once in a while to trade beets for flour and sugar. He'd stop at our place to trade some beets for some of Mim's homebrew. He would be huffing over carrying his knapsack full of beets. It was hard for him as he was 80 years old if he was a day.

Mim always had me carry his knapsack home for him. Old Beets would fuss and complain, "I don't want to be no bother, me," but he'd give in and I'd carry his supplies home, with him puffing along behind me.

One summer day, Ella D. and I didn't have anything else to do, so we decided to go visit Lolly and Old Beets. They always had a batch of kittens we could play with, or a puppy or two.

We got there about 3 p.m. and spent a couple of hours playing with the animals. Time went fast, and it was suppertime before we knew it. Lolly had supper on the table. She said she'd set two places for us, and she wouldn't take no for an answer. Ella D. whispered to me, "I'm not eating any pink puke," but still she walked with me to the table.

Lolly had cooked one of their old chickens and made dumplings and gravy. The dumplings were bright red, swimming in pink gravy. The chicken was pinkish with bright red spots where the beet coloring had soaked in deeper. The bread and butter were their usual pink tinge. The mashed potatoes were pink, and there were boiled beets, pickled beets and beet hash. All that was white was the milk, which was in a pink pitcher with big red roses on it—a nice touch.

That table was a beautiful sight to behold in every shade, from pink to red. Ella looked at it in amazement. It was okay until it hit her that she was supposed to eat it. Old Beets was already cramming it in. Between gulps, he managed, "Come on, kids, and get your iron." I looked at Ella. She turned pink just like the table, and she kept swallowing hard. I think it was the red-spotted chicken that did it. She started panting and croaked out, "I gotta go." I heard her gagging quite a ways down the path as she ran for home.

Now Ella and I were two different stories. Ella's father worked in the pulp mill down in Ticonderoga. He made enough money so they ate three squares a day. I was lucky to get one square meal a week—at the best, cod fish gravy over potatoes—and this was chicken. I had never seen anything like it, but it smelled like chicken! I sat down.

Lolly heaped my plate full while I kept my eyes on the kerosene lamp hanging over the table. I took a small bite. The dumplings melted in my mouth. It didn't matter that they were bright red. The more I ate, the better it tasted, and the less pink it got. I felt sorry for Ella. She didn't know what she was missing.

Then suddenly, Lolly fell off the chair and was gasping for breath. We got her into the bedroom and onto the bed. She lay there like a little ghost. I wanted to run out and get help, but Lolly said no, she'd be better in the morning. I went out and started picking up the table. Old Beets came out and said to stop, to run along home. He said, "I'll do the dishes. I don't want to be no bother, me." Lolly died a few days later. Men had to go in and carry her out. Old Beets had tried to do it, but he didn't have the strength. He felt bad about this and kept saying, "I don't want to be no bother, me," as they took Lolly away.

The last time we were visited by Old Beets was late that fall. He stopped at our house and got his usual homebrew for beets. He said he was fine. Mim gave him a big piece of a slab of bacon, which we could ill afford to do. But that didn't matter. Mim was like that.

As usual, Mim told me to carry his knapsack home, but Old Beets said, "No, I don't want to be no bother, me." We knew he meant it. The last I saw of him, he was shuffling into the woods dragging his knapsack behind him.

That winter was very stormy and very cold. We always kept a big pot of tea simmering on the back of the stove. We could never get enough wood to keep the stove hot to keep the tea more than lukewarm. We considered this our worst hardship of the winter. With good hot tea you can stand a lot. Scrambling around to keep warm, we didn't think much about anything, including Old Beets.

Well, spring came late, but it came. The snow was four to five feet high in places, but it was beginning to melt. Dodger Wright was walking along the road near where you went into the woods to go into Pink Paradise. He noticed a big odd hump of snow. He reached down and brushed some of the snow away, and he found Old Beets. They put Old Beets in a big pine box, lifted it up onto the back of Wright's truck, and Old Beets was on his way to join Lolly.

We knew he had lain down and frozen to death out by the road so no one would have the hard job of going back into the woods to lug him out. In his mind, he had made it as easy for everyone as he could.

We knew this because Old Beets had left a note pinned to his shirt. It said, "I want to be with Lolly and I don't want to be no bother, me."

I'm sorry to say, Old Beets' "beets for iron" theory didn't catch on. I haven't eaten any pink chicken with red spots in it since those Pink Paradise days.

Ernest

Ernest was the oldest of the Lichfield boys. I first remember him when I was about six years old, and he must have been at least 80. He was a small man, quick and agile as a boy of sixteen. He was the cleanest-looking man I ever saw. His short sandy hair and moustache were always neatly trimmed and combed. His very pink complexion always looked scrubbed, and his small, very bright eyes were a very clear blue.

Ernest was always immaculately dressed, except he never wore shoes! Now, some people considered that this proved he was crazy. Not to me, it didn't. I never wore shoes, either, if I could help it.

Some people said Ernest was childish. He forgot things, and he giggled too much. That didn't bother me, either. I just figured that he was happy.

Ernest never walked—he skipped. No one took him seriously. He realized I accepted him as he was, and we became fast friends.

He always came down the hill in the early morning and would call out, "Come on, little gal," and away we'd go down to the brook or into the woods.

Some of my happiest childhood hours were spent with Ernest. He always had a smile on his face, and he showed me many wonders—where bluebirds nested on the red fence down back of Wrights' hayfield and where an old pickerel rested in the heat of the day in the pickerel grass on the edge of the river.

We called the fish "old monster," and he did look ten feet long to me. Ernest and I never threw our fish lines near him.

We seemed to have a mutual agreement. If we didn't touch the water, we could watch "old monster" all we wanted, and he would just stare back at us, unafraid.

Ernest showed me where an owl slept in the daytime and where the bats hung during the day in an old half-fallen-down chimney where a house had once been. He loved to tell stories about his home in Vermont and how he was going back "after a while."

Finn, Ernest's brother, had told me that an old family farmhouse had burned, and it had been deserted for years out in that part of the country, but Ernest never listened or believed. To him, it was still there and he was going back someday. As I listened to his stories, I always thought it was strange that he considered Vermont "home." He said he had left there when he was fifteen years old and never went back. But if that's the way he wanted it, it was okay with me. I don't know if he ever lived there or not.

Some people questioned my mother about her letting me go with "that simple old fool" into the woods. How did she know that he might not "bother" me? Mim started to talk to me, and young as I was, I understood.

"Mim, he's good to me. He's my friend." Mim hugged me and said, "I know." She always knew. So let people talk! Ernest and I were friends still. We skipped happily through the fields and over the hills for the next couple of years.

One day in our last spring together, Ernest took me over the brook and up through some poplars on a hill. We skipped down into a quiet little valley, and there were hundreds and hundreds of yellow lady slippers growing. Even then, lady slippers were rare and protected by the state. We sat down in the middle of the flowers. The sun seemed to settle around us as those beautiful yellow blossoms nodded in the slight breeze. We sat there a long time while Ernest told me stories of Vermont, of home. Every time I was with him, Ernest talked more of going home.

One morning in June, Ernest called, "Come on, little gal," and we went up past Roster Pond to a little clearing in a growth of maple trees. There in the deep grass were two adorable little fawns. They were the only twin deer I'd ever seen. I wanted to hug them. They were so cute, with big black eyes and spotted coats.

But Ernest said, "No, we must not touch them. The mother might not take care of them if the smell of humans is on her babies." So we just watched them, and he told me about the little deer he had for a pet when he was a boy. He used to put salt and hay in the apple orchard for it. After a while, many deer came to the apple orchard for food during the long Vermont winters. Ernest wondered what had happened to them after he left, and more and more he talked of going home.

Berrying time came. One morning I heard him call, "Come on, little gal," and up over the mountain we went and way back in the old clearings. There we found the biggest, most luscious blueberries I ever saw, big as the end of your thumb. We picked all day, and he told me those berries weren't anything like the whoppers that grew in Vermont. He said he'd send me some from there someday—someday when he went home.

Then came that last late summer morning. Ernest came down the hill and joined me where I was fishing at the brook by the side of the road. He looked his usual perky self—except for one thing. He was carrying his shoes slung over one shoulder.

We talked about our flowers and animals. He told some more stories about Vermont. He stressed more and more about how beautiful it was there. He seemed sad, but excited, as he talked. Finally he said, "Today is the day. Little gal, today I'm going home!"

He stood up and squeezed my hand. His small eyes looked teary instead of their happy bright blue. Then, with his usual smile, he turned and skipped down the dusty road. He waved once before he disappeared from sight over Chilson Hill.

I heard different stories now and then—that Ernest had ended up put away for good in a crazy house, that they had found him dead in an old barn by the road, that they had even locked him away in jail. I never asked Mim because I didn't want to know for sure.

For me, Ernest always skips free, down the road and over the hill, going home.

Little Coat

I loved cats. Anyone could pawn off cats on me—any size, kind or amount. In farm country, there were always plenty of cats being offered for the taking. So any cats offered to me, I took. I considered that the people who gave me the cats had done me a favor. Mim always made me lug them back where they came from. She didn't consider cats any favor.

One Sunday morning, coming home from Sunday school, I was just loafing along. I scuffed my feet on the dusty dirt road. The day was warm, and I felt so good. Summer was coming, school would be out, and there was much to be done.

Anyway, I was scuffing along, dreaming my dreams, when I heard *meow, meow* behind me. I turned around and following me was a little old cat. It was scroungy. It was dirty. Its legs bowed out. If a cat can have rickets, it had rickets. No matter, it was a cat. It swirled around my feet as I petted it.

The cat had one redeeming feature. Its coat was four different colors—brown, black, white and reddish tan. In Sunday school that morning, we had read about Joseph and his many-colored coat. So "Joseph," I said, "come home with me now," and down the road I went in seventh heaven with Joseph close behind.

I walked in the house. Mim smiled at me, and then she noticed "it" at my feet. She said, "What is that? Don't tell me, I know. Take it back." But for once I had her stumped. I couldn't take it back. It didn't have a home. It had just been there in the road.

I started to try and wiggle some tears out of my eyes, but Mim had given up at last. She sighed, "All right, you can keep this one." I spun around the kitchen and then ventured the great news, "His name is Joseph."

Mim kept slapping the dough she was getting ready to put in the pan for bread. "That cat can't be named Joseph. Boy cats are never four-colored. That cat's a girl!"

I had to think fast. "Okay, her name is Little Coat!" Mim laughed and said, "All right, but remember if she has any kittens, out they go!" I knew what "out they go" meant. It was into a paper bag and down to the brook. But I figured I'd worry about that when the time came. Little Coat was mine, all mine.

I took off my jacket and started feeding Little Coat. Bread, milk and raw hamburger, then more bread, milk and raw hamburger—could that cat ever eat! Her sides blew up like a balloon, but still she kept on eating.

This was Sunday, and every Sunday after dinner, Uncle Sharpe came over to take Mim, Bubby and me for a ride. Now, to own any car in the spring of 1934 was a big deal, but to own a big shiny new black car was really living. Uncle Sharpe owned just such a car, and he was justly proud of it. He polished it often, and he kept fresh flowers in the vases on the inside walls.

Most Sundays I couldn't wait to go for a ride in that car, but this Sunday was different. I didn't want to go. It would mean leaving Coat behind. That was a terrible thought, so I got brave and asked Mim if I could take Coat along with us. "Absolutely not!"

Well, while everyone else was busy talking and getting into the car, I sneaked into the backseat with Coat hidden under my jacket. No one noticed and Coat was very, very quiet as the beautiful shiny car sped along.

We were riding along the dirt road near Paradox when we came to the beautiful little spring of water. Most everyone in those days stopped for a drink there as they went by, and we were no exception.

We were just about to open the doors to get out when Little Coat exploded. She streaked around and around the inside of the car screaming bloody murder. I didn't blame her, though, because she was vomiting and having diarrhea at the same time.

Over Uncle Sharpe's bald head she flew, squirting from both ends. The flowers in the vases on the walls drooped as she spattered by. Over Uncle Sharpe's head she sailed again, only this time she didn't quite make it, and her claws left a long scratch in the mess on top of his bald head.

We were all yelling and hollering at once. Finally, Mim got her door open and Little Coat sailed free. She landed by the edge of the spring. She sat there looking very relieved. Why not? She had left all her troubles behind on the inside of the car and on us.

It was very quiet in the car. I didn't know where to look, so I just kept looking out my window. I saw Little Coat lift one of her paws and start licking it. She sure was a cool cat!

I sneaked a glance at Uncle Sharpe. He looked like he would suffocate. He was all purple-colored. He was trying to wipe Little Coat's mess off his head with one hand and clean off the wall beside him with a piece of newspaper in his other hand.

We all got out and Mim started to try and clean up the car. She said, "I thought I told you not to bring that cat." I thought it best not to answer that.

Finally, we had cleaned up as well as possible, and we were ready to go. I found the nerve to call, "Come here, kitty, kitty." Mim roared, "Leave that cat alone!" She said, "You have two choices. You can leave her here, or Uncle Sharpe can bash her head with a stone and that will be that."

I jumped in the car quickly. I didn't want to give Uncle Sharpe a chore he would so obviously enjoy.

As we turned around, I looked out the back window. Little Coat was already walking up the road toward a farm she had spotted. I knew she could take care of herself, but my heart stayed with her as we drove away.

Uncle Sharpe never asked us to go for a ride again on Sundays in his beautiful big shiny car. I didn't care for it myself, but I felt bad for Mim and Bubby. So much later I was happy to hear that, though Uncle Sharpe tried every cleaning fluid known, the faint odor of Little Coat lingered on, and on, and on.

About My Very Own Dog

One morning we opened our front door and a small black dog was sitting on our doorstep. We didn't know where he came from. The minute I saw him, because of the white patch on his chest, I called him Spot.

It was an especially cold part of the winter, and food wasn't too plentiful. No one seemed enthused about Spot's arrival but me. There was something about him that I loved, and he sensed it.

Spot was nice to Bubby, but he stayed close to me all the time. Mim said Spot sure belonged to me. I sneaked him some of my food, and Mim gave him whatever table scraps she could. Spot also roamed around the neighborhood eating anything that he found loose, so he fared as well as most.

Mim said Spot moped around when I was at school. About five minutes before the school bus was due, Spot would go sit on the knoll in back of the house. He was watching for the bus. When we'd come around the bend, way over on the knoll, all I could see of him was the white spot on his chest.

When the bus stopped, he'd come running to meet me. We played together until bedtime, and he slept every night at the foot of my bed.

Spring finally came. We hadn't had much meat to eat that winter, so Mim decided to plan ahead for the following year. Later that spring, she figured the answer was to get some chickens. They could scratch outdoors and feed themselves all summer and fall. Then in the winter we could eat them.

Mim had $1.50 to spend. She checked on little chicks. Baby hens were six cents apiece, but baby roosters were only three cents. Of course, she settled on the baby roosters, and fifty of them came through the mail.

Cowboy put some chicken wire around a small section of the yard and up to the house. He tacked the wire onto one side of the house. The little chicks could not get out of there. Then Cowboy cut a small hole in one bedroom wall and the little chicks could go in and out. They always came in and slept under our bed at night. When we had a thunderstorm, it was such a comfort to hear those little chicks peeping away as we fell asleep.

We fed the little rooster chickens mash and water. They thrived, and soon they were big enough to turn out in the yard. They really scratched the fields finding their own food, but we did throw out cracked corn every evening, so they'd come home to our yard at night.

Roosters sat up in the trees and all over our house. You think one rooster crowing at 6 a.m. to wake you up is something. You ought to try fifty of them! A few people made some snide remarks about Mim's "herd of roosters." Mim didn't care. She said they were just envious. The roosters wouldn't be going into their stomachs next winter. She did say we would get baby hens the next year. They wouldn't be so noisy early in the morning, and we might get a few eggs.

We kids had another bonus. The roosters' manure was excreted in loose gray, green, and black piles. Now with fifty chickens in a yard, there are a lot of those piles. We kids always went barefoot all summer, so there was a great opportunity to have an interesting contest. If you plopped your foot down on the manure pile with your big toe and your second toe held just right, the manure would squirt a great distance. So we had a running race to see who could squirt the furthest. We had many a squabble over that, and it removed the monotony on lazy summer afternoons. Afterward, you could always go down and wash your feet in the brook, if you wanted to.

Now Spot watched all this. He would sit and growl softly at the roosters. I think he was jealous of them and considered them to be trespassing on his territory.

One day, a rooster was found dead and half-eaten. In a few days another chicken was found mauled and dead, then another and another. Mim was very upset. What was doing it?

Me, Bub, and Spot, my very own dog.

A raccoon? A weasel? Finally, my darling Spot was careless and got caught in the act killing a chicken.

Mim said Spot had to go. I begged to keep him, and at last, Mim said I could, if he were tied up. I tied him out by the old elm tree and begged him not to kill any more chickens. He hated those roosters, and I knew he enjoyed getting rid of them.

Spot stood being tied up for about a week, then he had had enough. He chewed the rope that tied him in two pieces. He went right for the roosters and killed four of them to make up for lost time. Mim discovered what he was doing too late.

When I came home, Mim was tying him up again. She said he had to go this time for sure. I didn't say anything. When something was killing off your winter food, there was nothing to say. If we didn't have those chickens, we would be a lot hungrier next winter. It was survival.

Just the same, I thought Mim might forget and Spot could stay. But next day when I came home from school, Spot was gone. Mim said she gave him to a man who wanted a dog, and he would give Spot a good home. Besides, the man didn't have any chickens, so Spot would be free from temptation.

I knew Spot was gone all right, gone in a hole in the ground somewhere. Nobody would want a chicken-killing dog but me. I never asked any more questions because, in my secret heart, I hoped that Mim might just be telling me the truth. Maybe Spot would run away and come home.

For a long time after that, every afternoon coming home around the bend, I looked out the bus window toward the knoll. Hopefully, the little white spot would be sitting there. Of course, it never was.

The chickens did help us from going hungry that winter. I relished eating them. I knew Spot would be happy. For me, every rooster cooked was a blow struck for him, my very own dog.

Cousin Henry and Strawberries

Cousin Henry was a couple of years older than me, so he'd always been part of our family as far as I was concerned. We thought he was "not all there," but it was just because he was stone deaf that he did things differently from us. He could not hear us, so, of course, he could not talk, only scream like a fire engine when he didn't like what was going on. We thought he was just "hollerin' dumb," but I realize now he was just so frustrated trying to communicate. Even the grownups didn't realize it. We were the dumb ones, not Henry.

Henry loved grasshoppers. He would take a cardboard box and spend all day out in the dirt road catching them. Cars would come up behind him and toot and toot, until one of us came out and got Cousin Henry out of the road. That always made him mad, and he'd go streaking up a pine tree and sit at the top, screaming. It looked so easy, sometimes I'd rush over and try to go up the tree like he did, but I could just about get off the ground. I really envied him being able to do that.

When he could, Henry outshined us. We kids had the job of picking potato bugs off the potato plants. We didn't have any pesticides in those days. You could probably buy them, but we couldn't afford them anyway. We called the potato bugs "potats." We also had to gather the plums off the few trees when they were ripe, another job we hated. Now Henry seemed to sense that we hated those two jobs, so he could get our attention and pats on the back when he did those chores. He had the fastest hands I ever saw, and he could beat any kid for miles around picking potats and plucking plumbs.

Now we could laugh at Cousin Henry, or play little jokes on him, but no one was allowed to physically hurt him in any way. We ran a loose ship on the farm, but there was one ironclad rule—no one was to hurt Cousin Henry. That was okay with us kids because we loved him, and we would never let anyone hurt him if we could help it.

When strawberry time came, we kept track of Mr. Bernard's big patch that he grew down over the hill from us. We kids knew when the berries were ripe because we could smell the scent of them wafting up the hill on the breeze.

After supper, we youngsters (cousins, neighbors), about six of us, would put on our swimsuits. The grownups thought we were going down to the creek for a swim, but first we'd swing around to Mr. Bernard's strawberry patch for a snack. It would be about dusk. Mr. Bernard was wise to us, but he had to milk his cows, and when we saw his lantern's light coming through the window of the barn, we knew he was milking.

But he caught us quite frequently, and he'd holler and rave and come after us with a pitchfork in his hands. I don't know what he would have done with that pitchfork if he'd caught us, but we never stayed to find out. We were under the fence and away before he got to us.

When all you have is lumpy cold cornmeal mush for supper most nights, nothing is going to keep you from having a few luscious, sweet strawberries for dessert, so we braved Mr. Bernard's wrath.

Once, he let his bull out in the field to come after us. For a couple of days after that, we stayed away and gave him a chance to calm down. Then we were right back at his strawberries. We figured he wouldn't sic the bull on us again as he had torn up a few of the strawberry plants when he was out to get us.

We never took Cousin Henry with us to the strawberry patch, but one evening we did. The grownups had gone to Ticonderoga, and we were taking care of Henry. We sat him in the woods behind the fence. He stayed there and watched. When we finished our strawberry repast, we brought him some and he squashed them into his mouth. You could see the delight on his face as he ate them. He ended up happy with his face all stained with red strawberry juice around his mouth. For some reason, Mr. Bernard didn't see us that evening. Maybe he'd gone to Ticonderoga too.

A couple of evenings later, we had our swimsuits on ready to take our detour through the strawberries to the creek when we heard Cousin Henry screaming, coming up the back path. His nose was bleeding and there was a big whack mark on his cheek. His shirt was torn, and his shoulder was getting black and blue. Someone had whopped him good.

Cousin Henry was so terrified that he ran in and crawled under his bed, and we had some time pulling him out so we could fix him up. The adults were boiling mad. They kept asking us if anyone had hurt us, or if we'd seen anyone strange around. Of course, we couldn't say anything. They'd keep asking us questions, and they'd find out about our strawberry thefts and our taking Cousin Henry there. There would have been hell to pay, especially on the seat of our pants. But we knew who did it, and what happened, because Henry's mouth was all red strawberry juice-stained.

Mr. Bernard came up to the farm the next day to borrow some all-purpose crates from Grandpa. Mr. Bernard was bragging about his great crop of strawberries and how the next day they'd be just right for picking, and he was going to make a big profit off them.

Grandpa asked him if he saw any stranger around and told him how Cousin Henry got beat up. Mr. Bernard looked amazed and couldn't imagine who would do such a thing to him. We knew, and the old liar was going to pay. If Mr. Bernard had caught one of us kids and whopped us good, it would have been fair and square, but no one hurt Cousin Henry, no matter what he did.

That evening, we went down to the strawberry patch, determined to eat every strawberry in sight. We ate our fill, but it didn't make a dent in those strawberries. We had to do something else to get even with Mr. Bernard, and we only had that evening to do it.

We saw the lantern light in the barn window shift. We scurried back in the woods at the end of the strawberry patch and waited for it to get a little darker. Finally, we could just make out the rows of strawberries, but it was dark enough so Mr. Bernard couldn't see us from his house if he looked our way.

We each took a row of strawberries. We lay down and rolled the whole row down. Then we rolled back over it the other way. There being six of us, it didn't take too long to flatten the twelve or fourteen rows of berries. Then we were off to the brook to scrub ourselves stark clean of telltale strawberries, juice and stains. Later on that night, it rained, and what strawberries we hadn't got were covered with mud and ruined when they lay on the ground; also any foot tracks were destroyed.

The next morning we heard a commotion out in the yard. It was Mr. Bernard, all excited. He had his shotgun with him, and he said something awful was loose in the woods, come and see what it had done!

The men climbed in the Wrights' truck, and they went to check out the strawberry patch. Monty Hall, the oldest of the lot—he was ninety-two if he was a day—said in all his life he'd never seen anything like the mess in that strawberry patch; nothing human ever did that!

The men were all jittery. When they got home, they each checked and cleaned their guns. Grandpa scoffed at "the wild beast nonsense" as he called it, but I noticed he checked his shotgun too.

Not one man really wanted to go, but they couldn't admit it, so they went into the woods and made a show of looking for "the monster."

Clarence (who was old enough to go with them, but young enough to be in our group that flattened the berries) told me that he'd never seen anything like it. The men were very jumpy, and if a leaf fell, they'd turn or jump around and aim their guns at it. They sneaked around and wouldn't walk last in their line, which was strung out searching for "the monster." Clarence volunteered to be last in line. They couldn't believe how brave he was. Of course, they didn't know why he willingly walked behind—he knew who "the monster" was.

For about a month, we kids watched the men and how they shied away from the woods. We began to think maybe there was "something out there." Even today, for all I know, that monster could still be wandering the woods of Chilson. No one ever did catch it.

Junior, Little Boy Lost

A house was being built in the field between the Covells' and our house. Bub and I watched them build it. It didn't take too long, and soon Joe, Effie and Junior Oscier moved in.

Junior was about my age, maybe a year older. He was a very pale blond little boy with freckles. He was very quiet, different from Bub and Clarence and all the other kids I knew. They were always roughnecking, wrassling around, or playing cowboys and Indians. Junior never did any of that, so though the kids were nice to him, they never bothered with him much. He was too quiet for them. Now I was a real tomboy. I played as rough as any kid around, but there was something about Junior. He was polite, and he treated me like a girl, not just somebody to wrassle around with. That intrigued me, so once a week or so, I'd go over and play with him.

Junior had a brown-and-white bird dog named Lindy. Lindy was very old, and he had long floppy ears and big feet. He was always with Junior. He never let Junior out of his sight if he could help it. Junior had a little wagon with stake sides on it and a harness. He would hitch Lindy to the wagon and we'd go round and round the field. I can still hear Junior as he hitched up Lindy: "Okay, Lindy, now back up just a hair." Lindy would slowly push his rear up to the wagon, and Junior would hook him up. Sometimes Junior and I would take turns riding on the wagon, but the one who wasn't riding would always push so it wouldn't be too hard for Lindy. He was awfully old.

We had a playhouse too, in the middle of the field. Well, it was really only a spot where we had stomped down the grass. We had a big stone for a table and little stones for chairs. We pretended we lived there, and Lindy was our horse. It was our farm. We pretended we were two cowboys living there. We couldn't pretend we were a farmer and his wife because Junior said he couldn't marry me because he was Catholic. I didn't know what that had to do with anything, but no matter, Junior, Lindy and I played together happily many a long summer afternoon.

Once, when we were playing, it started to rain, so I asked Junior over to my house to play cards. He said he couldn't come in my house. I said, "Why not?" He said because he was a Catholic.

I went home and asked Mim what that meant. She said Junior couldn't come in our house because Catholics believed different. So I asked, "Could I go in his house?" She said, "Yes." And I asked, "How come?" She said, "Because we are Methodists, and we believe different." So I asked, "Do we believe anything alike?" She said, "Yes, we're all Christians." I gave up. It was beyond me.

Then one day, Junior got very sick. His parents took him to Ti to see Dr. Cummings. He stayed in the hospital for a few days. Dr. Cummings said it was very important that Junior have an operation as he had appendicitis. Effie said, "No." No one was operating on her son, and they brought Junior home, still sick.

Mim was awfully worried. She made up her mind. She was going to talk to Effie. Mim, with me skipping along at her side, went over to the Osciers' house and knocked at the door. Effie opened it, and they started talking. After a minute, Mim said, "Effie, Dr. Cummings knows what he's doing. If he says Junior needs an operation, please let him have it." Effie looked mad. She said, "No one is cutting into my child. Father Smith is coming tonight to pray, so I have to get ready. Goodbye," and she slammed the door in our faces.

We walked slowly home. Tears were running down Mim's cheeks. I asked, "Will the priest make Junior better?" Mim said, "No. Junior has to have an operation or he could . . ." She stopped what she was saying. I asked, "Or he could what, Mim?" She didn't answer, just went into the house.

I looked over at the Covells'. Junior was sitting on the steps with Lindy close at his feet. (The Covells were Junior's grandparents.) I decided to go over and see how Junior was doing.

When I got there, I asked him to come and play house or hitch up Lindy, and we'd go round the field. He shook his head listlessly, and I knew he didn't even feel like talking. He looked so pale, worn-looking, and sad. I tried to sound cheerful as I said, "Okay, then, maybe tomorrow." He nodded his head slightly, and I walked away.

After a few steps, I turned and looked back at them. Junior looked like a little ghost sitting there. I had an odd feeling that, even though I could see him, he was gone. It was scary. I ran home fast.

The next day Mim told me that Junior had died early that morning. They had rushed him to Ticonderoga Hospital, but it was too late. His appendix had burst and he was dead. The neighborhood seemed very quiet and gloomy. I saw Lindy lying by Junior's little wagon out back of their house. I went over and petted him. His tail moved slightly, but he never lifted his head from the ground. That dog knew Junior was dead. Lindy wouldn't eat, and he never moved from that spot. Old Lindy just lay there and died of a broken heart.

Mim took a cake over to the Osciers' for the wake. What could I do? Then I knew. I picked some buttercups. They were Junior's favorites. I put the buttercups in my jacket pocket. I'd drop them on Junior's coffin when we said goodbye at the grave. I knew Junior would like that.

We, Junior's classmates, went on the school bus to the funeral. It was in a big stone church. A person stopped us as we started up the aisle. We had to sit way in the back of the church because we were Protestants.

We could see Junior's coffin way up front, and the priest and his assistants were walking round and round.

The priest was talking in Latin, and once he held up a silver cup. All I could think of was Junior being up there. Everything looked so stark and cold. I wanted to run up and tell Junior that I loved him.

Then the priest walked round and round Junior's coffin, swinging a container of incense. The smell filtered back to us, and it made me feel suffocated. To this day, I can't stand the smell of incense.

Finally it was over and they wheeled Junior's coffin down the aisle and out a side door. I jumped up quickly to follow. I wanted to be with Junior to the end, and I still had to place the buttercups on top of his coffin.

As I hurried toward the door, someone grabbed me and asked, "Where do you think you are going?" I said, "With Junior." Then someone said, "Oh, no, you're not. You can't go through the cemetery gate. He's going into blessed ground." Blessed ground? I was only a little kid. I didn't understand. I only wanted to say a very last goodbye to Junior. But I could only stand there, sobbing outside the gate, as Junior disappeared from sight.

So, Junior, if you can hear me, I want you to know, they could stop me from sitting close beside you in church, and they could stop me from following you to the blessed ground, but no one could stop me from keeping you in my heart. It's more than seventy-five years later, and you're still there.

At Last We Got a Car

Mim had somehow saved enough money for a car. There was only one secondhand dealer in Ticonderoga, at least that we could afford. He was Double-Talking Charlie, and his place of business was just below Chilson Hill, this side of Ticonderoga. Need it be said, Charlie was a slick operator. Once he made a sale, that was that. Charlie never took a car back or made a bad car good. With him, you never won. Of course, Mim knew this, but it was deal with him or go without.

Charlie's place was four miles from home, and we would have to walk. It didn't matter as most of the way was downhill, and we would have a new car to ride home in. Mim made a picnic lunch. We would stop halfway down the hill by the spring and eat.

It was a warm sunny morning, and we were so happy. What a festive affair was ahead! Each of us took our share of lunch to carry, and we sang as we strolled over the top of the hill. We reached the spring, and we had a great time eating our lunch. Bubby would have taken a nap, but Mim said we'd better keep going as we still had two miles to go. She wanted to get "our car" and be home early.

Finally we reached Double-Talking Charlie's. We weren't as jaunty a threesome as had started out four miles before. But soon we forgot our sore feet as we began to look over the cars Charlie had for sale. There weren't many, and they weren't too swift-looking, either. Mim kept returning to one little coupe with a rumble seat. It was small but it was shiny. Someone had outdone themselves buffing that car. It was set up on a low platform where the first sucker who came along couldn't miss it, and we were right there. Boy, were we there! The tag read $85. Now Mim only had $65. I'd seen her counting it.

Charlie came out. Mim played it cool. She looked at two or three other cars while Charlie bragged them up. But Mim's eyes kept turning back to that little coupe. After a few minutes, Mim walked over that way and said, "How much for this little car? I didn't see it before." Charlie said, "$85." Mim said, "How many miles on it?" Charlie was very vague—in fact, extremely vague—on all these points, but it didn't matter. Mim had decided that was her car when she first saw it. She said, "I'll give you $65 down and have to owe you $20." Charlie snapped, "I'll take it," so fast that it should have put Mim on guard, but she was too much in love with her car to notice. She signed a paper while Bubby and I climbed into the rumble seat. Then Mim sat down in the front seat and tried to start the car. At first, the car only made a funny noise, but after a few tries, Mim got it started. The car backfired, there were clicking noises in the motor, and something rumbled now and then. However, the car slowly moved off the platform and onto the road. Charlie waved a cheerful goodbye from his yard, then disappeared into his garage, fast. We got across the flat with only a couple of backfires, then we started up the hill.

I was in seventh heaven. I always wanted a puff-sleeved dress, a baby goat and a car with a rumble seat. I never got the puff-sleeved dress, I never got a baby goat, but here I was in our very own rumble seat. Joy! Joy! Joy!

We ground along. After the first grade, something began to happen. The car started wheezing and coughing. Steam came out the front. Mim stopped by the spring to let the car cool off. Then she went back and forth, back and forth, filling the radiator with the dipper from the spring. When it was full she said, "There, guess that was all it needed, a little water."

The car groaned and belched along. We had to stop at two different houses along the way to get more water. At last! The last grade of the hill! By this time, "Car" was making funny whining noises. A banging backfire had become very frequent. Add these to the *clickety-click* and the *rumble, rumble* in the motor and you could hear us coming for a mile up the hill. Of course, the Wrights were out in their front yard to see what was coming. When they saw what "it" was, they broke out in cheers and howls of laughter. Mim was a little put out. She stuck her nose in the air and tried to sail us by. Well, we only lurched by, but no matter, we had a car. We turned triumphantly into our driveway. Car choked, blasted a big cloud of black smoke, and died right there. She just settled into the dust.

Mim sat there. Then she said, "We're taking this car right back, right now!" She tried to start the car. Nothing happened. Not one groan, moan or even a squeak out of that motor. It had gone to its reward. Mim said, "Okay, everybody out," and we pushed that car around and shoved it back over the road to the top of the hill. The Wrights were dying to make some remarks. What a chance to have some fun! But one look at Mim's face was enough. They kept their big fat mouths shut.

Mim said, "Get in!" Bubby and I climbed in the rumble seat again. Mim shoved the car and it started slowly moving down the hill. She jumped in the front seat, slammed the door, and we were off! We went down the first slope, rolled across the little flat, and stopped. We had to push the car across some of the flats. But the car was light and it rolled along easily.

Finally, we came to the last slope. It was a lot steeper than the other slopes. Mim was riding the brakes. The only thing that car had was brakes. It must have been an oversight on Double-Talking Charlie's part. As we flew along, you could smell the brake pads burning. Thank God they were thick. I was hanging on for dear life, but Bubby was having the time of his life. He was a mere four years old, what did he know? Two years make a lot of difference, but I felt a lot older than six when we shot over the last grade of good old Chilson Hill.

We flew over the flat and into Charlie's yard. Mim brought the car to a jerking halt about three inches short of the garage doorway. Double-Talking Charlie was standing in that doorway looking out. His mouth popped open, and his crummy old cigar fell out. He stood there frozen in shock with the smell of burned-out brakes all around him. Mim climbed out of the car and went inside the garage with me stepping on her heels. I wasn't about to miss anything.

Mim said, "Charlie, I want my money back. That car's no damn good and you know it." He said, "I don't have to give you nothing. A deal's a deal." Mim grabbed a long-handled monkey wrench and said, "Give me my money, or I'll crack your thick skull." I couldn't believe my ears. I knew Mim would never do that, but Charlie didn't.

Charlie sat down quick and said, "All I got left is $30. They delivered some gas and I paid them $35." Mim said, "Let me see." Charlie plunked open his old cash register. Sure enough, there were only three $10 bills plus a few coins. Mim scooped up the $30. She left the coins in case Charlie had to make change for someone who came in for gas. Mim was always fair. She straightened herself tall and swept out of the garage with me close behind. Bubby was taking his much-belated nap, still in the rumble seat. Mim grabbed him up and we were off once more.

It didn't matter that we still didn't have a car. It didn't matter that we were $35 light. It didn't matter that we had to trudge four miles up the hill home. Mim had gotten something back out of Double-Talking Charlie, and that was a prideful thing.

Rock of Ages

I used to love to go to church with Grandma. Any Sunday morning when I was at her house, she'd always take me along. Grandpa never went with us, even when she asked him to. I asked her once, "Why not?" She said Grandpa wasn't much of a church man, but he was an awfully good man, and going to church couldn't make him any better. Then she added quickly, "But don't tell him I said that."

One weekend, I was staying with Gram, and she made me a new dress. She measured me, cut out the cloth, and sewed it up on her Singer foot-pedal sewing machine. I loved the noise that machine made, purring along. The dress was white with a full skirt. She sewed pink rick-rack around the neck, sleeves and hem. To me, it was the loveliest dress ever.

I asked if I could wear it to church the next morning. Gram said I could, if the weather was nice. It had been raining hard for two days. Everything outdoors was wringing wet, and big puddles of water were everywhere. I went to bed praying the rain would stop so I could wear my new dress.

And lo and behold, the next morning, the sun came out to stay just before it was time to get ready for church. I could wear my pretty new dress.

The church was about a mile and a half down the hill, over the flats, up a hill, turn down another dirt road, past the cemetery and across another little flat. The little white church stood there with its brave little steeple reaching to the sky. Even when we walked through snowdrifts in the winter and we were very cold, catching sight of that little church made me feel warm all over.

That morning I skipped along beside Gram, holding her hand. She was always awfully busy on the farm. Sometimes, of an evening, she'd play checkers with me, but mostly she just worked and worked. But on those walks to church, Gram was all mine, and she talked to me and paid attention to me, and I knew she loved me. Of course, that morning I had on my new dress, so I was doubly happy and very proud.

We were walking across the flats, getting around mud puddles as best we could, when a car drove up beside us. It was some young guys on their way to church down in Ti. They knew where we were going.

Right beside us, the driver stepped on the gas hard. Mud and dirty water flew all over us. They stopped a short way down the road laughing back at us. I said, "Gram, I'm scared." She held my hand harder and said, "Just keep walking. Don't ever let bullies know you're afraid of them."

Suddenly, those guys shot off in their car, out of sight. I looked down at my ruined pretty dress, and the tears started. I said, "Is that all they're going to do to us?" Gram said, "Yes, they have to hurry or be late for mass, and if they miss that, they believe they'll go to hell for sure." I asked, "If we don't go to church, will we go to hell?" Gram said, "No, but if we believed

My favorite road—to Grandma's house.

Me and my Grandma.

Grandma Granger's house.

that, our church might be a little fuller on Sundays." And she smiled. I wanted to ask more, but we were at the church, and we went in, dirty clothes and all.

I don't remember what the preacher spoke about. I was still scared and feeling sad over my ruined pretty dress. When he finished, Mrs. Fred Moody started to play the old pump organ. It always wheezed and coughed until it finally got going, then it really could belt out the hymns.

Mrs. Fred Moody played two or three hymns, then it came time to play the last one. For that one, she always picked someone in the congregation to choose it. This time, she pointed at Grandma, who said softly, "Rock of Ages." That hymn swelled out of the old pump organ and settled all around us. I looked up at Grandma, and she smiled at me. I moved a little closer to her, and my ruined pretty dress didn't seem important anymore, and the scared feeling went away. I was with Grandma, my Rock of Ages.

And she still is my Rock of Ages, though she's been gone more than sixty years.

With Love to Our Catholics

When we got home, I was going to tell Grandpa what happened to us on our way to church, but he was out in the barn. However, some of my cousins were there, and I told them. Grandma said, "Forget it. I don't want to hear any more about it." But we kids didn't forget it, and we told some neighborhood kids too. A couple of nights later, after dark, we decided to go up to the Catholics' house and tip over their backhouse. This was a dig deal as it wasn't even Halloween.

When we got to the house, their grandmother's rocking chair was sitting on the front porch. One of the boys crept up and got it. He gave it to me and told me to throw it over the bank beside the house and be sure it broke. I just took the rocker and sat it over the bank. I didn't break it. That meant I was soft, but no one knew it but me. As soon as the boys finished tipping over the backhouse, we got out of there.

There was a little chewing back and forth among the grown-ups about who had tipped over the three-holer, but no one could prove who did it, so things quieted down.

～

Down on Eagle Lake, Herb Moore had a dock and beach. He had boats for hire for thirty-five cents a day, and he sold ice cream and candy. Of course we couldn't afford to hire the boats, but sometimes we had a penny or two for candy. Herb Moore was a very kind man. He treated us kids swell, no matter how we got in his way when he was busy with his boats. His beach was so nice and long and sandy, and we spent quite a lot of time swimming there.

One nice summer day, six of us kids went down to Herb's beach to fool around and swim. As luck would have it, four Catholic kids were down on the other end of the beach. We ignored them, and they ignored us, so we were getting along just fine.

Sometimes a group of kids from over Schroon River way came over and swam on Herb Moore's beach too. They were rich kids "up for the summer." They looked down their noses at us, but it didn't bother us any. We kept out of each other's way.

This day, about ten of them came down the road and went up to the Catholic kids, who were nearer to them than us. They said the Catholic kids were in their place on the beach, and they started mouthing off and pushing the Catholic kids around. They knocked a couple of them down. What could they do? There were nine or ten of those bullies to their four.

We watched this for a minute or two, then it hit us. What the hell did they think they were doing, beating up on our Catholic kids? Down the beach we six kids went as fast as we could run. We lit into it good. The Catholic kids, seeing they were not alone anymore, pitched in like wildcats. Boy, did we fight a royal battle, and when the smoke cleared, all we saw were nine or ten pairs of heels disappearing down the road.

That left us and the Catholic kids standing there grinning at one another. Together we went home, arm in arm, singing, "It ain't gonna rain no more, no more, it ain't gonna rain no more. How in the hell can the old folks tell, it ain't gonna rain no more?" We were now close friends, and we had many good times together from then on. Mim said she thought she'd never see the day, but we'd turned into good Christians. Well, pretty good ones.

All those kids are gone now. Time caught up with them as it'll soon catch up with me. I like to believe I'll catch up with the kids, and we'll have more good times together.

No More Make-Believe, Virginia

Bubby and I were running through the field and over into the woods. That day we went a little farther over the ridge than usual, and suddenly, I tripped and fell over a rock in the dirt. It didn't look like a regular rock. We pushed back the leaves and dug out some dirt and found that the rock had a rounded top. It had a very worn surface and something was written there. It said, "Virginia (something) . . . 8 yrs . . . 1833." I said, "Oh, it's a little girl buried here, Bubby, a little girl of long ago."

We sat down under the old oak tree near the little stone. The sun filtered down to us and felt warm. A crow cawed from further on up the ridge. We sat there dozing in the dappled sunlight. I thought, "It's so lovely here in your spot, Virginia."

That was it! I was talking to you, Virginia. I always wanted a sister, and now I would have one. I said, "Bubby, we're going to get her out." Bubby was always gung-ho for anything I wanted, so we started digging right away with our bare hands.

Every day, whenever we could, Bubby and I would scurry back into the woods to dig. We imagined how it would be when we reached you, Virginia. We were sure you'd have laughing blue eyes and yellow curls and that your dress would be beautiful velvet of old. The dirt was very sandy. We dug with our hands, and then we brought the old shovel from the barn. It went much faster after that. When we got tired, we took turns. One would lie in the sun while the other scooped and dug.

It couldn't be much longer, Virginia. We had dug down about three feet already. We were going to have such fun together. Bubby and I had it all planned. It was hot work, and sometimes, when we were thirsty, we drank from the little brook that gurgled along just over the knoll. We were going to go wading there, Virginia, and play hide-and-go-seek in the field. We'd jump in the hay in the barn and sneak you into the house and no one would ever know. No one would believe it anyway, but you were going to stay with us forever. As Bubby and I scooped and dug, we made more and more plans about the things we were going to do.

Oh, Virginia, we were digging, and we thumped on something. It was wooden. We scuffed off more dirt, and it was a top of a box. The wood looked water-soaked and rotten in places. There was some kind of an old lock falling apart over on the side. All we had to do was lift up the top!

We climbed out of the hole and sat looking back down on where you were. The sun was just the width of a board away, Virginia. After a hundred years, you were going to be in the sunshine again. We sat there waiting to get our breaths back, huffing and puffing from all our hard digging. Then Bubby fell asleep. Such a cute little boy curled up there in the soft sun. Bubby could fall asleep anywhere in a split second, so I was alone to finish, to lift off the boards.

But I had to grow up then, Virginia. Make-believe was over, and I didn't want to see what was under those boards. Slowly I pushed the dirt back, Virginia. It had been fun playing make-believe with you. Faster, faster went the dirt. Filling up the hole went much quicker than digging it had. Then I patted down the dirt and spread oak leaves over it. Your little stone stood guard. "Virginia . . . 8 yrs . . . 1833."

Bubby woke up and was running on ahead, off on a new adventure. I was going, too, but I turned to look back at your spot, Virginia. The old oak stood firm with the sun filtering down over your place. I thought, "Little friend, I wish . . . but I have to grow up now, Virginia. Goodbye and I love you."

The Bums

I went to the store and I asked for some bread.
  And the lady said, "Bum, Bum, the baker is dead."
Hallelujah, I'm a bum. Hallelujah, bum again.
  Hallelujah, give us a handout to revive us again.
I went to a house and I knocked on the door.
  And the lady said, "Bum, Bum, You've been here
    before."
Hallelujah, I'm a bum. Hallelujah, bum again.
  Hallelujah, give us a handout to revive us again.
Oh, I don't like work And work don't like me.
  And that is the reason I am so hungry.
Hallelujah, I'm a bum. Hallelujah, bum again.
  Hallelujah, give us a handout to revive us again.

"The bums are coming! The bums are coming!" Bubby came slamming around the corner of the house to where Mim and I were hanging up the wash. We rushed out back and looked down toward the meadow.

Sure enough, there was Old Abe looking the ground over and seeing if the place was in halfway decent shape for the overnight. No one else would let the bums stay on their property when they passed through, heading south for the winter. But Mim always let them stay down back in the meadow. Bubby and I were jumping for joy. It was a real outing for us. It was already ten o'clock and there was a lot to do. All the bums would be here by evening. Usually ten to fifteen showed up.

Now the bums were bums, but they were a special bunch of bums. They only came into our lives one night a year, but Bubby and I loved them all. They were men who had seen better days. They were from good families and had educations. You could still see it in them. They were polite and never mean, even when they were stinking drunk. And that was the bond they all shared. They were all far-gone drunks, hardcore alcoholics. They were fine if no one interfered with their drinking. Families and professions had done that, so these men had cut out from everything.

They wandered north in summer and south in winter. On the way, they slept any place, bummed food, stole just enough to survive, and drank everything they could get from rubbing alcohol to Bay Rum. When they stopped in our meadow, Bubby and I were in heaven. And when they came, we had a lot to do.

First, Bubby and I sneaked over in Joe's cornfield with a bushel basket and picked it full of corn. We didn't figure we were stealin'. Joe was so mean to us that everything we took from him we believed we deserved. Then we took another basket and went over to the Wrights' place. We helped ourselves to the fattest and best potatoes from the piles they had stored in back of the barn. We always went along the brook and up in back of the barn, so they never saw us. They had killed our dog, Bigness, so we assumed they owed us plenty. We took the two full baskets down to Old Abe, and he'd be delighted to see us. Shorty would be there, and so would Limpy and Stuttering Sam. They greeted us, "Hello, little lady and little gentleman." That's the way all those bums treated Bubby and me, even when they got roaring drunk as the evening wore on.

Mim sent down some red cloth pieces from old underwear and some fishhooks and twine. Two or three of the bums would head for the swamp to catch bullfrogs. You put red cloth on a fishhook and dangle it in front of a frog, and he'll snap it every time. Before the bums stopped frogging, they'd bring in three pails full. Every time they caught a frog, they'd whop it quick over the head with a stick so they were out of their misery before they got eaten.

Most every bum, as he came into the clearing, would drop on a pile a chicken or duck that he'd snitched from some coop along the way. A big fire would be roaring in the middle of the field, and a bed of hot coals would be forming to cook the food on.

Another smaller fire would be going over to one side to warm the "canned heat." One of the bums would be going around collecting ten cents from each of the others. If you didn't have ten cents, okay, but if you had twenty cents, you put it in. If they got $2.40, it was great. They'd give it to Bubby and me, and we'd go down to the store and get a case (twenty-four cans) of the "canned heat" and lug it back to the small fire. Oh, yes, canned heat was some kind of fuel that people lit to boil coffee over when out hunting overnight.

Anyway, a couple of the bums would heat up the cans to make their contents liquefy and then they would strain and squeeze the contents of each can through a handkerchief. The liquid that came through was a dark red color, and they'd have two or three quarts of it when they were finished. Someone had to be left to guard it until the food was ready. Then someone had to be left to watch the guard. Any one of them would have stolen it and run. It was their favorite drink.

About five o'clock, we'd throw everything on the fire, the corn in their husks and the potatoes in their jackets. The chickens and ducks were propped up on sticks to sputter and cook in their own juices. The frogs were stuck through their mouths on sticks and laid over a stone to simmer awhile. When they were done, you only ate the legs. Mim always sent down a big crock of homebrew. Most everyone had a bottle in his hip pocket. Everyone kept nipping away and getting a real glow on.

It would be getting dark as the food cooked. Amid the lush smells and the glow of the fire, the bums would be talking and laughing, harmonicas would be squawking, and we'd clog dance and sing. When the food was ready, and never did food look so good, the bum called Preacher would stand up, wave his bottle in the air, and yell, "The Lord will provide." Someone would yell, "Oh, yeah? And the Lord helps those who help themselves!" A big laugh, and then we'd dig in. What a feast. Food never tasted so good! Now and again, Fiddlin' Joe would fiddle up a tune to which we'd get up again, swirl around and dance, and then head back to the food and eat some more. This would go on for a couple of hours until Mim would descend on us, and Bubby and I would be whisked off to bed.

We snuggled down in the blankets and listened to the party going full blast now. I would drift off to sleep to the sounds of their favorite song:

Hallelujah, I'm a bum. Hallelujah, bum again.
Hallelujah, give us a handout to revive us again . . .

Late next morning, when Bubby and I woke up, they'd all be gone, till next year.

The Stones

They moved into Chilson one day. They went up to an old farm way up at the end of an old dirt road.

From the beginning, there was a mystery about them. They stayed by themselves completely. Lots of stories went around. They were from Pennsylvania. They didn't talk much to anyone. They didn't come to Sunday school. Oh, they belonged to *some* church, but it was a stern, cold, no-smiling one far away.

Finally they came to school. That is, Harry, Sid, Roxy and Hilda came, and there were a lot of little ones at home. They were very clean blond pudgy-looking kids. They were very quiet. You had to say hello first, but they always smiled back.

But we could not figure out why they always stayed by themselves. Their father was a tall stern-looking man who cut hay up on his acres of field and sold it to the other farmers around. Their mother, no one ever saw.

There was a lot of visiting between farms in those days. What else was there to do? No one had any money for entertainment. "Visiting around" didn't take money, and besides, it was fun. But the Stones never extended or accepted any invitations to visit.

We kids figured there had to be "something" hidden in the Stone family, but no matter what we did, no one was invited to their farm. Finally, the novelty wore off, and the kids quit trying to get asked to their home, but not me! I was more determined than ever to go there.

I kept asking Roxy to come visit me, without results. Then one Friday, she hesitantly asked me to come over that Sunday afternoon. I was so excited, then I got scared, but I was going! Sunday came, and I found myself going up the rutty side road, off the main dirt road to their farm.

I came into the yard. The red house was more paintless, and more boards were coming off than I had remembered. Some of the roof had fallen down over one side of the house, but it was such a big house that it didn't matter. There was still plenty to live in.

Kids came running from all sides. A couple of dogs came over, sniffed around me, then settled back on the dusty ground with their tails slowly wagging. Mr. Stone looked out from the barn for a second, then went back inside.

The kids pushed me inside the old house to meet their mother. She was a pleasant plump blonde lady with a very clean look about her. She smiled at me and then told the kids to go out and play.

Then I noticed it! Out of the big old wood stove on the other side of the kitchen came one of my most favorite smells of all! My Grandmother Granger made it. It was one of my favorite foods—apple crow's nest. Oh, the cinnamon and apple smell, warm and luscious! I stood there staring at the stove.

Mrs. Stone had turned to put more wood in the stove. Next, she opened the oven and pulled out that crow's nest! It was in an enormous black iron pan. It was getting brown on top and it was steamy and bubbly. Oh, that hot cinnamon smell!

I looked at the kids and they said, "Mom's cooking dinner." There were no other pans on the stove. Great! If that was dinner, fine! Imagine having a whole meal of nothing but my favorite dessert!

We went out in the yard and threw sticks for the dogs to fetch, and we climbed the apple trees around the house. There were small knotty, wormy green apples on the trees. I thought they must have a magic tree hidden that they used to make crow's nest. Only big juicy red apples could make that smell coming from the house.

Mrs. Stone came outside. I was dismissed to go home. I'd had no breakfast, and the smell coming from that open door was torture. I would have to drag myself out of there. One never asked to stay for dinner.

Then Mr. Stone came out of the barn. He walked quickly by me. He caught up to his wife, and as he went by her, he said, "Invite the child to lunch, Elly." She stopped with the oddest look on her face and said, "Oh, yes, come along inside." With one leap, I was up beside her.

The kids were around the big old rough table. The apple crow's nest sat in the middle. Each kid had a big dish full, and they were shoving it into their mouths like crazy.

I shut my mouth hard, or I would have screamed, "Give me some! Give me some!" even though Mrs. Stone was dishing some up for me. She handed me my dish. The kids stopped eating to watch me take my first bite. They were so happy they couldn't wait to see my enjoyment.

I took a deep breath. Oh, Lord, how delicious it smelled! I filled my spoon and closed my eyes in pleasant anticipation. Into my mouth it went. Oh, God—my jaw snapped sideways and went slack. My nose stopped breathing and my eyes slid tears out the sides. Never had I tasted such a sour, bitter mess!

I sneaked a glance at Mrs. Stone. She was standing to the side of the kitchen by the stove. Our eyes caught and held. Oh, the pleading look she gave me—there was no sugar! They had no sugar and the apples were the sour green ones from the trees beside the back door. Their apple crow's nest always tasted like this, and the kids didn't know the difference. To them it was delicious.

Somehow, I swallowed that first bite and smiled with my mouth all puckered crooked. Then I took another bite and let it go down without chewing. The kids laughed. It was good. They were so happy their friend could have some of their crow's nest. They started slamming it into their mouths again.

I looked at Mrs. Stone. "Thank you, thank you," she said with her eyes. She knew and I knew and I would never tell. I know now why the Stones never invited visitors to their home. They were so poor that they couldn't even buy sugar to put in the tea that was always served to visitors. They were proud and didn't want anyone to know.

Somehow I finished the dish. The kids clamored that I should have more, but I said I was too full. Mrs. Stone helped me out by saying it wasn't polite to push people to eat more than they wanted. She patted my head and I knew she would always be my friend. We had a secret!

When everyone was full, the boys pushed the old tables and benches over in the corner of the big kitchen. Mr. Stone got a fiddle off the shelf. He leaned an old chair back against the wall on its hind legs and sat down.

He started playing "Come Around the Mountain," "Oh, Susannah," "Turkey in the Straw," "Hoe Down," "Little Brown Jug," "Nellie Grey," and on and on and on.

We started dancing, stamping our bare feet on the old rough wood floor. Backward and forward. Backward and forward. Round and round. For an hour or so, no one spoke. We went backward and forward. Round and round. The music went faster and faster. We slapped and stamped our feet. Backward and forward. Round and round!

Then abruptly, Mr. Stone said, "Chore time." He put the fiddle back on the shelf and the older boys scurried out the door after him.

I knew it was time to go. The children and Mrs. Stone came out to the yard with me. Mrs. Stone put her hand on my shoulder and said, "Come again, little girl," and the kids screeched, "Yes! Yes! Yes!"

Then Mrs. Stone said, "Laddy, walk her down a ways." The old dog and I sauntered down the path. He sat down firmly at the gate. He panted and smiled up at me, but that's as far as his world went. I turned and waved goodbye to the group waving back from the yard. Then I skipped out the gate.

The sun going down shone warm and orangey on the oak trees on the hill as I flew along. My bare feet slapped faster and faster over the dusty dirt road. The two miles home went quickly. The world was mine. Because the Stones liked me. They liked me, and I could "Come again!"

On Swimming Holes and Pigs

One spring morning Mim decided we should get a couple of pigs. Cowboy bought a couple of half-grown ones from his father who lived up in Hague. His father raised a lot of pigs, so Cowboy said they'd be good ones. He put them way down back in the field. He put up a pen run-yard for them from some of the old boards Mim always had lying around.

Bubby and I named the pigs Goof-Goof and Oink-Oink because of the way they yelled when they got real hungry. They always were fed, though, even if some days it was only big armloads of pig weed that we pulled in the fields and threw in to them.

When no one was looking, Bub and I rode those pigs round and round their pig yard. We always were thrown off into the pigs' mud hole (waddle hole), but give us an A for effort. We always went back for more. We never did break those pigs "to the saddle," but they never hurt us or offered to bite us. They never seemed to get mad at us climbing on their backs. Sometimes they even seemed to be laughing at us. We would end up covered with mud everywhere but our eyes. Then we'd have to get cleaned up before Mim saw us.

So over we'd go to the swimming hole to wash up. It was a part of the little brook down back. We had dammed up the brook with visions of having a nice swimming hole for the summer.

In the spring, the melting snow really had that brook looking like a promising summer cooling-off place. But alas, by the end of June, when school was out, so was the brook; our pool would be half water and half mud. We never gave up on this, though.

Every spring, we always put back any part of the dam that was broken away. You never knew—that summer there just might be more water.

Lack of water didn't keep us from using the pool, however. We swam with gusto. We never looked much cleaner after washing there to get rid of the pigpen dirt. We just exchanged that mud for the mud of the brook. But at least the pool mud had a quieter, deep-down musty smell—not quite as bad as the stink of the pigpen mud. Of course, we had ringworm and impetigo every summer.

When the ringworm or impetigo, or both, got bad enough, we would complain to Mim about it. She'd scrub the sores with green soap, get the scabs off, and put on thick yellow sulfur-smelling ointment. That helped control the itch some, and after cold weather came, it would go away anyhow. Mim said there was something in the cold air that made it go away.

Me and Bub ready for a busy day with our swimming hole or pigs.

We never thought much about it or connected these diseases up with dirt. We thought all kids had ringworm, impetigo, or both, most every summer when they were growing up.

When late fall came, it was time for "pig slaughters." Bub and I always went to these events in the neighborhood. There was much bustling around gathering old tires and wood to make hot fires. Big iron kettles full of water were put over the fires to boil. After they were killed, the pigs would be dumped up and down in the hot water to get their bristles off.

The best place to see what went on was up on the rail fence around the pigpen. Bub and I would climb up on the fence, hook an arm around the top of a fencepost, and watch.

Finally, a big fat hog, so fat it could hardly walk, would be driven to the middle of the pigpen. The fatter the pig, the better in those days. It showed what a good farmer the pig's owner was and that the pig contained lots of grease needed to fry donuts and potatoes.

Three or four men would get in with the pig. One had a big, long sharp butcher knife that we had watched being sharpened on the grindstone wheel. Sometimes the men allowed Bub and me to put water over the sharpening stone as they were using it. This kept its grinding stone cool so the knife would be sharpened just right.

Anyway, when the men started walking toward the pig, it always seemed to know what was coming. It would dart this way and that, and the men would try to grab it. What a performance! Wrestling, rolling, grabbing, kicking, swearing, and screaming!

A pig, at that time, had the most fascinating, horrible scream I ever heard. You could hear it a mile away. At that point I always wanted to run, but I was frozen on the fence. My eyes were glued to the pig's throat.

When, finally, the men were able to slash the pig's throat, it would sigh and gurgle and gurgle. One of the women would run over and hold a tin pail under the stream of blood to catch it for use in making blood pudding.

Then men would stand around wiping blood off their hands and look important as though they had conquered the world, while the poor old pig just lay there and gave up the ghost.

I always felt awful sorry for the pig then, and I hated those men. I always swore that I'd never go to another pig killing. That would at least register my disapproval. However, at the next "hog slaughter," I was there.

Except one. It still hurts to remember. It was Goof-Goof's and Oink-Oink's time to be killed. Bub and I were up at dawn gathering wood and old tires in a pile as Mim told us to do. An awful sick feeling was coming over me.

The men came, and I could see scorn in their eyes for our long, lean old pigs, not hardly an ounce of fat anywhere. How could they be fat? Bub and I had played with them as horses, round and round the pen every day all summer. They never had any time to lie around and get fat.

I wanted to chase the men out of the pigpen, but they would only have swatted me away. When the screaming started, I ran over the road and into my beautiful grove of poplars. I fell on my face on the ground. I remember kicking my feet on the ground and putting my hands over my ears, and I cried my heart out. And I kept saying, "I'm sorry" to Goof-Goof and Oink-Oink over and over again.

Pigs sure get under your skin, especially when they're friends. Needless to say, I never went to another pig slaughter.

Gypsies and Good Luck

Occasionally Gypsies would come through Chilson. When they were first seen starting up Chilson Hill, the word was passed along. Everyone locked up their chickens and pigs, except Mim. She said if the Gypsies wanted your belongings, they'd get them anyway, so why bother?

The Gypsies liked Mim because she always let them make camp in the little grove of poplars out in our field. They never stole anything from us.

Having the Gypsies there was an exciting time for me, and I watched them a lot. Their wagons were built up like little houses. They took good care of their horses, which were old, but loved. The Gypsies' clothes were very colorful. They weren't always the cleanest, but their bangles and earrings made up for it.

Mim went over to their camp sometimes when she was through work for the day. It was usually after dark and the Gypsies' campfires would be going. Mim would take them some corn or potatoes, sometimes even a chicken, and I'd go with her.

We'd sit by a campfire, and the Gypsies would play music on guitars, banjos and jute harps. The music was so different. I would snuggle down beside Mim and close my eyes and listen. Their music was sad but exciting at the same time.

There was a girl named Tilly who wandered around Chilson. She had just sort of drifted in from somewhere. Sometimes she stayed overnight with us, and Mim gave her something to eat. Tilly would go over and stay with the Gypsies when they came. She even slept by the campfire at night.

One day, Tilly and I were walking down to the brook to wash up. I told her I liked Roni, one of the young boys in the Gypsy group. Tilly stopped dead in her tracks. "Has he ever touched you?" she asked. I thought she meant had he touched my hand, so I said, "No." Tilly said, "Good, but what Gypsies want, Gypsies get, so you have to have some protection." Protection from what? But I said okay.

Tilly told me she'd have the protection for me the next day, but it was going to cost me a dime. A dime! Where was I going to get a dime? It was Saturday night, and sometimes the Wrights asked Bub and me to go to the cowboy movies in Ticonderoga with them. As luck would have it, they asked us to go that night. It cost a dime apiece to get in. We teased Mim to let us go. Finally, Mim gave us two dimes that she was saving for milk money, and we were off to the movies with the Wrights.

We never sat in a group at the movies. We kids sat with friends we met there, so no one noticed that I didn't buy a ticket. Everyone else went into the movie. I sat around the lobby and spent some time sitting in the ladies' room. I even spent some time sitting on the car running board.

When the movie was over, we climbed into the car and went home. I hadn't seen the movie, but I still had the dime. I considered myself very lucky.

The next morning, Tilly came over to our house. Mim was out hoeing potatoes. Tilly had a little bottle in her hand. I asked what it was and she said, "Turpetine." Turpentine? What for? Tilly said if any boy touched me, to take a slug of the turpentine. Then I wouldn't "get caught." I thought Tilly very clever and smart to know this. (I still believe that she really believed it.) Then Tilly said to really be sure it would work, I had to give her the dime so she could have a spell cast on the turpentine. I gave her the dime, and she went over and up into one of the wagons. After a while, she came back and handed me the little bottle of turpentine. She said, "There, you're all set."

I took the turpentine home and hid it in my very secret place—under my underwear in my top drawer. I felt really grown up. I usually told Mim everything, but somehow I didn't think I should tell her about this.

The next day, Billy Moore came by, grabbed my arm, and tried to force me to get under Cowboy's truck with him. I got away from him by kicking him good, but he had touched me. I rushed in and took a little slug of my turpentine. I sure didn't want to take any chance of "getting caught."

The next day I told Tilly what happened. She said, "Good God, did he touch you?"

I said, "Yes, on the arms."

Tilly said she knew I was lying. She said she knew I had gotten under the truck with Billy and that he had touched me, and more than just on the arm. She also said that the turpentine was just a backup, and not "getting caught" was mostly luck. I didn't argue with her. Knowing I was always lucky was enough.

Meanwhile, when I went over to the Gypsies' camp, Roni was smiling at me more and more. He had a cough that seemed to be getting worse, but he skept smiling at me more and more, and I liked him smiling at me more and more. In fact, I was smiling back at him more and more.

Then came the day I wouldn't mind if he touched my hand, maybe he'd even kiss me, which would be better yet. I knew it was going to happen soon, maybe tomorrow.

However, when I woke up the next morning, the Gypsies were gone—lock, stock, and barrel. Mim said some of the neighbors were complaining of a pig missing or a shovel gone, etc.

The Gypsies had left in the middle of the night. Tilly had gone with them, and of course, Roni went too.

I felt bad that he hadn't got to kiss me before he left, but I knew he would when he came back.

Late the next summer, the Gypsies came again. I didn't see Roni, but Tilly was still with them. I noticed she was coughing quite a bit and was very thin.

The first chance I got, I asked her where Roni was. She told me that during their wanderings that winter, Roni had died of tuberculosis. I cried for Roni. Now he would never kiss me. Without even knowing it, I had lucked out again.

P.S. A year or so later, I heard through the grapevine that Tilly had died of tuberculosis. I don't know what happened to the Gypsies as they didn't come through Chilson anymore, though I vaguely remember hearing that the police wouldn't let them go through Ticonderoga anymore and, thus, Chilson Hill.

The Fourth of July

The Fourth of July! We didn't have any money and our car was broken down. Some combination. It meant that we couldn't go to Ticonderoga for the fireworks. Bubby and I had looked forward to that all year, and now we couldn't go. Mim gave us hotdogs for supper as a treat. We had a few sparklers, and when it was dark enough, Bubby and I lit them. We stuck some in the ground and swung some around our heads. For Mim's sake, we pretended we were having fun, but I was very bored. Bubby had some caps, and we banged them off between two stones. Then there was nothing else to do but go to bed. I was an unhappy little girl as I tried to go to sleep.

Cowboy had parked his big old truck in the yard near the house. I knew he couldn't make his payments on the truck, so he was going to lose it. I also knew he had something called insurance on the truck, and I'd heard him talking to Mim about it sometimes. I never could hear all he was saying, but once or twice, I heard her say, "You better not."

After lying sleepless in bed for about an hour, I heard a muffled noise out beside the truck. I carefully crawled out of bed so as not to wake up Bubby. I sneaked over by the window, kneeled down, and peeked out. It was pretty dark, but there was someone by the truck, all right. When he moved around, I could tell it was Cowboy. He had a rubber tube in the gas tank and was siphoning gas into a can. He took the tube out and put the cap back on the gas tank. He threw the tube in on the floor of the cab. Then he took the can of gas and poured some around on the grass under the truck, and then on the cab, inside and out. Next he threw a match on the grass under the truck and jumped back. Poof! It exploded, and flames leapt up, around, and into the cab. It burned fast and furious. Suddenly the horn started blowing. Neighbors came running from all directions. Soon there must have been 30 people milling around our yard. All the neighbors' dogs had come swarming to the fire too. They were barking, snapping at everything, and having a great time. Litchfield's tied-up old dog, Rip, was roaring up on the hill.

The truck was parked under the electrical wires that led to our house. The wires caught fire and the fire crept along the wires toward us. Mim was screaming, "Get the kids out!" I took Bubby's hand and we calmly walked out the front door. Mim grabbed us and ran across the yard to the old apple tree. She told us to stay put and went hurrying back to where the excitement was. I put my arm around Bubby and we watched.

The sky was all lit up by the fire. The truck was burning furiously and the horn was still blowing like a siren. Dogs were running around barking, chasing each other, and getting into fights. The noise and light had confused the chickens in the coop. The rooster was cock-a-dooing, and the hens were squawking. The cow was mooing and kicking the walls of her shed, and in their pen, the pigs were squealing. People were running around yellin', "Get some water." "Get some pails." "Bring some shovels." "Anybody got an axe?" "Turn off the switch box." "Get the kids out of the house." Everyone hollering orders, and nobody taking them! Then some people were bringing water from the brook. Others would grab the pails before they were full and throw them toward the fire.

The fire started past the house. Instead of going into the house, it went along the electric wire that went to the little storage shed out back in the field. That old wooden shed burned quickly. I held my breath. I knew Mim had some dynamite sticks stashed away there. It was only a minute before the shed blew up. *KABOOM KABOOM*! Burning boards and sparks shot high in the sky, and also quite a few whiskey bottles. Someone yelled, "That's those goddamn liquor inspectors! Liquor inspectors!" A few people stumbled out of the yard to run home and get their bathtub gin and homebrew better hidden. Mim came screeching

Cowboy and his truck.

across the yard, "My kids! My kids! Oh, you're okay." And back she went into the fray.

Finally some men had formed a line from the brook, and pails of water were quickly passed along the line to throw on the fire. But the men were excited, and water was being thrown everywhere, on everything, and in all directions as well as on the fire. Eventually the flames were beaten back and smothered. The animals quieted down and people went home. Mim shooed us into the house and we felt our way to bed. I was tired, but content. Best Fourth of July I ever had.

And So We Had Milk

Mim was rabid on the idea that Bubby and I would always have milk, and so we did. But first, Mim went over and made arrangements with the Wrights. They were to deliver one quart of milk in a little gray enamel pail with a top on it (they furnished the container) once a day. It was to cost ten cents upon delivery. Where Mim planned to find this ten cents a day, I don't know, but she would, and she did. When the milk was gone, we kids would rinse out the container and take it back to be filled the next day. The enamel pail always looked dirty. It got dirtier and dirtier on the outside. I don't think it ever got washed except for Bubby's and my rinsing, but no matter. We drank the milk, and Mim never noticed. She was too busy putting up and taking down parts of our house.

As the summer wore on, the milk seemed to get thicker and thicker, but it tasted okay so we drank it. Finally, it was almost too thick to come out of the pail, so I showed Mim. She turned purple. "Oh my God, gargety milk. They're feeding my kids gargety milk!" She grabbed that pail and over she went to the Wrights. Mim met Clayton in the yard. Her arms started waving around and flying in the air, and she was yelling. I couldn't hear what she said, but the air was blue. Finally, Mim threw the pail on the ground at Clayton's feet. She came stomping home, mad as a wet hen. Mim would show them! She'd go over to the Covells, our neighbors in the other direction, and get our quart a day from them. Mim washed her face, combed her hair, cooled down, and took off.

Mim and me, thinking things over.

The Covells made the same deal. One quart of milk per day, delivered, for ten cents. And they also would furnish the container, only their pail was shiny tin. Never had I seen such a shiny tin pail. It always looked that way, and Bubby and I never had to rinse it out, either.

When Carl brought the milk each day, Mim would check it out as he watched. She was always satisfied. This went on for about a month. Then Mim began to check the milk every other day, and then only once a week, and finally not at all. She had become busy putting in a root cellar, and besides, the milk was okay.

Gradually, the milk got thinner and thinner. I noticed, but never said anything. It didn't seem important. At last, the milk was just thin bluish water.

One evening, Bubby was pouring some from the pail and Mim noticed. She grabbed his glass and held it up to the window. "Skimmed, no, double-skimmed milk—those cheatin' rats!" Mim grabbed the shiny tin pail with the skinny milk in it. Over the road she went, with blood in her eyes, to the Covells' house.

She went in, and we watched. Suddenly, the Covells' door opened and banged shut behind Mim. She stormed home. Her wrath had descended upon the Covells' house, and it remained very silent and deserted-looking for the rest of the evening. Not a single person was seen to poke his head out a window or door.

Well, Mim was not about to give up yet. Up went some kind of a lean-to against the side hill by the house. Then, one afternoon when we came home on the school bus, there stood a cow in that shed. Not too young a cow or a very fat cow, but a cow. Mim's kids were going to have milk. All the rest of that fall and winter, we did.

There was one thing, though. The dung hill grew by the side of the shed. Every night, as we came over the hill on the school bus, I swear I could see that it had grown taller. It was always steaming and, when it was really cold, it looked like it was smoking. I lived in horror of the day we'd come over the hill and that dung hill would be shooting blue flames! No one ever mentioned the pile to me, not one kid ever laughed, or I would have died of embarrassment. Maybe no one ever noticed it, but it haunted me, and I cringed in my seat every day as it came in sight over the hill.

But we did have milk, until one day, a New York State agricultural inspector was going around Chilson doing tests on cows. He did ours, and he said she was tubercular. I'm still sad to think about who sold that cow to Mim. He was a very close relative and had known the cow had something wrong with her before she was sold. Mim was heartsick, and mad. The cow disappeared. Mim watched us and worried for a long time that maybe we'd get sick. But we were lucky and stayed as healthy as pigs.

Mim finally gave up on milk and started buying White House evaporated milk, at ten cents a can in the store. You mixed it half and half with water, and it was "whole milk." I never did learn to like the taste of it, but at least it was "safe." That's what we drank for a good many years. *And* what a relief when the old dung pile finally sunk down below the view from the bus window.

Candy Bar

Lonson's was our nearest store. It was about two miles from our house, near Eagle Lake. It was closer than Ticonderoga. That was six miles away.

About once a week, Aunt Dean would stop at our house on her way to Lonson's to see if we needed anything. Even if Mim didn't, I would ride down to the store and back with her. I always went in with her while she bought what she needed.

The store was a small room with shelves along the back wall. There was no self-service in those days. The storekeeper waited on you. There were only a few cans of everything on the shelves. No fresh produce or meat could be bought. Lonson's didn't carry any. Who could afford to buy it? People in Chilson raised their own or went without.

Lonson's had a small case containing candy on the first two shelves, pretty and bright-colored, but the third shelf fascinated me. That's where the five-cent candy bars were. They were just as accessible as the penny ones to me.

There were four Hershey bars, two Baby Ruths and three Milky Ways on the shelf. At first I wanted any one, but then I started to concentrate on a Milky Way. How I wanted one! Every weekly visit, I stared and stared at them.

Then one week, there were only two Milky Ways left. Someone had bought one. I dreamed on about the other two. A couple of weeks later, when I went to stand in front of "my" candy bars, there was only one left! I felt sick. I'd never know what a Milky Way tasted like. When that last bar went, I wouldn't even be able to dream over it. I had to have it! Where would I get five cents? I worried about that all the rest of the week.

The next Sunday morning, I was picking up bottles, cans, and junk in the driveway after Mim's Saturday night dance. She always had a square dance on Saturday nights. It was one of my chores to pick up the yard on Sunday mornings. I kicked over a bottle, and there was a nickel. I grabbed it up and stood there, unbelieving. I could get my Milky Way!

I went in and pestered Mim to let me go to the store. Bubby helped me pester her. He wanted some candy, too. Finally Mim said, "Oh, all right, but come right back." I started trotting down the road. All the time I was praying, "Please don't let anyone have bought my Milky Way!"

I walked in the door of the store and went slowly over to stand in front of the glass case that held the candy. Mr. Lonson was sitting in the sun in his old rocker by the window. He was nodding, half-asleep. The flies buzzed lazily on the warm sunny window beside him.

First I looked at the first shelf where the penny candy was. I could buy ten of those for five cents. The hard balls were three for one cent—fifteen of them for my nickel! I pretended I'd buy six of those, and four of that, but I knew there was one piece of candy I would end up with. Finally I dared sneak a look at the top shelf. Was it there? It was there! No one had bought my Milky Way.

Mr. Lonson yawned slowly and stretched with his arms over his head. He scratched his belly and got up slowly out of his chair. Then he ambled his big bulk over in back of the counter.

He knew today was different. Whether he had seen my nickel clutched in my hand, or whether he could tell by my controlled excitement, he knew today I would buy something. He knew today was not just a looking day!

His face was empty. He showed no impatience, and I stood there soaking up the look of the candy. He knew I would buy, so he let me have my moment.

It was only a nickel, but in the hot, dry summer of 1934, a nickel was a nickel, and so he patiently waited. Finally, dreaming was over, and I did what I knew I would always do. I said, "I guess I'll take that Milky Way."

He slowly opened the drop-down door on the back of the case. He slowly took out the Milky Way and set it on the counter. Then he pushed out his hand for the five cents. I dropped it in his palm, and with his other hand, he passed me my candy.

I said, "Thank you," and turned to walk slowly toward the door. Slowly, slowly, for at last I had bought something. For once, I could leave with dignity. I went off the store porch and down the dusty road. Slowly, slowly, then my feet began skipping and dancing, and I was running, running down the road. I didn't even bother to glance back to see if Mr. Lonson was looking out the window. All I wanted to do was get home.

Across Eagle Lake Flats I went, around the bend across Mud Flats, up Mud Hill. I didn't even stop at the spring there for my usual drink of icy water. Across Heustis' Flats, through Scary Hollow, past Ed Latrell's burned-down shed. Ed was a cripple who had burned to death in that shack. For once, his presence didn't chill my soul or scare me as I skipped. Maybe it was because it was such a happy, sunny day, but I think it was the candy in my hand.

I went around Dead Man's Bend and over Home Flats. I flew in the door and hollered, "Mim, Mim, Mim, I'm home!"

Mim was at the stove. She turned as I placed the candy in the middle of the kitchen table. Bubby came running in the back door. "Did you get it? Did you get it?" Mim smiled and took a flat-sided knife out of a drawer.

She opened the paper on the candy, and there it was! A shiny brown rectangle of chocolate. There were white veins on top of it because when the hot sun hit Lonson's candy case, the candy would melt, then firm up again when the sun was gone. But no matter, it was beautiful!

Mim slowly cut that small candy bar into three equal parts. She picked up my piece between the knife blade and her finger. She held it toward me. Just as I reached up for it, Clarence, Francis, and Jean (neighbor kids) walked through the back door.

Mim drew back the candy and put it back on the table. Then she cut each piece of candy in two equal parts. I didn't feel hurt or cheated or resentful. Sharing was something you always did.

Then Mim handed each of us one of those pieces of candy. Mine was lying on the palm of my hand. Instead of two bites, it was now one, but it was mine! I slowly brought it up to my nose and smelled. Ahh! Then I put it in my mouth. I closed my eyes. Slowly I let it melt on my tongue. For one moment, pure, pure heaven!

Down in the Narrow

After the January thaw, the whole flatland swamp along the Corduroy Road would be flooded from the main roadway back for miles toward Ironville. Then really cold weather would return and freeze the water solid.

For about half a mile from the main road, ice would form, smooth and clear, until the land narrowed from the width of the swamp to a very narrow ice strip. This strip went for one hundred fifty feet or so before going out into the wide frozen swamp again. In the "narrow," as you went through, the bushes gently touched you from both sides.

Every Friday night when it was clear, we kids would grab our skates and any long stick we could find and head for the flatlands. About a dozen kids, and most every dog in Chilson, would be there.

We used a tin can for a puck and we'd get a noisy game of "stick-can" going. The idea was to get the tin can to yourself and head down the swamp with it with everyone in wild pursuit.

It sounds easy, but hardly anyone could get that can away from the pack. We'd slam and push and shove each other around, and so did the dogs—them yapping and kids yelling.

With tails up and hind legs slipping sideways on the ice, their front leg toenails digging and clawing into the ice, the dogs didn't care where the can went as long as they could get it. So it made for a wild yelling, yapping free-for-all. I don't know who had more fun, the dogs or us kids.

One night I especially remember. We reached the ice about 6 p.m. Over on a side of the ice we built our usual bonfire with old

134

boards and tires that some of the bigger boys had lugged there in the afternoon after school.

We were well into our stick-can game when we had to get off the ice and gather over by the bonfire. We had to make way for Grandpa and Tweedle Armstrong, who were coming over the ice with a load of wood on a sleigh pulled by Tweedle's horses. They had been cutting wood down in the narrow and had to go right through our skating spot as it was the easiest place from which to get onto the main road. Grandpa and Tweedle waved hello to us and kept going for home.

The moonlight was almost as bright as day. The flats and the mountains in the distance looked very serene and restful. I slipped away from the game and skated toward the narrow. The noise from the rambunctious stick-can game became dimmer and dimmer behind me. I loved the free feeling of skating along with the only sound breaking the quiet being the stroke of my skate blades. Here and there, the ice would sparkle in the moonlight. I believed the sparkles were fairies touching their wands for a second on the ice.

Skating dreamily along, and about seventy yards from entering the narrow, suddenly I stopped dead in my skates. Did I see something ahead of me, or did I hear something down in the narrow? I didn't know, but I didn't think so.

After a minute, I started skating a few strokes again toward the narrow. It looked gloomy, dark, sullen and oh so very quiet. Goosebumps went over me. I turned quickly and started skating toward the distant light of our bonfire. Something warned me not to go down through the narrow that night.

I was skating along when I met Marion. We stopped, and she said she was going to take a whirl through the narrow and would be right back. I said, "Don't go there tonight." Marion asked, "Why not?" I couldn't tell her why not. "Just don't go there tonight." Marion looked at me oddly but turned around and skated back to the bonfire with me.

It was about 8:30, and it was getting colder and starting to snow, so we decided to call it a night. As we and the dogs were leaving the ice, Grandpa and Tweedle came walking back carrying kerosene lanterns.

Grandpa said he had lost his wallet. He was sure it had happened when they were loading the wood on the sleigh down in the narrow. They were going back to look for it. We took off for home. Grandpa and Tweedle kept walking down to the narrow.

Mim was away working, so Bub and I were again boarding at Grandma Granger's. When we got there, Gram gave us some cookies and hot chocolate. We were slurping that up when Grandpa came into the kitchen. He said he had found his wallet and then asked, "Did anyone of you go down through the narrow tonight?"

I answered, "No. I almost did but turned around and came back before I got there." He said, "Good thing, because when we got there, there was blood all over the ground. Whatever happened must have been between 7:30 when we left the narrow and nine o'clock when we got back there."

During that time was when I would have been skating through the narrow, if I'd kept on going.

I went to bed and pulled the feather blanket way up over my head. If something was going to get me, at least I wouldn't see it coming.

No one ever found out what had happened down in the narrow that night.

I Am a Lily, Easter 1934

Things were going along fairly well. Mim was busy building and adding more onto Top of the Hill. She had Saturday night dances, and Cowboy was working, so we were eating pretty regularly, and Mim had managed to buy Bub and me a few new clothes. With our new affluence, Mim decided to get us involved in Chilson's social life, such as it was. But where to start?

Mim decided the church would be a good place to begin. She joined the Ladies' Circle, and we kids were to go to Sunday school every week. At first, Bub and I didn't think too much of that, but as we got into it, we enjoyed Sunday school and all the things that went on there.

It was a couple of weeks before Easter, and Mrs. Hunston, our Sunday school teacher, handed out poems for us to learn. We were going to put on a program for the grownups on Easter morning.

I said my two verses over and over so that I would have them down pat. I was excited about our program, and I was going to make Mim proud of me.

Easter morning, Mim got Bubby all scrubbed up, dressed and eating his breakfast. Then it was my turn. I even had a new dress and a big hair ribbon. My excitement was growing as I was to do the "Easter Welcome." I would be the first one to speak. I couldn't eat anything and told Mim.

She said, "Okay, but pour yourself a big glass of apple juice and drink it. You have to have something," and she proceeded to hurry and get ready. As usual, we were running a little behind.

Now in the closet were two jugs of apple juice. One jug was sweet for Bubby and me. The other contained "hard apple juice." In other words, very strong cider. That jug was for Cowboy and Mim, and we knew we were never to touch it. Of course, I was waiting my chance to take a sample, and as Mim was in the bedroom, my time to try it was here.

I poured myself a big glass of the very hard cider and drank it down. It was sizzly and stingy, but extra good once you caught your breath again. So I poured another big glassful and downed that. Then I tipped up the jug and took a long swig, then another. Bubby watched but said nothing.

I was innocently putting on my coat when Mim came into the kitchen and hurriedly got us into the car and away.

We were in the church, waiting for about twenty minutes for things to begin. Bubby and I were sitting over to the side of the stage with the other kids. The church filled up quickly. Thirty or 40 people must have been sitting in the pews. Mim had charge

Chilson Methodist Church, circa 1938.

of the refreshments. She had hurried out to the kitchen to get things started.

It was very hot in the church, and I felt flushed and sort of dizzy, but I didn't pay any attention as I was so excited to get the program going. It was time! Mrs. Hunston motioned to me. I grabbed the Easter lily that I was to hold and jumped up to go and make my welcoming speech. I started hiccupping and burping very fast as I hurried to the center of the stage. I started:

I am an Easter lily—*hic, hic, hic*—sent out to welcome you—*hic, burp, hic*—To give you all a nod and smile— *burp, hic, burp*—Easter wishes, too—*hic, hic, hic.*

At this point, sneezing came over me. I sputtered and coughed and sneezed for about a minute. My pretty hair bow fell down over my nose. By this time, I was holding the Easter lily only by the stem. The pot fell off and it and all the dirt crashed to the floor.

I hiccupped a few more times then went bravely on:

Now every Easter lily wants to do just what is best— *hic*—So I will bow and take my seat—*burp, burp*—And listen to the rest—*sneeze, sneeze, sneeze.*

My speech was over, but I couldn't bow as I felt as if I was falling through space. My feet wouldn't move, and the *hics* kept coming. But what the heck, by now I was having a good time, so I loudly started up again—"I am a lily"—but someone had gotten Mim from the kitchen, and she snatched me off the stage.

The church was very quiet. People sat wondering what was wrong with me. Drunk? Never, not in church.

As Cowboy and Mim were carrying me out the door, Bubby proclaimed at the top of his voice, "Yada sneaked and drank up all the hard cider." That did it. I was now a total disgrace.

After that, I didn't want to go to Sunday school anymore, but Mimmie made me trot off every Sunday. She said I had "to live it down."

Only Cowboy found my performance hilarious. He said I was off to a great start, and by the time I was ten I'd be Chilson's most illustrious "Wino/Cidero." Mim told him to shut up and not to encourage me along my downhill path.

For a long time after that, the good ladies of the church clucked their tongues over me and wondered what would become of Mim's "cross to bear."

Lake George Vacation

Only once did my biological father come see us in Chilson. He took Bub and me on a boat trip on Lake Champlain from Ticonderoga to Lake George and back.

I don't remember too much about the trip except at the hotel, Dad gave Bubby a bath. Then he wanted to give me one, and I absolutely refused. I made it plain that no one gave me a bath. I'd take one when I got home. I could be very stubborn and not the sweetest of little girls.

The other thing I clearly remember was walking the railroad tracks from Baldwin to Ticonderoga. We had to cross a high narrow railroad bridge. I was very afraid of heights. Some big boys were there, throwing stones at us and calling us names. Dad hurried on ahead of us. Bubby and I were scared, but we made it over the bridge and ran hard to catch up with Dad.

In an old book he sent me a few years ago, I found the following account that Dad had written about this trip.

I thought it interesting because of the cost of things back then:

A Four-Day Vacation During the Depression

August 9, 1934
Thursday
10:30   Drove W. Plains to Harmon, left car at garage
11:54   Train
4:14 pm   Left Albany
7:43 pm   Arr. Mt. Calm

Friday
Gloria, Harland and Father
12:30 pm   Lake George Boat
3:30 pm   Arr. in Lake George
Stayed at Hammond House
Had own private beach
Fine food—chicken, lamb and fresh lake trout
And did they eat!
Went to movies
11:15   To bed
Took some pleasant walks along the lake. Children enjoyed the swing and wading.

August 11
Saturday
9:30   boat
12:30   Arr. in Baldwin
Walked RR tracks to "Ti." Ate lunch and taxied home.
Left Sunday 1:53 pm train from Mt. Calm

August 10th
Shoeshine	.25
Coca Colas	.20
Taxi to Baldwin	.75
Lunch in Baldwin	.90
Boat tickets	4.00
On boat eats	.25

At Lake George Village:
Cones	.15
Room	3.00
Supper	2.75
Magazine	.25
Movies	.80
Cones	.20

Dad, Bub and me, ready for our boat trip.

August 11th

Breakfast	1.75
On boat	.30
Lunch in Ti	.70
Toys	.64
Cones	.15
Candy	.15
Taxi	.75
	17.94
Gas	.88
Lunch	.50
Car fare	10.15
Albany	1.75
Car from Mt. Calm	2.00
Beer	.70
Taxi	.25
	16.23

*To Mary (Mim) $5.00
                        ─────
                        21.23
                        17.94
                        ─────
                        39.17

Spent
39.17 (4.00 left)
Garage 1.25
40.42

The Wedding Reception

Josie had stopped running around. She was finally going to marry Bill. She'd been running around with him off and on for years. All of her other boyfriends were very skittish when she coyly mentioned marriage, but not Bill. He was old faithful, so Josie settled for him. Maggie D. had always had a crush on Bill. She was always trying to "get him." Maggie felt badly and at last gave up on Bill when Josie snared him.

Mim and Josie were good friends. Mim never ran around like Josie did. She always married her mistakes, or so she said. Anyway, Mim was having the wedding reception for Josie at the Top of the Hill dance hall. No invitations would be mailed out (couldn't afford it). It would just be word of mouth. It would be held from 6 p.m. until?

People brought money to Mim, from fifty cents to $5 to help pay for liquor. It was during Prohibition, so when about $30 was collected, Cowboy took off over the Canadian border to get "the good stuff." Mim wasn't going to have any low-grade bathtub gin at any affair she gave.

For music, there would be Carl (Jew's harp), Cowboy (bones) and old Herm (fiddle). Herm kept complaining that he wasn't too sure he'd play because his arthritis was so painful. But Mim knew with three or four homebrews in him he would be in fine shape, without a pain in the world.

Aunt Sadie would play the piano. Mim really would have liked to ask a better piano player, but she didn't want to hurt Aunt Sadie's feelings. Besides, she was going to give Josie one of the best wedding gifts she would get. It was a newfangled large white galvanized chamber pot, crack-proof, no matter how cold the weather got. Aunt Sadie was also including a big bottle of CN deodorant to take care of deodorant problems.

We didn't have to worry about flowers. Bub and I would gather wildflowers out in our field and put them around for decoration. Aunt Dean had some streamers left over from last year's Fourth of July. We planned to string them up too. It didn't matter that they were red, white and blue. Oh, it would be festive when we got done decorating.

Food was not a worry, either. At any affair in those times, people always brought something—salads, bread, cakes, etc. You never thought about having to ask. Mim was cooking an enormous ham that Archie Wright was donating from his store in Ti. We had plenty of hot dogs and rolls. Mim ordered them every week for the Saturday night dances. That week she just added on five dozen of each to her order. All that week, I dreamed about that ham.

Cowboy donated three gallons of fresh oysters from his car trunk business. He used to put ice in his car trunk, pack the gallon cans of oysters in it, and go around selling them from house to house—a pint, a quart or whatever you wanted. He only had to pay $1 per gallon for the oysters, so his price was right. In the hot summer, hardly anyone had refrigeration, so they had no really cold food. Cowboy was known far and wide for his really cold oysters.

Kids were all included to come to the reception. No problem—you either brought them or stayed home. No leaving them this time with grandmas. Grandmas were coming to the reception. Bub and I could hardly wait. Me, I had my eye on that ham.

Everything was all ready. Josie and Bill got married that afternoon by a justice of the peace down in Ti. No church for Josie. She said no church would let her in, anyway.

Six o'clock in the evening came. The newlyweds and guests began arriving. I always hated the beginning of our social affairs. Every time they started out so prim and proper. The music was boring waiting for things to get going. But once enough home-brew had been poured down enough throats, the music took off, and so did everyone.

Oh, the dancing and the drinking. You might be someone's worst enemy tomorrow, but that night everyone was everyone's best pal. Except Benny. He was an old flame of Josie's. We could see he was mad that she had married Bill. Benny didn't want Josie, but he didn't want anyone else to have her. Cowboy was keeping an eye on him as he was glaring all the time at Bill. Benny was also loading up on homebrew and the good Canadian stuff. He could bear watching.

I couldn't wait for the buffet to be opened so I could get to that ham. When Mim called out, "Okay, come and get it," all the big people pushed to the buffet table ahead of me. Everyone filled their plates with ham. They'd eat the other stuff later. By the time I got to it, the ham was all gone—my one unhappy memory of that wedding reception.

Suddenly, Benny grabbed Bill and slammed him out the door. We went running to see what would happen. They were pretty drunk, but they got in a few swings at one another. Finally, Benny ended up down on the ground, and Bill went back in to dance with his bride. We went back inside too. Benny could sleep it off right where he was. He'd see it differently in the morning.

How the dancing and the feasting and the drinking went on! Nothing interrupted the fun and good times for the next few hours. Around 4 a.m., the food and drink were all gone. The musicians, half-slopped, were falling asleep in their chairs. People started drifting toward their cars. Some had to be carried. Homebrew and Canadian good stuff were a potent mixture.

When Bill looked around for Josie, she was nowhere to be found. She'd taken off with another guy on this, her wedding night, so Bill took Maggie home with him. What the heck, it had been a slam-bang party, and everything would get straightened out in the morning, maybe.

P.S. I'm still mad about that ham!

Elmer Clanged

The three Litchfield brothers, Ernest, Elmer and Finn, lived in the old house on the hill above us. Ernest and Elmer were in their eighties, but Finn was younger. He was sixty-three and the baby of the family. There had been other children in their family, but they lived in Vermont. I only met one of their sisters, a lonely old lady who visited occasionally. She would try to clean up their house and "straighten them out," but they would fight and carry on so that she never stayed long.

In the wintertime, after Ernest had gone away, Elmer had to stay alone because Finn was away all week working in the lumber camp. Elmer hit the bottle but good, if he could get it. He was so fat that he couldn't get out without Finn to help him on the icy road.

Elmer had a cowbell in his coat pocket at all times to "clang" in case he needed help. It was my job every night about 9 p.m. before I went to bed to put on my coat, stand outside the door, and listen. If I waited five minutes and didn't hear the bell, I figured Elmer was in the house, safe.

One very cold night, just as I was about to go back in the house, I heard *clangity, clangity, clangity!* Elmer was in trouble. I rushed inside, put on my overshoes, called to Mim, "Elmer's in trouble," and over the road to the Osciers I rushed for help. Joe and Carl got their coats, and we rumbled and lurched up the hill in Joe's old winch truck.

Sure enough, as we drove around the yard, we could see Elmer's large hulk lying in front of the backhouse door. He was mad as a wet hen. He roared that someone had deliberately put that icy spot on the privy's path where he'd have to step. Elmer was pretty well-oiled. He had bribed one of his cronies to get him gin on Friday night instead of Saturday when Finn would be home to watch him.

I held the lantern while Joe and Carl got a rope around Elmer. They winched and winched until he was up and hanging with his boots about three feet off the ground. We were going to try and pull him little by little to the house when he said, "Wait a minute. I was going in, not coming out of the backhouse. Get me down out of here. I gotta go!"

Carl, Joe and I looked at each other. No way could we let him down. We'd never get him up again. There was only one thing to do. Carl went over and unbuttoned Elmer's fly. Boy, was Elmer mad, but he had to go bad. So there he was, swinging and swaying and swearing and spraying as he kicked and twirled round and round in the air. We kept back out of the way. Finally he hollered, "Get over here, Joe, and button me up. The cold's gonna snap the damn thing right off!"

That over, we pushed, pulled, and half-carried him down the path and, eventually, into the house. All the time, he was swearing about getting even with the bastards who put the ice there. We put him into his favorite chair by the table. He grabbed the bottle of gin and downed what was left. I was glad it was gone, but I knew he'd be really slopped now.

There were a couple of old horse blankets hanging on pegs on the wall. I dropped them over Elmer. He was really shivering. When Joe and Carl saw that he was settled, they went home. They had to get up early to go to work, but they would stop and tell Mim that I'd stay with Elmer until Finn got home.

I stoked up the wood in the kitchen stove, then sat down to wait for Finn. Elmer was deep in song by this time: "Down by the Old Mill Stream," "There's an Old Spinning Wheel in the Parlor," "Rock of Ages." Occasionally he'd rouse up enough to inquire, "How's that, little gal?" And on and on we went for a couple of hours.

Finally, Finn came in, bringing cold air rushing behind him. His cheeks were scarlet, and he stamped his big boots to get the chill out of his feet. He had to walk three miles out of the woods to get home from the lumber camp, and it was twenty degrees below zero that night. I made him some hot tea and warmed up some biscuits on the old stove. Finn grinned and patted my back. He was a big man, six feet, three inches, and he never talked much.

Then he pulled a wooden doll that he had whittled out of his pocket. It was about 18 inches long, and its arms and legs were jointed so that they moved. He had penciled a face on it, and a red bandana was wrapped around it for a dress. He handed it to me. "Oh, I love it. I love it." I hugged it close and spun around and around the room as he watched. Then I ran up and gave him a big smack on the cheek. He beamed and said nothing.

Well, Finn was home, so Elmer was safe. I pulled the blankets more evenly around Elmer's massive shoulders then put my coat on to leave. I thanked Finn again for the doll. Elmer interrupted his singing long enough to roar out, "Good night, little gal," and I went out into the cold, frosty moonlight.

Hugging my doll closely, I trotted down the hill. Until I went in and shut the door, I could still hear Elmer's song bellowing through the night from above:

Let the lower light be burning
send the gleam across the wave.
Some poor heartsick suffering seaman,
you may rescue, you may save.

Afternoon at the Carnival

The carnival was in Ticonderoga for a week, and Cowboy had a job working as "jack of all trades." He worked all over the carnival on any job where he was needed, and he collected late rent on the tent and booth spaces.

One afternoon, Cowboy took Mim and Bub to the carnival. Someone had to stay at Top of the Hill so no one would steal anything, especially Mim's homebrew. We didn't have any locks on our windows or doors. I was elected to stay home and keep the homebrew safe.

The only reason that I let Mim and Bub go to the carnival without me and did not throw a screaming fit was because Mim made me a promise. She said that I could go to the carnival with Cowboy when he went to work the next day. I could stay there all afternoon and come home with Cowboy when he was done with work. Wow! I couldn't wait.

The next morning, Mim put cardboard in the bottoms of my Buster Browns to reinforce the soles. Then she took some lard and shone up the shoes. She checked my one good dress to see if it was okay, and she picked out my least-holey pair of bloomers to wear. I put on the clothes and then laid my head on the ironing board, and Mim twisted some curls into my hair with the heat from the iron. She gave me a dime, and I was ready. I considered myself a gorgeous sight as Cowboy and I took off for the carnival.

When we got to Ticonderoga, Cowboy, instead of pulling up in the carnival's big parking lot, turned off on a side street and parked behind Peck's Auto Repair. Cowboy turned the car around and faced it toward Chilson before he stopped it. I asked why we had parked there, and he said he didn't trust somebody. I didn't ask who he was talking about.

We walked up the hill to the carnival ground. We walked around a while, then Cowboy said to behave myself, and he'd meet me at 5 p.m. by the carnival's front entrance. He had to go collect some overdue booth rent.

Did I ever feel grownup and important! I had a whole dime and all afternoon to figure out how to spend it. I went down the midway and the barkers were out in force. They were showing little tidbits of their shows—just enough to get you to spend your money to go inside. Most every show cost a dime to get inside the tent.

One show was called House of Giants. On his stage, the barker had a tall man of about 30 who had high heels on his boots. The barker said he was the *little* brother, and I ought to see the other giants inside—"Only a dime, little girl, only a dime"—but I kept walking.

The next was a fat lady who was supposed to have bigger, fatter relatives in her tent. She didn't impress me much. We had Elmer up in Chilson who was three times as big as that lady. I kept walking.

The freak tent was large, but no freaks were to be seen except two poor cretins whom the barker was playing up as wild people. He was ordering them around and making them do tricks. I felt sorry for them, and I kept walking.

The next tent had a weird woman onstage who was chewing on dead snakes. She had a box of half-eaten and live snakes at her feet. That was too disgusting for me, so I kept walking.

I walked by quite a few stands of ring-throw games and shooting games and guessing games, but none interested me.

Then I came to the tent of the hootchie-cootchie dancers. They were up on their stage, swinging their bodies around to music. They had on flimsy kimonos over their skimpy outfits. Some young guys were whistling at them. I was entranced. I didn't see the women's bored faces or the smeared makeup or the sweaty-looking clothes they wore. I thought them very glamorous and decided right then and there to be a hootchie-cootch when I grew up. I would have spent my dime right there to get in, but I was too young (no one under twenty-one), so I had to keep walking. A kid standing nearby told me that girls never went in that tent anyway—only men were allowed. That made me feel better, and anyway, I knew when I became a hootchie-cootch I'd get in, no problem.

I was getting hungry. I followed my nose to where a great smell was coming from—a roasted-peanut-in-the-shell machine. I sure wanted some of those peanuts, but I didn't want to spend my dime on them. A lady with a little boy walked up, and she bought him a bag. They walked away, and as they went, the kid was dropping peanuts out of the bag clutched in his hand. I walked along behind him and picked up the peanuts as they dropped. They were delicious. I wished he'd dropped the whole bag, but he didn't.

Then I went over to the rides. The swings looked too fast and the Ferris wheel too high. But the merry-go-round! Never had I seen such a thing! I had to ride on one of those horses! I reached for the dime in my pocket, and it wasn't there! I had lost it somewhere. I went running back all over where I had been, looking all over the ground. To no avail. My dime was nowhere to be found. I went back to the merry-go-round and stood there, brokenhearted.

Two women came along with about twenty kids. They must have been a church group from somewhere. The women bought long strips of tickets and handed them to the merry-go-round operator. He didn't even bother to count them. He just told everyone to get on. So I sidled over to the group and got on the merry-go-round too. No one noticed. I climbed on the beautiful white horse I'd had my eye on. Round and round, up and down we went in a circle while the music blared. That ride was worth it even if I got caught and sent to jail, which I thought was surely going to happen. When the ride was over, I couldn't believe no one grabbed me by the shoulder as I walked away.

I walked quickly along and came to a spun-candy machine. I watched the candy spin around, and my back teeth were hurting for wanting some so much. There was a happy-looking short lady spinning the candy. I never saw anyone chew gum as fast as her.

As I started away, she said, "You're Cowboy's kid, ain't you?" I nodded my head yes. She said, "Yeah, I saw you with him before." Suddenly she thrust a big twirl of red spun candy at me. I started to protest. She said, "Hey, that's for you." So I walked away stuffing red fluff in my mouth. It melted instantly and left the sour taste of strawberry food coloring behind it, ugh! But a gift was a gift, and I was going to eat it, no matter what.

Ticonderoga Pulp Mill's horn let out its 5 p.m. moan, and eating my spun candy, I started out to find Cowboy. When I met him, he looked nervous and said, "Stay close to me. I have to see my boss before we go."

We went in a tent, and the boss was there. Cowboy handed him a roll of money and looked quickly over his shoulder. I think he figured someone was following him.

The boss said to Cowboy, "I'm not giving you none. Why should I?" Cowboy's hand shot out like a rattlesnake and grabbed that money out of his boss's hand. He said, "Run, Yada, run."

The boss was taken by surprise. He started after us but realized immediately he'd never catch us. No one could catch Chilson Hillers when they had a good reason to take off, and as I saw it, we had a good reason.

The boss hollered to two burly-looking men across the midway, "Head 'em off in the parking lot!" And they took off. Little did they know that our truck wasn't there.

We kicked up our heels down the hill, around the corner, out of sight, around back of Peck's garage. Cowboy said, "Stand still," and he kept peeking out. In a minute, a car sped out of the carnival's parking lot and went by us, really moving. The boss and the two men were inside. They took a left turn and sped up toward Hague. They thought they'd catch us on that road as Cowboy had told his boss he lived out Hague way. He never said a word about Chilson.

We got in the truck and took a right turn, over the flat and up Chilson Hill. I put my feet up on the dashboard and resumed eating my spun candy.

We knew they'd never catch us now. Cowboy said, "Don't tell Mim about this." Then he grinned and said, "At least, we'll eat for a while."

We were belting out *"Buffalo gals ain't ya comin' out tonight, comin' out tonight?"* as loud as we could when we chugged up over the last grade of good old Chilson Hill.

Mim and Bub heard us coming, and they were standing there waiting when we pulled into the driveway. They wanted to hear all about the afternoon at the carnival. I had a long tale to tell, only what they heard and what really happened were two different stories, and the truth was not in me.

Circus Time

The circus was coming. As I remember it, it was to be located in a field just a ways out of Ticonderoga. They were picking the most outstanding public person from each community to be guests of honor at the circus. They picked Aunt Bonnie as most important person from Chilson. Now, no one begrudged her that. In fact, no one "gave a damn." It was what she did that bothered people. She went around telling everyone and bragging, even down to Ticonderoga and over to Schroon Lake, that there wasn't another person cultured enough in Chilson to be chosen for the honor. She was probably right, but she didn't have to rub our noses in it.

Aunt Bonnie stopped in to Top of the Hill to tell Mim about the honor bestowed upon her. She asked Mim if we were going to the circus. Mim said we kids were going, but she wasn't. She said she had some important work to get done, and besides, she'd seen circuses before. I could see Aunt Bonnie was dying to know what the important work was. Well, Mim was building a privy. She didn't tell Aunt Bonnie what she was doing and that she wasn't going to the circus because we only had fifty cents—just enough to get Bub and me in. She didn't have another quarter for herself.

Mim called us in from play about noon. We had an apple and a piece of cheese for lunch. Then Mim dunked us into a big tub of hot water. She scrubbed hair and feet. She cut fingernails and toenails. She put on our best clothes, but it was the middle of summer and we didn't have any school shoes yet, so we had to go barefoot. Mim said not to worry, no one would notice. Then

156

she put a little tie around Bubby's neck, and she tied a great big red ribbon in my hair. It made us feel a little better, not having shoes and all.

Bub and I were the cleanest we'd been in months when we took off with the Wrights, in their old truck, for the circus.

When we got there, I noticed some of the boys didn't have shoes on, but all the girls I saw did. However, I didn't see one beautiful big red bow tied on any head anywhere, so I stuck my nose a little higher and plopped my bare feet right through the crowd. (And, Mim, thank you for always helping me to come out ahead, at least in my mind.)

We bought our tickets and went inside. Of course, we could afford only the cheapest seats and had to sit up high in the bleachers, but we could see everything okay.

Down below us were the reserved seats. They were level to the circus ring. They had a blue ribbon across them so no one would make the mistake of trying to sit in them.

The tent filled up quickly. There must have been two hundred people, a big gathering for those times. I saw quite a few people from Chilson.

Finally, being seated last, came Aunt Bonnie with the elite group. The master of ceremonies, resplendent in shiny black boots and high hat, walked them across the floor and cut the ribbon. Then he bowed to Aunt Bonnie and company, and they sat royally on their thrones. No one from Chilson missed this entrance, but no one let on they noticed. We were too mad at Aunt Bonnie for putting down Chilson Hillers.

The music started with a bang. Clowns, circus performers and animals paraded around the ring, and they all bowed to Aunt Bonnie's group as they went by.

Act followed act. Acrobats, bike tricks and trapeze acts, and they all bowed to Aunt Bonnie's group when they finished.

Hawkers were running up and down the aisles selling their wares. Each one had something different. They had birds on a string, balloons, Cracker Jack, spun candy, cigarettes, cellophane dolls-on-a-stick all dressed in feathers and hot buttery popcorn. The Wright kids, Bub and I pooled the pennies we had and came up with enough to buy a bag of popcorn. We ate some, but it was more fun to pop someone down in front in the back of the head with a big hard half-popped kernel. They would turn around and yell, and you would be looking the other way, or you would look very innocent and pretend you didn't know what they were yelling about. Then someone would pop you from behind. Oh, it was exciting! You never knew when you popped someone if he might have enough beer under his belt to come back and start a brawl. Yes, it was exciting!

I had a couple of favorite acts. One was the dogs that came running out. They walked on their hind legs and jumped through hoops of fire. The lady and man with them had the dogs counting numbers and playing throw and catch. The dogs stood on their hind legs and pushed a doll carriage around, and they pulled a wagon with their teeth. At the finish, the dogs went over and danced around in front of Aunt Bonnie and company. Then they stood still and let them pet them before they ran out the tent. How I wanted to pet those dogs. Boy, was I jealous!

Then there was the horse act. They did tricks. Next, a lady ran out and jumped on a big black horse's back. As I watched them galloping around the ring, the lady standing on one foot on the horse's back with her tutu sticking out around her middle and with one leg stuck up in the air, my resolve to be a hootchie-cootch faded a little. Maybe I'd become a lady bareback rider instead.

Oh, came the finale—the elephant we'd all been waiting for lumbered into the ring. Around she went, standing on her hind legs, standing on her front legs. She did dance steps and twirled around in circles. A lady climbed on her back and did somersaults and back flips. Then the elephant's trainer set a great big jug of fizzing soda right in front of the elephant. The elephant picked it up with her trunk, held it to her mouth, and gulped it down. Then she walked, weaving around as though she was drunk. Everyone was delighted.

The band gave a fanfare. The elephant sashayed over in front of Aunt Bonnie and company. She was so big. She sort of frightened me, and I didn't know if I liked elephants.

Suddenly, the elephant did something that wasn't part of the act. She started sneezing and burping. Then she vomited right at Aunt Bonnie's feet. A whole big bunch of gunk gushed out of her mouth and splattered all over Aunt Bonnie and company.

Aunt Bonnie and company bolted out of their seats and were yelling and dry-heaving and clawing for their handkerchiefs and trying to wipe off their faces. The whole place was in an uproar. I've loved elephants ever since.

Great-grandpa Hall

Grandma Granger told me once about her father, my Great-grandpa Hall. He lived with her a couple of years after he was done working in the lumber camps.

There was an old house way up over the hill, past Flannigan's, and half a mile or so down the river. One day, some women and a man moved in there. No one knew where they came from.

After a while, people noticed men sneaking through the woods or over the log road leading there. There was a lot of talk, and finally, Gram said, the old house became known as the house of ill repute. I didn't ask what that meant, but I thought it meant that the house was haunted.

Anyway, Gram said that Great-grandpa Hall used to go over there and "scratch around." No matter how she hollered at him, he'd still go. She said he was a fine-looking old man and kept himself spiffed up. He talked and led you to believe, if you didn't know, that he had money.

Well, if he didn't up and marry the lady who ran the house of ill repute! One day he came home all dressed up and told Gram they were married. It was too late to do anything about it, so Gram just hoped for the best.

Great-grandpa Hall moved down to the house. For a couple of weeks it was quiet, then Gram saw him come down the hill with his suitcases. They had a fight, and he'd moved out. He went back in a few days, then left again. Then back and forth. Finally, he was thrown out for good.

He brooded over this for about a month. Then one Saturday night, after many snorts of hard cider, he decided he was going down to that shack and clean house. He had taken all he was going to take, and "they" were going to get thrown out of there. All except his wife. He and she were going to stay there and make a go of it. Gram couldn't stop him. He said that he would see her the next day, and away he went with blood in his eyes, up over the hill and out of sight.

He didn't show up the next day, or the next, or the next. Finally, Gram got Grandpa Granger to go look and see what he could at the house of ill repute. He went and found out that the people who lived there had cleared out in a hurry. It looked like there had been a big fight. Windows were broken out and whiskey bottles had been smashed on the ground. Some of the chairs were broken, but no one was around. It was very deserted.

No one saw or heard from Great-grandpa Hall. Gram knew he would never go away and not say a word to her. Rumors

The "house of ill-repute," as I knew it.

started. Then people began to believe he had been killed and was buried in the swamp, but nothing was found.

Weeks went by. After a while people forgot and no one looked for Great-grandpa Hall to come back anymore. But Gram said she knew he couldn't come back. He was in that swamp. That's what was believed by all the old-timers.

Of course, this fascinated me, so every chance I got, I went flying up the hill, through the swamp and down to the house of ill repute. The windows had no glass left. They were only black holes. The stairs leading to the second floor were broken, but I went up them anyway. The bedrooms were so quiet. I used to wonder what stories they could tell. I'm sure not the kind of nice stories I was thinking about happened there! Sometimes a rat would scurry between the walls and scare me, but mostly I loved it there in the quiet. Whatever happened, it hadn't ended there in the house of ill repute. It was in the swamp where I felt the "chills down your back" feeling.

Once I was through the swamp, I'd swear to myself that I'd never go back again, but something drew me time and again through the swamp to the house. I'd stay playing around the house all afternoon and start home at almost dark. Going through the gloomy, sullen swamp, maybe I liked the scary, excited feeling. I don't know, but I couldn't stay away.

I wasn't afraid of Great-grandpa Hall. It's just that I felt a brooding, waiting presence in the swamp. If I went by the right spot, a bony hand was gonna jump up and grab me. I would have dropped dead right there. I thought maybe he knew that and he didn't want to hurt me, so he did nothing.

I'm going back someday and walking through that swamp. Maybe now that I'm old, he'll know that dropping dead doesn't bother me anymore, and he'll grab my arm.

Pros and Cons of Red Twine

During haying time, I used to love to go over to Wrights and watch them cut hay. One day I noticed a red string around Clarence's neck and a red string around Clayton's neck, and Joe had one around his neck too. I was dumbfounded, but I didn't dare ask what the red strings were for. I watched day after day as those strings got dirtier and dirtier. The men worked hard, and sweat and dust from the hay got into the creases of their necks, and as the strings were in one of the creases, they got blacker and blacker.

One day I got up enough nerve to ask Clarence what the string was for. He said that red string kept you from getting a nosebleed. I said that the red string was black now. He said, "Yes, but it's still red underneath."

I ran home and told Mim that I wanted a red string around my neck to keep from getting a nosebleed. She laughed and said, "No." But I insisted I didn't want to have a nosebleed. I might bleed to death. Mim said I'd have to take my chances.

When Mim wasn't looking, I snitched a piece of white twine. We didn't have any red. I ran over to have Clarence tie it around my neck. He said white twine wouldn't work. It had to be red. So I threw away my white twine and reluctantly gave up the idea. I knew we didn't have any red twine, and I sure couldn't ask the Wrights for any. That would have been begging.

If that red twine worked or not, I cannot say. I did keep my eyes open, and I never saw Clarence, Clayton or Joe have a nosebleed, but then, I never had one, either.

Politics, Country Style

It was the summer of 1936. Franklin Roosevelt, Democrat, was president. Chilson was mostly Republican. The New Deal and all of FDR's "give-away" programs weren't for us. For Chilson Hillers, if you didn't work hard and earn what you got, you went without—which is usually what we did, but no matter. We had our pride. Of course, with few battery-run radios and only the *Glens Falls Times* that filtered into Chilson sporadically, we really didn't understand about bank failings and other things that were going on in the outside world.

But Alfred Mossman Landon from the Sunflower State of Kansas was running for president against Roosevelt. We were going to get Alf elected. He was Republican and would "straighten out the country."

Aunt Bonnie took charge of the campaign. She held rallies and meetings. She even went over to Schroon Lake and Ticonderoga to speak at their rallies and meetings.

She and her husband, Uncle Ray, had built a real nice house. They even had a toilet in it. There was running water that went out through the ground, no more slop pail under the sink to empty when it got full. They even had electric lights.

The floors were shiny polished wood, and the walls were "finished off" and painted. That was a miracle to me. Aunt Bonnie never let us kids in as we'd "track up the floors," but I peeked in the windows every chance I got.

Uncle Ray was a boxer. He went all over to boxing matches and made money. He won a lot. He also worked as a carpenter and helped on his father's farm. Whatever little work there was, he was there. He worked awfully hard. Aunt Bonnie wore silk dresses and always looked like she'd never done a day's work in her life. She snubbed people and considered herself to be "high society." People snickered at her and "her airs" behind her back.

However, Aunt Bonnie worked hard to get Alf elected, and she planned to have a big victory celebration at her home the day after he won. She never once considered that Alf might lose. Election Day came. The grownups went to vote.

We kids, Bub and my cousins Amy, Jimmy and all the very little ones, Dick, Whitney, John and Maureen, were corralled on the porch off the kitchen at Aunt Bonnie's. Our mothers were helping Aunt Bonnie get ready for her big shindig. They were cleaning her already-shining house. They had baked lots of cupcakes and cookies and made big potato, macaroni and gelatin salads early that morning, but Aunt Bonnie was making the sandwiches. She said they had to be very fresh and made just so.

We kids could watch through the kitchen door if we kept quiet. I stayed there because I was always hungry. I hoped she might offer me something, but she didn't.

They fascinated me, those sandwiches she was making. She sliced the bread in strips and was putting cream cheese and other spreads that I had never seen on the bread strips. She said they were "finger sandwiches," and they were for the "genteel people," who were coming to the party. She said we were not to dare touch those sandwiches, or even look at them. She might as well have waved a red flag in my face because I'd get one of those sandwiches, even if I'd die trying.

The next morning, the day after Election Day, came the bad news that Alf had lost. He got only eight electoral votes. Of course, New York votes were not among them, so Chilson's hard-fought campaign had amounted to nothing. Aunt Bonnie was in shock, but it was too late to cancel the party. To save face, she said it wasn't a victory party, anyway. It was just a get-together to thank people for working so hard on the campaign.

About 4 p.m., people started coming in for the party. They were very subdued. The house was full of people, but it was very quiet. Then Uncle Ray rushed in with a big package that someone had left at the post office for Aunt Bonnie. Everyone gathered around, and she, very importantly, took her time opening up the package. She lifted out a great, big wilted sunflower. Aunt Bonnie said, "Oh-oh-oh-ooooh," and sunk to the floor. Some men helped Uncle Ray lift her and carried her upstairs to bed where she stayed, staring at the ceiling, for three days.

Well, Aunt Bonnie was out of the way, and people started loosening up. Jugs of hard cider and homebrew appeared. The finger sandwiches were pushed to the back of the dining room table, but we kids kept our eyes on them.

Our musician, an old fiddler, arrived. He already had a "jag on," so he didn't have any qualms about making that fiddle squawk. He outdid himself, and the walls just rocked with his fiddling. Everyone was dancing with the strong homebrew they were slugging down having taken effect. Big boots stomped, and the pencil-thin heels on the ladies' shoes scratched and dug into the floors. Our dirty bare feet clomped right along with them. Aunt Bonnie's beautiful shiny polished floors became just a memory.

I noticed some "fine people" from Schroon or Ti standing on the front walk. They were hesitating about coming into that slam-bang party, but finally they started up the steps. Just then, old By Lightnin' Cross opened the front door and squirted a long stream of tobacco juice—*ca-splat*—right in front of them. I'm sure it sprayed them as it shot by. The "fine people" turned around and rushed to their car. They hightailed it out of there, and that was the last of the "upper crust" we saw that evening.

Things were really moving now. We kids figured it was time to make our move against the finger sandwiches. Jimmy and I sneaked under the table and slowly pushed the tray over to where we could grab it off. We didn't want to get caught, but no one saw us, or if they did, they didn't care. The grownups were too full of homebrew to eat. We gobbled up the finger sandwiches. They didn't taste so great to me. If that's what "genteel people" ate, they could have it. We ate the cookies and the cupcakes too. We were too full to eat the salads, so we set them out through the window for our dogs who were waiting there for us to go home.

The party was in full swing, but we kids were getting awfully tired, so we lay down in a corner of the living room and went to sleep. We could have gone up and gone to bed in one of Aunt Bonnie's soft shiny clean beds, but we were afraid she would find us and start grilling us. God help us if she ever found out what happened to her finger sandwiches.

Next morning, when we woke up, the house was a mess and smelled like a brewery. We crept out the door so as not to wake Aunt Bonnie and started home. Along the way, we passed quite a few bodies lying beside the road, "sleeping it off." In those days, that was a sign a party had been a good one.

Don't get me wrong, kids, about Aunt Bonnie. She really meant well, and I remember her with affection. She just tried to bring a little highfalutin' class to people. She never had a prayer.

Typical Late Summer Morning

Every morning, Bubby was up early, 5:30 or 6 a.m., as soon as the sun came up out of the valley over Lake Champlain.

Some mornings, I slept late, but mostly I was up too, especially when the sun's first rays hit directly on my eyes through the little window by my bed. It was always chilly in the house at that time, and I shivered as I put on my clothes. Just panties and dress. I didn't even comb my hair—it was a short boy cut anyway—and then I'd bolt through the door to the stoop.

As I stood on the stoop, the sun would warm my arms, but the field beckoned. I would run over, crawl under the old wire fence, and run, run through the beautiful sweet-smelling tall hay from one end of the meadow to the other. Sometimes the heavy dew made my feet and legs all wet, but as I was so warm from running, the cold water felt good.

Back and forth I'd go until, finally, I'd go over the hill at the far end of the field and down to the brook. Wright's old cat was usually sitting there fishing. She was a very dignified old cat.

The first few times I caught her there, she looked at me disdainfully and would walk away slowly. Finally, after a few mornings, she accepted me as a stupid necessary bother if she wanted to fish. We seemed to have an unspoken agreement. If I would stay back about 30 feet and sit quietly, Cat would allow me to watch.

As I'd sit hugging my knees, she would forget about me and go intently on with her fishing. Suddenly, her paw would sweep out, and a minnow, or chub, as we called them, would fly through the air in a silver arch and land on the bank. How the sun would shine on the sides of that fish and make it sparkle! Cat would slowly turn to see if the fish had landed far enough back up on shore so that it couldn't flop back into the brook. If she thought the fish might be too near the water, she would pounce, flip the fish farther back on shore, and return to her fishing.

When four or five of the three to four-inch chubs were up on the shore, Cat would slowly turn, sit up straight, and stare me right in the eye. I knew that I was being dismissed; fishing was over. Cat never allowed me to watch her eat her catch. She insisted on enjoying her feast in private.

So I'd be up and away, running back to the field. I'd grab an apple from one of the wild apple trees on the side hill. Munching my breakfast, I'd run for my car at the side of the meadow. It was an old car—I guess a Model A. The tires were gone, and it was sunk over its wheel hubs in the turf. The windows were all broken and stuffing was coming out of the old leather seat. But the stick shift was there and the steering wheel turned. I was in awe of that car. I thought it had been there forever.

Before I could sit on the front seat, I'd look carefully inside. Usually up in the left-hand corner, over the driver's seat, I'd see "Old Bud"—a great big fifty-cent-piece-size gray barn spider. I figured he moved over from the barn across the field. If he was there, I'd get a rock or stick and bang on the side of the car. Old Bud would scurry up under the torn edge of the cloth on the ceiling of the cab.

Why didn't I kill him? I shuddered at the thought of the horrible splash he would make. But mainly I didn't want to kill him. I liked him, but I had a healthy respect for the terrible bite he could inflict.

Soon I'd be in the seat with Old Bud peeking down at me. As long as I had warned him I was coming, he tolerated me and we never had any trouble. I'd take off the brake, put on the gas on the steering wheel, step on the floor peddle, and slowly, slowly the car would start moving. My mouth sputtered and puffed the noise of the motor. I'd hit the little horn button hard. I'd hear the *uga, uga, uga* as my mouth yelled the sounds. I'd throw open the throttle, and I was flying over the ground. The landscape flew by the windows. I went over hills, mountains, and through valleys.

Faster, faster, things flew by me. The sun was warm, the morning was beautiful, the world was mine, and I was free, free! Oh, the trips I took in that car!

Slowly I'd return to the meadow; the landscape fell back into place. The car crawled to a stop. I turned off the throttle. The roaring motor stopped coming from my mouth and I climbed slowly from the car. If I waited a minute and watched, Old Bud would come sliding down a thread and take up his business of checking his web for tears and flies.

I'd pick up my apple from where I'd dropped it on the ground and walk slowly toward the house. Just as I got there, the old horn on the lumber mill down in Ticonderoga moaned out 8 a.m. I felt so good that I twirled round and round. The world was my oyster. I was free, free, free and the whole beautiful day was ahead.

Reflections

We were getting up in the world. Mim arranged for Bub and me to take music lessons. Now I love music, but as for playing it, I don't have a musical bone in my body.

Mim got Ernie Meanne to come over from Hague to be our teacher. He sometimes played in the band that Mim had for the dances at The Top of the Hill. She paid him a quarter apiece for each of our half-hour-long lessons. We used the orchestra stand (stage) in the dance hall, and the piano was there too.

Bubby was the first with his lesson. He was so cute, standing there scurrying up and down his scales. The violin was as big as he was. You could see the relief on his face when he was done and could rush off the stage. Then it was my turn. Whenever I sat down at that piano with Mr. Meanne, I wished with all my heart that I had practiced during the week. He was awfully nice, and he tried to make my wooden fingers produce some kind of music. Nothing much ever happened, but he was very patient with me and I liked him a lot. He was an alcoholic. He really tried, but one day, he fell off the wagon and was off on a six-month toot, so Mim had to find another teacher. I was hoping she never would, but she did.

She heard about a Mrs. Twang, over Paradox Lake way. Mrs. Twang had retired from teaching music in a school when she got married a few months before. She was looking for some private pupils. She told Mim that she would come over to Chilson and teach us, if Mim could get a few more kids together as students. Then it would be worth her while. Mim talked some of the neighbors into letting their kids take lessons, and some of my cousins were joining too, so our musical group came into being. Mrs. Twang named us The Reflections. We met every Wednesday after school at the orchestra stand.

Mrs. Twang got along okay with all the kids but me. She could see that I had no talent, but worst of all, she knew I didn't care and hated playing the piano. She told me I had a tin ear, and would slap me or give me a shake when she thought no one was looking. Sometimes she pulled me off the piano stool onto the floor.

This went on from fall to spring. I didn't tell Mim because I was so humiliated and hurt. I know I was no prize music student, but couldn't she allow for me being eight years old?

In May, our lessons were almost over for the summer (thank God!), and Mrs. Twang said we were going to give a recital. By this time, my terror of her had turned into a deep-down hatred. Somehow I was going to make her feel the way she had made me feel. I figured out what I would do to her recital. I told Clarence what I was going to do. He was laughing, and thought it was great. He said, "But she'll kill you." I didn't care.

A couple of the kids did see what Mrs. Twang was doing to me, and they told their parents. They, in turn, told Mim, and they were all mad. They decided, in order not to upset us kids, they'd wait until after the recital. Then they were going to tell Mrs. Twang off and get rid of her. I didn't know any of this, but it probably wouldn't have made any difference anyway. I had made up my mind what I was going to do.

We were using the orchestra stand where we had our lessons for the recital stage. We nailed up a rope and put a big blanket on it that we could pull across for a curtain. Mim and Cowboy put rows of orange crates with boards across them in front of the stage. They were the seats for our guests.

Now we were ready for the big night. When it came, I kept peeking around the curtain to see parents, grandparents, and friends. My teacher, the minister and Aunt Bonnie hadn't made it. Knowing what I was going to do, I had been hoping those three wouldn't show up.

People settled down, and Mrs. Twang walked, all puffed up, to the middle of the stage. She said the musicians they were about to see were her representatives. She said that we had worked hard, but she had molded us and we were a reflection of her, and that's where we got our name, The Reflections. She thanked the audience, and our recital began.

Reflection No. 1 was Clarence W. He plunked out "Old Black Joe" on a guitar.

Reflection No. 2 was Bubby. He squeaked out "I Have a Little Pony" on his violin.

Reflection No. 3 was Marty F. He thumped away on a drum.

Reflection No. 4 was Mary B. She twanged the Jew's harp with "Yankee Doodle."

And so it went through about five more Reflections.

Then it was my turn. Mrs. Twang glared extra hard at me as I walked across the stage. I was supposed to play a couple of stanzas of "My Country 'Tis of Thee," and the audience waited for the notes to float out over their heads.

I started, "My count . . ." I stopped. Again, "My count . . ." and again, "My count . . ." then again and again until I was playing "My count, my count," over and over as fast as I could. At first the audience sat in shocked surprise. Then they started hooting, laughing and clapping.

Mrs. Twang, when she finally could believe what I was doing, jumped to her feet and pulled the curtain closed. Just because the curtain was closed, it didn't stop me. I kept on banging out "My count, my count" as loud as I could. The audience was still laughing.

Mrs. Twang came rushing over the stage at me and grabbed me by the back of my neck. I managed to bang out one more "My count" before she ripped me off the piano stool. She started shaking me and swatting me and saying, "You brat, you brat, you miserable little brat!"

Mim came rushing up and pushed Mrs. Twang away. She said, "That's enough. I'll take care of her now." Mrs. Twang's face was very red. She said, "You beat her! You beat her! You beat her good!"

Mim put her arms around my shoulders and walked me down the back stairs of the stage. We met Cowboy hurrying toward us in the back hall. He was grinning. He and Mim looked at each other and burst out laughing. They hurried me out the back door into our "sleeping house."

I thought Mim would beat me good, but it didn't matter, it had been worth it. She did not beat me. She hugged me hard and said, "Yada, what am I going to do with you?" I had no answer. I was only happy that my turn at being a Reflection was over.

Oh My God, Bedbugs

Mim had taken off on one of her disappearing acts again, but not before she'd taken Bubby to Gram Granger's to stay. Mim said Gram had boarders, so she could only keep Bubby. I had to stay home alone. She said I was nine, old enough to be on my own, just go to bed early and stay in bed late and time would go quickly. She also didn't say that there were only three or four apples left in the house to eat or how long she'd be gone. Well, at least this time she'd warned me. Usually she disappeared right out of the blue sky.

It was the 27th of December, Christmas vacation and bitter cold. Whether I wanted to or not, I had to stay in bed to keep warm. We had no heat in our sleeping house, nothing unusual.

I stayed there two days. The apples were gone, and I was getting pretty hungry. I decided I'd walk over to Gram's and visit Bubby. Maybe she would ask me to stay or at least give me a cookie and cup of milk. It was getting dark as I started out.

The snow was deep in the road. I slugged along around the bend and over Dead Man's Flats. My feet and hands were getting real cold, but I knew I had to keep moving.

The Heustises lived up over the bank of the road about halfway down Dead Man's Flats. Their house was low, not over nine feet high, and banked with horse manure and straw all around it to insulate it from the cold. It was really just a hovel, but smoke was coming from the old stovepipe in the roof, and the yellow glow from the kerosene lamps through the windows made me drool. I hadn't seen anyone in two days, and just the thought of people in there made me feel awfully alone.

I stood shivering in the road, looking enviously at their windows, when suddenly someone said, "My God, Yada, what are you doing out here at this time of night?"

It was one of the Heustis boys who had come up behind me. He picked me up and carried me into the hovel. He was hollering, "Ma, Ma!" Mrs. Heustis came running. They wrapped me in blankets, and Mrs. Heustis took off my galoshes and rubbed my feet to warm them. I said I had to get going. I was going to my grandma's. They asked if she knew I was coming. I said no. They asked, "Where's Mim?" I couldn't answer as I didn't know. They realized no one knew where I was and no one was looking for me.

Mrs. Heustis said, "You're staying right here, least till tomorrow." I cuddled down in the chair, so warm in the blankets, and fell asleep.

Next, Juanita, one of the Heustis daughters, was shaking my arm to come and eat. I went over to the table and sat down. They put a great big piece of meat on my plate. It looked like a big turkey thigh, and lots of turnips and beets. It looked delicious, and I asked Juanita was it turkey? She laughed and said they didn't have any turkey; it was skunk. At that point, I couldn't have cared less. It was delicious and I was terribly hungry. For dessert, we had big slabs of heavy gray bread (they had no yeast) with maple syrup poured over it. When I was done eating, I couldn't move.

I looked around the long room. There were snowshoes hanging on the walls and horse blankets and clothes. Their old grandfather kept getting up and spitting big streams of tobacco juice out the door. I thought it admirable the way he could shoot it way across the path before it landed on the ground. That way you never had to walk in it when you went out the front door.

One of the boys (there were about six or seven kids in the family) played the harmonica as Mrs. Heustis and the older girls picked up the table. I wanted to help, but they made a fuss over me and said no, stay in the chair and keep warm.

They were so nice to me, and everyone seemed so happy and good to one another. Even the dogs looked happy, lying around the old stove, chewing on their bones.

They were terribly poor, but I knew real happiness and affection when I saw it. I really wished I could stay with them forever. They filled up the old stove and we went to bed. I slept in my clothes with three other kids in the same bed. No one offered me anything to sleep in or paid any attention that I slept in my clothes. I slept in them for the three nights I stayed there. The only thing was, I felt something sting or bite me now and then. As it didn't happen in the daytime, I ignored it. After all, I was warm and full of food, and it was the middle of the winter. A rare treat indeed!

Waving back at them two or three times, over the road I went. Mim was there. She'd gotten some wood someplace, and our sleeping house was warm. Bubby was playing with his toy truck. Mim never asked where I had been or anything. I just came in and went on as if I'd never been away.

That night, I laid my clothes on the foot of the bed, put on my pajamas, and climbed in bed with Mim and Bub. We slept together in the big bed as we kept warmer that way.

Next morning, early, Mim got up and said, "Something just bit me." Bubby showed her two red bites on his neck. Mim pulled the covers off the bed and started looking. Suddenly, she grabbed something and squashed it between her fingers. An odd, disagreeable odor filled the air. Mim jumped back away from the bed and screamed, "Oh my God, bedbugs! I'm gone ten minutes (she was really gone a week), and you bring bedbugs home! Yada, what am I going to do with you?" As usual, I had no answer.

Bub and I helped Mim carry the bed, blankets, mattress, and pillows out in the yard. Mim poured kerosene from our one lamp over the bed and set it on fire. Bubby had some marshmallows that Gram had given him. We roasted them on sticks over the flames. We were never ones to waste anything, especially fire.

Mim finally asked me where I'd been, and I told her. She scolded me and told me not to go near that outfit again. She said we might not have much, but we were never going to live with bugs—pride, you know. Actually, if I hadn't known Mim would find me and snatch me home, I would have gone back and lived with the Heustises, bedbugs and all.

Just Another Day at School, or the Joys of Teaching

It was another Monday morning, and we were back in school as usual. Mrs. Forth, our teacher, was in a bad mood. Her husband was running around with a girl from Ticonderoga. The grapevine was going full blast over it. Mrs. Forth was in a real snit. We knew this from the way she glared over her glasses at each one of us as we took our seats.

Another school day had started. Mrs. Forth took roll call. Then she said, "Gloria, go over and sit with the third graders. You are skipping a grade. You don't seem to have enough work to keep you busy in second grade. Your mother has approved this, so take your things and get over there." Even though I didn't agree with this at all, I had no choice but to do what she said.

Over the weekend, the third graders were supposed to have written a report of two pages on different subjects that Mrs. Forth had assigned them. I knew most hadn't done it as I heard them talking on the way into school. They were hoping for one of Mrs. Forth's easy-come-easy-go days and that she'd let them get away without having their homework done. Too late, everyone realized that she wasn't going to be messed with that day.

We all had to listen to the reports. Mrs. Forth called it, "Being informed on current issues" time. Juanita Heustis was the first one called on to report. When Mrs. Forth called on her, we all knew her report wasn't done, but Juanita was so scared she took a couple of sheets of paper and walked up to the front of the room. She was to report on "Cows and Their Uses to Us."

Juanita looked at the first sheet of paper and started reading. She read about how important cow's milk was to us and how we used their meat for food. She went on to say how we used their hides for leather and their hooves for gelatin and glue. She also told how great the cow's manure was for fertilizer, and how, mixed with straw, it was good to put around the outside of houses to insulate them in the wintertime. After reading through each page, Juanita finished up the last page with, "That is why cows are so important to us. They are good friends, indeed."

Then Juanita smiled faintly at Mrs. Forth and started to her seat. She said, "Wait a minute, Juanita. Let me see that report," and she stared harder than ever at Juanita over her glasses. Juanita hesitated a minute, then walked over to Mrs. Forth's desk and handed her "the report."

Mrs. Forth looked at the papers a minute, and then she said, "Juanita writes with invisible ink," and she held the papers up so we could see there was nothing on them. She said, "Okay, Juanita, go write, 'I am a sneak,' one thousand times on paper and hand it in to me, and I want visible ink used this time."

We kids didn't dare breathe. Mrs. Forth called on Charles to go up next. He was a good choice because of anyone in the group to have the report done, it was Charles. He was always a very dependable kid. His report was "Why Corn Is Important to Us." Charles's voice droned on and on. I didn't hear a word he was saying. I was busy watching Juanita. Three times she raised her hand to be excused to go to the toilet. Three times Mrs. Forth said no. I'm sure she believed Juanita just wanted to get out of there and goof off.

Juanita kept squirming around in her seat and jiggling up and down a little. I knew she was desperate to go. I'd been in the same position myself.

Finally, Juanita turned very red, but the expression on her face was blank. She reached down for her old square dinner pail under her desk, took out the food, and put it on her desk. Then she sat the dinner pail, minus the cover, down on her chair. She pulled her bloomers down, sat on the dinner pail, and let go. The room was stark silent. Juanita had to urinate so hard that it sounded like thunder pouring into that tin dinner pail. When she was done, she pulled up her bloomers and sat the dinner pail back under the seat. She even put the top on it—very neat, you know.

Now Lois M. sat beside Juanita. Rose D. sat right behind Lois. Rose wasn't feeling well as her stomach had been upset all weekend. Juanita was awfully nervous and maybe that's why her urine had such an odor. The smell hit Rose's nose and she let go and up-chucked all down the back of Lois's neck. The silence in the room was deafening, except for Mrs. Forth's glasses, which at this point fell off her nose with a clatter.

As Lois was pawing at the back of her neck, I couldn't help it, and because I was trying to suppress it, it came out of my mouth worse than ever—a great, big snorting guffaw. I buried my head in my arithmetic book.

Mrs. Forth said, "All right, who laughed?" No one said anything. Then Mrs. Forth asked, "Frances, did you do that?" "No." Mrs. Forth asked three or four other kids, who said no. Then she asked Melvin M. He was a good kid, but scared of everything. He said, "No," but to be doubly sure she didn't think it was him, he pointed at me.

Mrs. Forth said, "Gloria, stand up." I did. "Did you do that—laugh?" I had to answer, "Yes, but . . ." "No buts about it," said Mrs. Forth. "You know where to go." I knew. I walked up front to the corner of the room and stood in the corner with my face to the wall. Mrs. Forth said, "That will teach you not to laugh." It began to dawn on me that Mrs. Forth and I did not agree on what was funny and what was not. Anyway, there I stayed in the corner facing the wall until lunchtime.

Lunch was uneventful except that I saw Mrs. Forth gulping down some pills. I think it was aspirin.

During noon hour, we kids decided Melvin shouldn't have told who laughed, no matter what. We all decided that he had to pay his dues. Carly had a bar of X-Lax that he'd been keeping until he could find a use for it. We took the outside paper off it and put it in its tinfoil cover on Melvin's desk. He found it and ate it right down. He didn't care where it came from. Any chocolate was a great treat in those days. Besides, Melvin wasn't too endowed. Any other kid in that school would have been suspicious and wouldn't have touched that chocolate with a ten-foot pole.

Noon hour was over. Mrs. Forth sat down and, still looking over her glasses, said we'd had enough nonsense for the day and we were going to get down to business.

We were well into our arithmetic class when Melvin stood up. He looked aghast, then "it" started squirting down his legs and out onto the floor. He squished from desk to desk, hanging onto chairs and grabbing at kids. "It" still kept squirting down his legs and out onto the floor, everywhere he went around the room.

Mrs. Forth said, "School's out. Everyone's dismissed." She knew Melvin's mother was down in Ticonderoga for the day, so she said, "Bob, go get your mother (Melvin's aunt). Tell her to come immediately. Melvin needs her," and Bob went running on his way.

We herded out of school. I looked back. Mrs. Forth was slumped in her chair, for the moment a defeated woman, and it was only Monday.

Tomorrow we'd be back in school, Mrs. Forth would be back in there slugging, and education would continue to march ever onward. I would have been proud to know someday I'd have a son who would "pick up the sword."

Angelo

The state road was going through at last. Men came from all over to work on it. Sully Martinelle came and brought his friend Angelo with him. They came up from New York City. Sully had a big dump truck, and they were going to haul sand and dirt for the new road.

They were looking for a place to board. Gram Granger had decided to take a couple of boarders. Someone told Sully about it, and the next morning, he and Angelo were there at the farm with their hats in their hands. Gram looked them over and decided to take them in for $4 each a week. That included all their meals and washing too.

Every night, Sully and Angelo came home dead tired and starving. After they sloshed around washing up out back at the wash bench, they came in to supper. Boy, could they eat! Gramp said it was a good thing that he'd put in enough potatoes so we'd have twenty or so extra bushels, or we'd never be able to feed them.

Sully was quite the ladies' man. He was busy courting Aunt Leona, so Angelo was left alone a lot. He used to go out on the back shed steps and sit there singing. He had a most beautiful voice and sang wonderful old songs in Italian. Of course, I couldn't understand the words, but I liked to sit on the ground in front of the steps and listen to him while Sully and Aunt Leona billed and cooed sitting on the swing on the front porch.

Once I asked Angelo if he was lonesome because he was alone so much. He looked surprised and said, "Oh, no!" He said it was the best home he had ever had, and that he was going to stay in Chilson forever.

No matter how much Angelo ate, he kept getting thinner and thinner. He never complained about anything, but one day he fainted while pushing a wheelbarrow at work. Sully finally noticed the way he looked and took him to Ticonderoga to see Dr. Cummings.

Angelo's sputum test came back positive, which meant he had TB and that he would have to go into a hospital for treatment. Angelo had no money, so he had to go back to New York City for treatment.

He cried all the time. He didn't report to the Ticonderoga health officers when he was supposed to, so they came up to the farm to pick him up.

When the health officers arrived, Gram took Angelo's suitcase to the front door and let them in. When she did, Angelo took off out the back door and ran through the woods to Gramp's sugar house to hide. No one could find him, so the health officers had to leave without him. They said they'd be back in a week to ten days, and Angelo had better be there. But he wouldn't come back to the house when I told him.

No one knew where he was but me. Angelo had told me once that if he was ever missing, he'd be in the sugar house and not to tell anyone.

I sneaked him donuts and fried pork belly for breakfast, and he gathered berries and ate them.

Angelo became sicker and sicker. He was coughing a lot, and I kept begging him to come home and go to New York for treatment. Besides, it was awfully cold sleeping on the floor of the sugar house. After about a week, I couldn't stand it any longer, so I told Grandpa where Angelo was.

Grandpa went over to the sugar house with me. It was a good thing I told because Angelo was awfully sick and couldn't stand alone. Grandpa went and got the horse and wagon, and we carried him back to the house. Gram sent Sully to Ticonderoga to tell the health officers to come get him as he was real bad off. They came right up.

They put Angelo in the back seat of their car. He tried to fight them, but he was too weak. He kept crying and crying. We told him to get better and come back as soon as he could. Angelo looked surprised and he said, "You really want me to come back?" We all said, "Yes, yes, as soon as you can." That perked him up a little, and between sobs he kept calling out "I'll be back. I'll be back" as they drove away.

I don't know what happened to Angelo as he never did come back, and we never heard from him again.

Old Alice, or My First Halloween

Finally I knew I was old enough to go "Halloweening." I waited a long time to get to be ten. You start doing a lot of things when you're ten. Mothers just let you somehow.

We never heard of "trick or treat" in those days. We just went out to scare a few people and maybe soap a few windows or turn over a backhouse. I put on some lipstick and an old blouse of Mim's and wrapped an old sheet around my waist for a skirt. There I was, a hootchie-cootchie dancer.

The other kids arrived at our house and hollered for me to come out. I grabbed a hunk of soap and was off. The wind was brisk and chilly. For a while, we wandered around, soaping a window here and a window there. Then we decided to go up to Mrs. Brown's. Sometimes she gave us apples. We went over the back road that led to her house. We cut across the field and through the graveyard, then up the hill to her house.

The kerosene lamp shone brightly from the kitchen window. We knocked on the door, and Mrs. Brown opened it. She smiled and asked us in to sit down. The kitchen was warm and cheerful. She gave us sweet cider and donuts.

As we sat eating, someone said, "Please tell us a story, Mrs. Brown." She thought a few minutes. Then she said, "Did I ever tell you about Old Alice?" That rang a bell with me. Grandma Granger told me things now and then about "Old Alice." From what I had heard, I didn't want to hear any more about her, but I also knew I couldn't help but listen.

Mrs. Brown seemed to look far away as she started talking. "I remember her when I was a little girl. No one ever knew from where Old Alice came. She was just always there living in her old house up on the hill. There's nothing there now, just a cellar full of fallen-in stones and briars. Old Alice was a tall ramrod-straight woman, always dressed in black. I never saw her smile, and I never heard her speak. There was one thing, though, that I'll never forget—the swish of her long gown as she walked. You could be walking down the road in the middle of the night. It could be so dark that you would have to ask who was passing to know who it was, but you'd always know when it was Old Alice by the *swish, swish* of her gown.

"Peddlers with packs on their backs used to go through here. They went from farmhouse to farmhouse peddling their wares. Old Alice's house was far enough along the route through the valley that the peddlers would arrive just about dusk at her door. People would see them go in, in the evening, but no one ever saw them come out in the morning. Some said she killed them and buried them in the cellar, but I don't know. No one ever proved anything.

"One evening, a peddler went in her door, and later that night, her house burned down. The next morning, no one could find Old Alice, so they started probing around the wreckage. They found a man's body on top of the old cook stove which had fallen through the floor into the cellar. But where was his head? They moved the old stove, and there was the head, slick as you please, under it. Now how could a head fall, then a stove fall, then a body fall, in that order, into a cellar, unless someone had cut the head off first? But no one ever proved anything, and Old Alice still roamed.

"No one knew where she slept now. She just wandered the night, *swish-swishing* her black skirt. Old Alice hated kids. She would stare at them when she walked by. Her mouth would be tight and grim. They say now and then, a child would be missing from the countryside, gone without a trace. But no one could ever prove anything. Old Alice still roamed—*swish, swish* she roamed.

"Then one morning, she died while in Crown Point Church. They made a coffin and buried her in Chilson Cemetery, and people didn't walk by there for a long time. Then some said they saw her now and then, walking through the graveyard, and that's where she stayed."

The story was over. It was getting late, almost 11 p.m., but I didn't want to go out into that night. If I could only put Old Alice to rest for good, for sure. So I said, "Lots of Sundays I've gone to the graveyard to put flowers on my Grandpa Hammond's grave, but I never saw Old Alice." Mrs. Brown smiled and said, "Oh, she only walks at night." That did it. There was nothing more to say. We had to leave that bright warm kitchen and go home. No way but down the hill and through the graveyard.

We started out in a tight, jittery bunch. Just as we reached the graveyard, I tripped. I screamed and the other kids were off. I yelled, "Hey, wait for me," but I was alone. I had to get through that graveyard. I tore off my long sheet skirt. I didn't want to trip again.

Under the old arch gate, up the short slope, and then I was there on the winding path through the gravestones. The wind

No way but through the graveyard.

came up quickly and started swooshing leaves around. They rustled around me like angry little ghosts. It was dark, real dark. I tripped again over a small marker at the foot of a grave, up and forward. Suddenly, the wind died and it was still. Too still. Then I heard it! Terror froze my spine. *Swish, swish* went her gown! Oh, God, I didn't dare look backward or sideways. Only forward. But I knew her mouth was set tight and grim. Somehow my feet moved faster. One, two, one, two over the ground. Something brushed my leg. Dear God, it had to be a branch fallen in the wind, and *swish, swish* went her gown. One, two, faster and faster went my feet. And *swish, swish* she came. Finally I saw the gate! I'm out! Run, run, run—finally the light of home. I wiped the sweat from my face and went in to safety.

I never dared tell anyone, but Old Alice had surely walked with me through the gravestones that night.

Did We or Didn't We?

Dot Chase, a widow, and her kids, John and Lil, moved into Chilson. I don't remember where they came from or why they came to Chilson. When Ron D. met Dot, he took a shine to her right away. They courted for a couple of months, then they got married. They moved into an old house half a mile from Bovine's Tavern. The house was very rundown and dilapidated, but it was all Ron could afford.

Lil and I became very good friends. We were always looking for something to do. (This really means we were always looking for some deviltry to get into, and usually succeeded.)

We went to school in the new one-room schoolhouse that had been built to replace the old two-roomer. The school went from the first to the fourth grades. Another new one-room schoolhouse was built down in the middle of Chilson Hill. That had grades five through eight.

Lil and I were in the fourth grade and felt pretty important being in the highest grade in our school.

That Friday, I was going home with Lil to stay overnight. We couldn't wait to get out of school to get started. At noon, we decided to go up over the cliffs in back of the school and "shoot the brook." It was late in the spring, but the brook stayed frozen even after all the snow was gone. As it ran steadily downhill, you could slide on your seat for long stretches all the way down. That was called "shooting the brook."

It took an hour to get to the top of the cliffs over to the brook. We only had an hour for lunch. There was no way we could make it back in time for the afternoon session of school, but we told ourselves we could, "if we hurried." When we got to the top of the brook, the school bell clanged out that lunchtime was over. We would be late by the time we got back to school, so we figured we might as well skip the rest of the day. We shot the brook with no ill results, except frozen butts. We went through the woods so as not to be seen from school and made it to Lil's house.

No one was home, but the old kitchen wood stove was still going, so we opened up the oven, backed up to it, and stood there toasting our rears and thinking about what we could do next.

Ron and Dot were on relief. They were on their weekly trip to get their food allotment. They borrowed any car they could to get there, and they stopped at Wright's store as they went into Ti. You were only allowed to buy food when on relief, but Mr. Wright would let the relief people have anything they wanted, and he'd mark it down as food. That's how Ron and Dot got their two cartons of cigarettes every week.

Lil said, "I know what we can do!" And she climbed up in the closet where they kept their cigarettes and brought down a couple of packs. We lit up and started smoking. Lil was an old hand. She had three lit up and smoking all at once while all I could do was choke along on one. Then Ron and Dot were at the front door, coming in. We had been so busy smoking that we forgot to keep an eye out for them.

We couldn't get the cigarettes out before they'd catch us, so Lil said, "Here," and she threw the cigarettes down between the open portions of the wall going upstairs. I threw mine there too. Ron and Dot went on into the kitchen and never caught on to what we had been doing.

We had supper, and Ron said he smelled something, like a fire smoldering. He looked all around but didn't find anything. We went out and sat on the steps until about 10 p.m., listening to the music coming from Bovine's Tavern. Then we went in to go to bed. Ron sniffed around and said he could still smell something burning, but probably it was from the kitchen wood stove that was almost out.

About 3 a.m., John hollered, "Fire, fire," and jumped out the hallway window. Ron and Dot slept downstairs, so they ran out the back door. There was smoke all over and flames were shooting out of the wall in back of the stairs, but I wasn't jumping out of any upstairs window. I hollered "Come on" to Lil, and we went down those stairs, three at a time. We were lucky kids, because we made it, but the bottoms of our bare feet were tingling from the hot step boards.

There was nothing we could do but stand out by the road and watch the house burn. It went fast. The nearest house was far away. Nobody saw the fire and nobody came.

When it was pretty well out, it was awfully dark. We went over to a back shed, went in, lay down on the floor, and went to sleep.

When Mim and Dot found out from Mrs. Forth that Lil and I had skipped school, they scolded us good. Mim asked me the usual, "Yada, what am I going to do with you?" And I had the usual no answer.

Lil and I talked about it at school, and we were feeling guilty about throwing the cigarettes into the wall. But look how mad they were at us for skipping school. What would they do to us for burning down the house?

Just *maybe* something else had caused the house to burn down. Just *maybe* our lit cigarettes thrown into the wall hadn't caused the fire. We gave ourselves the benefit of the doubt and swore to each other that we'd behave ourselves from then on. And we did until the summer picnic, but that's another story.

The Summer Picnic

Lil was going to stay overnight with me. That morning, after she got there, we were standing in front of Top of the Hill thinking about what we were going to do when four boys came strolling by. These four were always together. They had a club-house built up in a tree down by the river and they called themselves The Toughs. They were on their way to go fishing at Rooster Pond. Anyway, they were just moseying along, and Lil and I said hi to them. We wanted to talk a little, but The Toughs just looked right through us as if we weren't there.

Sure, they were fourteen or fifteen years old to our ten or eleven—real big shots and we were small fry—but we thought they could at least acknowledge our presence. They left us standing in the road, knowing they'd handed us a real putdown.

Lil and I were seething, and we decided we'd fix them. We went over in the Wrights' pasture and collected a bunch of horse manure balls in a cardboard box. We brought them home and hid them under Top of the Hill.

The next morning, when The Toughs came by, we were out front waiting. When we said hi, they again ignored us, so we pelted them with the horse manure balls. If they swore at us or even socked us, we expected it, but again they ignored us completely and acted as if they didn't see or feel any horse manure balls being thrown at them.

Now when someone ignores your horse manure balls, you know you are pretty low on their totem pole. The ultimate insult.

Lil and I were madder than ever. We began immediately trying to figure out how to take The Toughs down a peg. We couldn't think what to do, but we knew in time we'd come up with something.

The next Sunday was our summer picnic. When Lil and I arrived that noon, the tables, all in a row, were set up with so much food that it seemed they would buckle under their loads.

There were Gram's long pans of beans with brown sugar and bacon. Also Mim's six-inch-high homemade rolls and her melt-in-your-mouth johnny cake. The Wrights brought an enormous whole sliced ham, covered with pineapple. Archie Wright ran a store down in Ticonderoga, and he was the only one who could afford such a thing. Aunt Nellie had brought her famous banana cream pies, which I had a slice of at once—no way would I chance missing that! Aunt Dean brought fried green beans and creamed onion casserole. Aunt Ethel brought blood pudding and upside-down cakes. There was too much to tell, but every lady there brought her best. Salads, macaroni and hot sausage, codfish balls, corn chowder, split-pea soup, etc., etc., etc. Everyone knew who brought what and everyone was praised accordingly. It was a prideful thing, you know.

And I must not forget Charlie Fox. This was the only public social event he ever attended. I asked him why once. He said it was the only doings that didn't leave him smelling like the inside of a whiskey barrel when he left. He said after he left the other doings, it took him a week of standing upwind of Bear Pond just to blow the stink off him, and he'd had enough of that.

Anyway, Charlie Fox brought rhubarb and crabapple pudding, pickled eel and fried rabbit with gooseberry sauce—a whole knapsack full. Some stuck up their noses at his stuff until they could be coaxed into tasting a little, and then they wolfed it down. But I knew how good his food was, so I was way ahead of them getting his goodies under my belt.

Lil and I finally had to quit eating. We couldn't make a dent in that food because there was so much. When you're hungry most of the time, as we were, you try to eat enough to carry you through the next week. We walked away groaning. We'd come back for more as soon as we could hold it.

There were a lot of people there. We looked the crowd over, and who did we see?—our "horse manure ball" boys walking nonchalantly toward the back of the field. They went across this open space about twenty-five-feet wide before you got into the woods.

If you went across that twenty-five feet, it meant you were going to only one place, down to the rocks to go swimming. There was no other way in or out of there. People who swam there had to jump off the rocks to get in the water. It was very dangerous. You could crack your head open on those rocks. It was definitely off-limits to the Sunday picnickers. Well, the boys had made it with no one seeing them, and we knew how smug they must be, going down to swim.

Lil and I walked slowly over the twenty-five-foot clearing, and we were surprised that no one called us back. So there we were in the woods, and now what could we do to get even with The Toughs?

We sneaked down and looked over the rocks. Yeah, there they were down in the water, fooling around, skinny-dipping. All their clothes were in neat piles right beside us. We hesitated, but the temptation was too great. We grabbed up the clothes and ran with them.

Don't ask me how, but we got across the clearing again, this time with armloads of clothes, with no one seeing us. Or, if anyone saw us, they didn't question what we were doing as we were walking along so quietly and innocently. We veered over to the right into the parking lot. The first car we came to, we opened up the back door and flung all the clothes in on the backseat and floor.

Then we went over to the tables and ate all we could hold again. We had time because the boys would be swimming a while before they discovered their clothes missing.

Next, we sauntered over and climbed up in a big pine tree beside the clearing and waited. The Toughs had to go by us to get away. After fifteen minutes, we saw the boys sneaking along through the trees. They came up to the edge of the clearing and stopped. Lil and I sat very still. Of course, The Toughs didn't have a stitch of clothing on them anywhere.

The picnic was going full blast. People were eating and talking. Some of the men were playing horseshoes. Others were playing croquet with their wives. Kids were playing blind man's bluff and tag. Three ladies were singing, and people were standing around listening to them.

Everyone was so busy that the boys gambled that no one would see them rushing across that land. They would have made it, too, but Lil and I yelled out, "Hey, boys! Hey, boys, where have you been? Where you going? Hey, boys!" They froze in the middle of the twenty-five-foot stretch. Everyone at the picnic stopped what they were doing and stared. For a second, the boys stood there. Then they took off and dingle-dangled across the rest of the clearing and into the lot. The last view we had of The Toughs was their bare white behinds bobbing up and down as they ran between the cars.

The picnickers were stunned. Then pandemonium broke loose. A couple of ladies fainted and fell to the ground. I didn't believe they really fainted for a minute, but it made a good show. Most of the men were hollering and running after the boys into the parking lot. Kids were laughing and some were bellowing. The mothers of The Toughs were arguing, blaming each other's sons for leading theirs astray.

Lil and I decided to get out of there. We dropped out of the tree and landed on our hands and knees. We'd gotten even with The Toughs, and no one was the wiser to what was going on. Just as I stood up, I glanced across the picnic area and met Mim's beady eyes glaring right at me. I knew that she realized whatever had happened, I'd had a part in it. Lil and I took off for our homes as fast as we could run.

When Mim got home, I was raking the chicken droppings out of the chicken house. That was a job we all hated, and I thought it might soften Mim up if I was slaving away in the chicken coop.

She came over and looked in the door. She said, "Yada, come out here," and then, "Okay, let's hear your story." There was nothing to do but tell her what we had done, and why. She listened, and then she said the usual. "Yada, what am I going to do with you?" And I had the usual no answer.

Mim said to go climb up in my bunk and stay there till Cowboy got home. I stewed in my bunk for a half-hour until I heard Cowboy pull in the driveway, home from work. I climbed out of the bunk and stuck my eye to a crack in the front door. I couldn't hear what they were saying, but Mim pointed at the sleeping house where I was, so I knew Cowboy was getting an earful. Then I felt a little better. I knew I'd probably be kept home a week or so, but it wouldn't be too bad since Cowboy was laughing so hard, and Mim joined in.

Now, you might think after what Lil and I did, The Toughs would be out to get us. Nothing of the kind. After that, when they went by us, they always grunted hello. All we'd done was get even with them, and they knew it. We fit right in with their "tough" standards—an eye for an eye, and a tooth for a tooth.

I'll Always Owe Beatty One

I always looked older than my age. When I was eleven, I looked fourteen. Mim said the women in our family developed quickly. She said it was too bad our brains couldn't keep up with our bodies, and that's why we always got in trouble with our looks, through no fault of our own. Well, I wouldn't bet on that all the time, but I'm going to tell you about one time when looking older than I was got me in trouble.

No one could figure out why Beatty B. married Mike Cooley. He drank too much, but he was good-looking and could be charming if he chose.

Beatty was beautiful. She showed her Indian blood. Beatty's family was mostly pure Indian with a little English thrown in. Beatty was tall and slender with lovely long black hair. She had snapping black eyes, and when she smiled, her teeth sparkled beautifully—at that time, a rare sight in Chilson.

People expected great things from Beatty just on her looks alone. But she up and married Mike, and they set up housekeeping in an old shack halfway up Chilson Hill.

Mike ran around on her right from the start. One day he saw me for the first time in a long while, and he did a double take. He said, "Well, you've turned into some little lady," and he grabbed me by the arm. I snatched away and didn't think any more about it.

One hot summer afternoon, I was skipping along home from playing all day at Marie Brock's. She lived on a farm almost to the bottom of Chilson Hill.

I stopped at the spring a third of the way up the hill and stooped over for a drink. Then Mike grabbed me. I hadn't seen him, for he was back of a tree by the spring, sleeping off a drunk. He laughed and said, "Now I have you, you brat!" He started to pull me close, but he didn't have me as he was drunk, and I was quick as a cat. I ripped away from him and ran up the hill.

He was roaring mad and started after me. He yelled, "You brat, I'll get you yet!" My feet flew, but he wasn't far behind. Then his shoestring tripped him. Swearing up a storm, he had to stop to retie it. I kept running.

Beatty was standing in the door of their shack. I pushed past her through the door. I couldn't think of what to say, so I said, "Can I have a drink of water?" My mouth was all dry, and I could hardly get my breath from running so fast.

Beatty looked at me and asked, "What's wrong with you, Yada?" Then she said, "I know. He's after you, isn't he?" Just then, Mike came up over the rise in the hill. He was swearing and hollering, "I'll get you, you brat!"

There was no way out of the shack but by the front door. The window in the back wall was too small to climb out. Beatty grabbed my arm and said, "Under the bed!" The "bed" was just an enormous feather mattress on the floor. Beatty lifted the side of it and pushed me under and dropped it down on top of me. She said, "No matter what happens, don't move and don't open your mouth."

Then she rushed over by the sink just as Mike came in the door. He said, "Where is she?" Beatty asked, "Who?" He roared, "That brat! I'm going to get her! Tell me where she is, or I'll kill the both of you!"

Beatty said nothing. Mike looked in the little closet. He threw chairs around. He crashed a looking glass that was hanging on the wall to the floor. Then he started beating Beatty around. All I could hear was *crash, bang, crash*. Next he threw Beatty on the bed and had his way with her and beat her some more.

All that time, I was under the feather mattress. I don't know how he missed feeling me there. I couldn't breathe from the feather dust, and the heat was terrible, but not for one second did I move or make a sound. I knew if Mike found me, Beatty and I were both dead.

Finally, Mike threw Beatty across the room and said, "Just because I've had you doesn't mean I'm not going to get her. Where is she?" He was swearing and storming around the room and he repeated, "When I'm through with you, I'm going to kill you both!"

Suddenly the thought hit him, "I know! She's gotta be in the barn!" Out he rushed to search the barn. It was a big one that belonged to a farmer up the road, and because there was a lot of hay there, it would take a few minutes to check it out.

Beatty pulled me out from under the feather mattress. I was gasping, and she quickly pumped a drink of water from the sink pump and made me drink it. All the while, she kept her eye on the barn through the little back window.

One of her eyes was swollen shut, and her nose was bleeding, and her clothes were torn. All I could think of to say was, "I'm so sorry." Beatty cupped my face in her hands and kissed me on the nose. Then she reached under the sink and pulled out an old rifle which she set by the door. She said, "Don't worry, Yada. He won't get you today," and her one good eye looked like black steel.

Then Beatty picked up the rifle again and pulled the trigger back. I didn't doubt for one minute that it was loaded. She said, "Yada, get up the road for home as fast as you can. Whatever you hear, don't look back. Run!"

I ran out the door, up the road a ways, and then glanced back over my shoulder. Beatty was standing by the side of the shack and the gun was on her shoulder aimed right at the barn. I knew Mike was a dead duck if he stuck his nose out the door before I was a good piece up the road, out of sight. As I ran, I didn't hear the gun go off. I've always been thankful for that. Beatty didn't deserve to go to jail over the likes of him.

I didn't go down Chilson Hill again. I knew Mike wouldn't come over the top of Chilson Hill because the Wright boys hated him for all he had stolen from them on their farm. They were lying for him and he knew it. I missed going down to Marie's, but I didn't dare. Carl told me that Mike told him and some of the guys that I wasn't so smart, and he would get me yet. So I knew Mike was down there somewhere, waiting.

I was going to tell Mim, but she was busy digging a deep ditch from our house out through the back field. That's so we'd be ready to put the pipe in when the town water line went through.

Mim was dynamiting the ditch to make it go quicker. She knew it was against the law, and she was working as fast as she could to get it done. But the loud explosions going off so often one day made someone complain, and the troopers came and made Mim stop. They couldn't arrest her because they couldn't find the dynamite that she had hidden in a box under the cow manure pile. They couldn't arrest her without the dynamite, but they told her that next time, they'd get her for disturbing the peace.

Mim was beside herself. She said they had no right telling her what to do on her own land. They said she might kill somebody, and she sputtered that the only one she might kill was herself, and that was her own damn business. Meanwhile, she kept digging and hacking away with a pickax and shovel. Anyway, you can see why I didn't want to upset her any more.

It turned out that I didn't have to. A week or so later, Mike was down in the "railroad tramp jungle." This was a gathering place that the tramps had down by the tracks just outside of Ticonderoga. Railroad tramps cooked and slept there and caught trains for any place out of there when they wanted.

Mike went down there a lot to beat up the poor older tramps and steal their cheap wine and liquor. This time, Mike really got loaded and passed out. Unfortunately for him, I heard through the grapevine, that he passed out right on the railroad tracks, and the next freight train coming along cut him right in two.

So that was the end of Mike, and I could skip freely up and down Chilson Hill again.

P.S. Nothing ever happened that I could do to pay back Beatty for helping me that day. She died a few years later of cancer. I'll always owe her one.

Charlie Fox

Our farm was located on Bear Pond Road about one mile from the main road through Chilson. If you went past our house where the dirt road ended, you went up a trail to the mountain for about a mile and you came to Bear Pond. That's where Charlie Fox lived.

Charlie's real last name was Hall. He was a relative of ours somewhere along the line, as Mim's mother had been born Etta Hall. But no one ever thought of him by any other name than Charlie Fox.

Charlie Fox was one of the last of a dying breed, a real mountain man. He was a loner, and some said he was mean and sneaky. He'd get the best of you in any deal. Hence the name, Fox. But when Bub and I went up to Bear Pond, he was always good to us. Mim said it was because Charlie had a soft spot that showed only when he thought no one was looking.

Mim decided she'd put up some jam for winter. Charlie Fox picked the biggest blackberries that ever were, and Mim decided to buy them from him. She had fifty cents saved, so this day she grabbed a knapsack, and Mim, Bub and I started up the mountain to Bear Pond.

When we got to Charlie Fox's camp on the edge of Bear Pond, no one was in sight, but some smoke was coming out of the chimney. Mim hollered, "Charlie, Charlie Fox." Finally he stepped out his door, and he had an old shotgun in his hand. He said, "Mary, you sure no one followed you?" Mim told him no one had followed us, and she told him what we wanted. We were going to get the berries and get out of there. But Charlie Fox said no. There was an awful storm coming. Lightning was flashing and thunder was rolling way over in the distance. It was going to get dark early, and he said that we could get lost going down the trail, or a tree could fall on us from the storm; we'd have to stay overnight. Bub and I loved that, and Mim had no choice.

Charlie Fox said he'd rustle up some grub for supper. He took Bub and me down to the pond to get some bullheads. He told us he never caught bullheads in his side of the pond—they were his friends. So we went to the other side of the pond in his leaky row boat. Charlie threw some bread on the water and bullheads swarmed and twirled in a circle. We thought he was going to catch them, but instead he pulled a trap out of the water that had bullheads in it. I said, "But aren't those bullheads your friends, too?" Charlie Fox said, "No, you gotta draw a line between friends and food," and he proceeded to "skin out" the bullheads in the trap.

We went back to his camp. He shook up his stove, which was some iron barrels with an old car side that he'd flattened out for a top. Charlie grew potatoes and squash in his little scrub patch of a garden, and onions too. He cut a lot of these up and put them in a pot of water. He threw a big piece of pork side belly in with them, and oh, the delicious smells that came out of that boiling pot. He said, "I'll fry the fish, Mary. You make the biscuits." Mim spied the old teapot Charlie had simmering on the back of the stove. The tea in it was black, so strong it would almost float a nail. Mim didn't have black tea too often. We couldn't afford it, but she loved it, so she warmed up to her task, and she whacked biscuits together out of the flour, lard, etc. that Charlie gave her.

All this while I'd been looking around Charlie Fox's camp. He had an old table and tree stumps for chairs around it. Odds and ends of dishes were on a shelf near the stove. He didn't have any sink. He washed his dishes and clothes out in the pond. Mim said he ought to get himself, at least, a dishpan, and Charlie said, "You can't improve on nature."

All around the walls of the cabin, furs and skins of all kinds were hanging—deer, skunk, coon, beaver and even a bobcat. His bed was a bunch of skins thrown in a corner.

Supper was ready. We gathered around the table just as the storm really broke. Charlie Fox looked toward the open door and said, "It's okay, boys, come on in," and in walked three fat coons and the strangest-looking cat I ever saw. Charlie said the cat was half wolf. That made Bubby sit up and take notice. Did we ever light into that supper! Coons and cat sat beside us getting scraps thrown to them. One coon got up in my lap and sat eating a wild leek that Charlie had added to our meal to "spice it up." I was in seventh heaven. We really pigged out.

Then the lamp went out. It ran out of kerosene, and Charlie hadn't brought up any more from the "settlement," as he called it. Charlie Fox threw some more skins around on the floor. The storm was raging, and it was very dark. So there was nothing to do but lie down on the skins and go to sleep, but not before Charlie gave me a coon skin to take home to cover my doll. He had already given Bubby a slingshot that he had made—good for plunking squirrels.

Charlie Fox snored up a storm, and Mim and Bub were to sleep. I lay there with a fat coon cuddled up on one side of me and that crazy-looking cat on the other side. My stomach was full, and we were warm and dry from the storm. I was such a contented little girl as I fell asleep.

Next morning, the storm was over. It was stark still out, clear and cold with the promise of a beautiful day ahead. Charlie Fox threw all the leftovers from supper in a big iron frying pan, even Mimmie's biscuits. Then he "het it up" on his old stove. That was breakfast; God it was delicious, washed down with his "nail-floating" tea.

It was time to go home. All there was left to do was measure out five quarts of blackberries and put them in our twelve-quart measure. Charlie measured out the berries and plopped them, one quart at a time, into our knapsack. When he was done, he shook the knapsack and settled the berries. Then he got down beside the knapsack and skimmed the berries with his eyes. He took out three or four and threw them back in his basket of berries. Then he put two berries back in ours and squinted across the top of the berries again. He said, "Nope, that's not right," and he took the two berries and put them back in his basket. At last he was satisfied. He said we had exactly five quarts, and he held out his hand for the fifty cents that Mim owed him.

Charlie Fox put the money in his pocket. Then he picked up his basket of berries and shook them into our knapsack until it was overflowing.

Mim said, "Charlie Fox, what are you doing? I can't pay for all those berries." Charlie said, "Those are for the young 'uns. It's gonna be a hard winter, and they'll need something to put on their bread." Mim said, "Charlie Fox, take those berries back. I can't buy the sugar to do them up." Charlie took the fifty cents back out of his pocket and forced it on Mim. He said, "That's for the young 'uns, and I ain't gonna hear another word about it." So there was nothing to do but pick up the knapsack and head for home. As we went down the path, we looked back, and there stood Charlie Fox waving goodbye with that weird old cat sitting on his shoulder.

Mim did make jam, and I helped her. We poured it into old jelly glasses and poured melted-down candle wax over it to seal it. Sometimes that winter, all we had was a piece of bread with Charlie Fox's jam on it three times a day. It kept us going.

We hardly ever have blackberry jam anymore. But when we do, I remember Charlie Fox, and I silently blow him a kiss. I believe the wind carries the kiss up and softly sets it down on Charlie Fox's grave, where he sleeps near our beloved Bear Pond.

Fertility

Mim and Cowboy were drifting apart. One day I realized Cowboy wasn't with us anymore, and he wasn't coming back. Mim left Bubby and me over to Grandpa and Grandma Granger's to stay because, without Cowboy's help, she had to work harder and harder to make ends meet. She paid a little each week for Bub's and my board.

I was lonely and feeling sad because of Cowboy. Bubby went down the hill to Tweedle's farm every day and played with his dog and any of his grandchildren who wandered in, but I never wanted to go. I'd go out into the barn and try to catch a cat to play with instead.

Every barn had cats. They kept down the rats and mice that were always after the grain stored in the barn for the cows and horses. All the farmers ever gave them was milk, so the cats had to catch the rats and mice or starve. Barn cats weren't very friendly, and they never were allowed in the houses close to people.

Every couple of years, there would be a "cat sleeping sickness" epidemic. The cats, when sick, would just lie down, go to sleep, and die. That happened at this time, so our barn was without cats.

Grandpa brought home a big mother cat that he got from someone down near Ti. I thought he was going to bring more, so I said, "But it's only one cat." Grandpa said, "Don't worry. She'll take care of that."

A couple of weeks later, I was out in the barn, and I heard faint squeaky little meows coming from under a corner of the hay in the haymow. I looked under, and there was the mama cat and four little kittens. I fell in love with one immediately. It was white and had a black ring completely around its neck like a collar.

Now when kittens were born, the farmers always drowned most of the females and kept only the males. Otherwise, the farms would have been more overrun with cats than they were. It sounds cruel, but it had to be done—part of the "survival practices" of the times. So I looked under my kitten's tail. Oh, no, it was a girl, and here came Grandpa into the barn. I couldn't let him see the kitten, so I quickly stuck it in a pocket and hoped for the best.

Grandpa saw me and came over to see what I was looking at. He said to the kittens, "You finally got here. Well, I better check you out." He picked each up and looked under their tails. Those three were all boys, so he put them back in their nest with their mother and went on about his chores.

After he left, I put my kitten back in with the others. I decided to call her Sam. I thought it might help to hide the fact that she was a girl.

After he checked them out, Grandpa didn't pay much attention to the kittens. Sam grew and thrived. When she was about ten months old, I went out in the barn one day, and Grandpa was looking down in the hay. There was Sam surrounded by six little kittens. She couldn't have had two or four, she had six—adding insult to injury for Grandpa.

He turned to me and stared me right in the eye. He said, "I checked those kittens. How could this happen?" And he stared me harder in the eye. There was nothing I could do. I had to tell him what I had done.

He shook his head and said, "Yada, what am I going to do with you?" A lot of people asked me that in those days.

I said, "Grandpa, do you have to check them out?" He said, "Yes, Yada, it has to be done, but I'll only take the girls." I knew he thought quite a few of them were female. He checked them out, but Sam and I had outwitted him again. Unbelievably, unheard of, but every one of those kittens was a boy, so Grandpa had to leave them all. He had promised.

I said, "I guess I can't call him (her) Sam anymore." Gramp said, "No, I guess not." I asked him to name Sam a new name. I was buttering him up. If he bothered to name her a new name, I knew Sam was staying. Grandpa said, "Sam is hereby christened 'Fertility,'" and he was grinning. I didn't know what fertility meant, and I didn't care. Fertility was here to stay.

The boy cats were strong and grew big. Of course, Grandpa had to tell his farmer friends what I had done. When they needed a cat, they'd come over and get one of Fertility's kittens. She was an awfully good mouser, so they figured her offspring would be the same.

I did notice that they always rechecked under the cat's tail to be sure it was a male, not a female. No one was sure that I might not try to sneak a girl through again.

Grandpa caught Fertility when she went into heat the next time. He locked her in the fruit cellar when she yowled and meowed and scratched the cellar way door to get out and go see her boyfriends. The noise drove us crazy. We could hear it, even in the house. I would have let her out. But Grandma was wise to me, and she warned me if I let that cat out and she went on a tear and came back full of kittens, I was a dead duck. The way Grandma said it convinced me she meant what she said. I didn't let Fertility go free.

Fertility ruled the barn. She was smart. All the cats sat around waiting for Grandpa to squirt milk in their mouths when he was milking. But Fertility would sit up on her hind legs and beg. She was so cute that she'd get more squirts of milk aimed her way, more than the other cats, and she knew it.

Over the next six to eight months, many things were happening. Mim had met a man named Bob Ford, and when she brought him to meet us, I instinctively knew he was going to take Cowboy's place. Then Top of the Hill burned down, and Mim was looking to buy a farm for us. She'd gotten some money from somewhere to buy one. When she found one, she came to get Bub and me. She said we were going to "start a new life" on the farm. I went out to the barn to say goodbye to Fertility, and Mim, Bub and I were off to our newfound utopia. I'm glad we couldn't foresee what the next few years would hold for us.

For a few weeks, it was quiet on the farm. Mim, Bub and I went slugging along, fixing things up and settling in. A couple more weeks went by. Then we went over to Grandpa and Grandma's house to visit.

I rushed out to the barn to see Fertility. I couldn't find her or any of the cats, so I asked Grandpa. He said that the cat sleeping sickness had struck again, and the cats had died. Fertility went too. I was heartbroken. Now, by some miracle, one little cat had survived. She was one of Fertility's kittens and looked just like her, all white with a black ring around her neck.

Grandpa said I could have the cat, and Mim said okay, because our farm didn't have a cat and we needed one. So Fertility II went home with me.

Fertility II and I had some great adventures. Sometime I'll tell you about them, but you're not going to believe me about the things that happened.

Special Friend

Bob Ford was really in our lives now. Mim was getting a divorce from my father, who was in Fort Blanding, Florida. Mim said Bob was going to be our stepfather, and he moved in with us on the farm.

At first he was nice to us, but his "nice to us times" came further and further apart, especially when he was drunk. He was a lumber contractor, and I will say that he knew his business. He got a job cutting pulp near Chilson, so we could stay right on the farm. He could work his pulp job from there. However, none of the local lumberjacks would work in the woods for Bob. They had worked for him before, and they knew how mean he could be. Most were afraid of him.

So Bob went up to Maine, where he used to live and work, to recruit some lumberjacks. He came back with five men. One was a colored man named Arnie.

Arnie was the first black man I'd ever seen. Of course, I was fascinated. He had the most beautiful white teeth I'd ever seen. We had no dental care around Chilson, and some people's teeth weren't that great to look at. I never found out why Arnie had come down to Chilson to work. I'm sure he'd seen bad times and had a hard life, but he was awfully nice to Bub and me and talked to us like we were grownups, not little kids.

The other lumberjacks stayed by themselves more and on weekends would go down to Bovine's and get loaded, but not Arnie. He would sit on the porch and talk to us and quote poetry. He knew more poetry and could quote it to no end, like no one I ever knew. He knew Poe's "The Raven" by heart and "Annabel

Lee," which was my favorite. He never lost patience, no matter how often I asked him to recite it.

He knew stories too. In fact, he could recite them like he was reading them from books. He could tell "A Tale of Two Cities," and I was right there fighting with the patriots. And "Treasure Island"—I loved Long John Silver, though he scared me. He told about "The Last of the Mohicans," and I was breathless, sneaking around with the Indians. I laughed over Dickens' "The Pickwick Papers" and cried over "David Copperfield." And how Arnie and I laughed over "Tom Sawyer" and "Huckleberry Finn." Arnie could tell all these stores from memory, and many more. He opened up a whole new world to me. He instilled the love of the classics in me that has lasted a lifetime.

Meanwhile, the men worked in the woods, and I did my chores and worked in the hay fields. My skin is the kind that tans deeply, so being out in the sun so much, I got darker and darker. The lumberjacks kidded me and said I was getting so dark that I looked just like Arnie. I was awfully proud of that. To me, Arnie was the greatest.

Arnie knew what was going on. He knew how Bob abused us, especially when Bob was drunk. Arnie never said anything, but he watched out for us. Of an evening, when Bob started swearing and hollering more than usual, Arnie would go make a big noise in the barn or the chicken coop. Bob would go running out to see who was after our chickens or whatever. Of course, Arnie would be out of there, and Bob would rave around the barn trying to figure out what was going on. At least, for the rest of that evening, Bob would forget to be mean to Mim, Bub and me.

One evening, Mim was getting supper. Bubby was setting the table, and he dropped and broke the catsup bottle. Bob insisted on catsup to put on his potatoes every night, so we knew we had to get some. We didn't have any money. Mim took a dozen eggs saved from our hens, and she and Bubby went running up over the back hill on their way to Lonson's store. Lonson would trade a bottle of catsup for the eggs. I stayed at home to keep the old wood stove going. The potatoes for supper were on it, boiling.

Mim and Bub had just disappeared over the hill when Bob drove in the driveway. He was drunk. He'd stopped off at the saloon, and he'd tied on a good one. He was in a really mean mood. He was madder when he found out Mim and Bub were gone, and he would take it out on me.

I was over on the side of the kitchen where I couldn't get out. The door was behind Bob. He smashed the end off a milk bottle and came at me with the rest of the broken bottle in his hand. He said, "You little brat, now you're going to pay for what your mother's done to me!" I sunk down on my knees and cowered in the corner. As Bob was about to slash me, a wild streak of fury came out of nowhere and crashed him over the head with a stick of stove wood. Bob fell to the floor unconscious.

It was Arnie. He picked me up and brushed me off, and he said, "It's okay now, little Yada. When he wakes up he will have slept it off."

Then he said, "I'll have to go, Yada." I knew what he meant. When Bob came to, if Arnie was still there, he was dead, even if it meant Bob had to take a gun to him.

Arnie got his razor and jacket from upstairs. He started for the front door. I knew I wouldn't be able to walk him down the road a piece. Bob might wake up and catch me. But I could give Arnie a kiss on the cheek, and I did. Arnie smiled his nice smile at me and said, "Good luck, little Yada," and was gone.

Young as I was, I knew I had lost a very, very special friend. I pray Arnie found a happy life somewhere.

Talking to Sarah

It was such a hot day. We were getting ready to go see you. No one was talking much. It was so hush-hush, but I heard Bob say you were dead. I heard him say they found you hanging from a tree up on the ridge. And I heard him say something about you "being in a family way."

Bob said that Mim shouldn't take me over to your house. All that sorrow. But she said I was going. I was glad, 'cause you were always nice to me, Sarah. Bob said, "Well, I'm not going." He started out to the garden to hoe the corn. Mim called, "You're going." He didn't answer.

Mim splattered down my hair and wiped my face. We went out the door, down the path, and out past Bob. I faced straight ahead but peeked from the corner of my eye. Mim glared as she sailed by. Bob slammed his hoe into the dirt and came along behind us. Mim didn't say anything.

We came to the old, old house where you lived. As usual, Ed, your bratty little brother, was sitting in the big old crabapple tree by the front door. As usual, he bopped me in the back of the head as I went by. *Bang*, sting! But this time I didn't turn around and holler at him. It was beneath my dignity. We had come to see you in sadness, Sarah. We walked in the door, through the kitchen, into the little side room on the left. It was darkened by a blanket that was hung over the window, but in a minute our eyes adjusted to the low light.

You were lying on a big board supported on each end by a chair. Your face was covered by a cloth. You had on your Sunday-go-to-meeting dress, and I couldn't believe it! My eyes

We went over the road . . .

. . . to the old house where you lived.

popped. You had on shoes like I'd never seen before. They were shiny new and black, with buckles on the sides. My bare feet itched to have something like that on them. I wanted to grab those shoes and run, but I stayed rooted by Mim's side.

Your grandma took the cloth off your face. She put it in a basin of water on the table near your head. Later, Mim told me there was alum in the water to keep your face from turning black. I glanced at your face, Sarah. You were so quiet. My eyes

213

snapped back to those shoes. Never in this world was there a pair like that.

Mim went over to your mom and kissed her on the cheek. She whispered something. No one else said anything. I could feel the sorrow and sadness hanging like a cloud in the air. I knew Mim told your mom that we'd be there tomorrow morning for the funeral. We walked slowly to the door. I glanced back. Your grandma was putting the cloth back over your face, but my eyes were riveted to those shoes, Sarah. They seemed to glow in the low light of the room.

Next morning, again, it was so hot. We walked swiftly as we went up the hill. We had to wait by the back door.

They were just carrying you in from the ice house. They kept you there overnight to keep you cool. After a few minutes, they had you settled in the house, but not before your old dog, Beanie, howled mournfully, loud and long, out in the barn where he was locked up. I knew he was saying, "I miss you, Sarah" and "Goodbye."

Next we walked slowly into the kitchen and sat on some chairs facing the little room where you were lying. Your shoes were still shining with a life of their own. There was no one but family and us. Everyone sat there with their heads down. Some I could see had tears on their faces. The cloud of sorrow and sadness was even heavier than yesterday. I felt like I was being smothered. Oh, yes, there was a minister going up front. I hadn't seen him before.

He started talking. I didn't understand all that he was saying, Sarah, but he wasn't saying the nice things I wanted him to say about you. I wanted to stand up and scream, "Shut up! Shut up!" but I didn't dare, Sarah. He would 'a squashed me but good. I'm glad you were asleep, Sarah, so you couldn't hear him going on and on. You looked so pretty lying there. You'll be glad to know that your shoes looked gorgeous too.

I shut my ears and closed my eyes, Sarah, and thought just of you. I remembered your pretty smile, and when we were pickin' raspberries by the creek. We sneaked into the water with just our underwear on. You were such fun, Sarah. I remember the big fat raisin cookie you gave me once and the kitten you gave me just that last week. I was going to call her Fluffy, but I named her Sarie. Thank you, Sarah, thank you.

The minister had finished, all sweaty and red-faced. I wished he would explode. Now it was so quiet. I could hear a mud hen clug-clug-clugging over in the swamp. A fly left the blanket-covered window, buzzed the ceiling a few times, and lit on one of your lovely shoes. I could see him, a dull spot twitching on the shiny leather. Then softly, Mim started to sing. *"Till we meeet, till we meet at Jesus' feet, God be with you till we meet again."* Then, slowly, everyone started singing, *"Till we meet, till we meet . . ."*

Oh, Sarah, my eyes were so full and my throat was so lumpy. I love you, Sarah. You were so nice to me. I still miss you. But God, Sarah, how I envied you those shoes.

To Get a Better Place

Our stepfather, Bob, was a little odd. As soon as the sun went down, you could feel him change. He'd get very stern-looking and wouldn't talk, just mumble to himself. Some nights he'd walk around and around the house for hours. Upstairs, downstairs, going from room to room in the dark. Then we would huddle very quietly in our bedroom. We wouldn't dare light the kerosene lamp.

One day, I heard Mim and Bob talking. They decided they were going to save money to move to a better place. Bob told Mim not to tell him where she would hide the money because he might take it and go get drunk. Then he started the savings off with fifty cents he'd been keeping. Mim worked as a waitress in Aunt Ann's restaurant. Tips from her work trickled into the jar in the cupboard over the stove. There was $9.81 in there, and that was enough to hide in a harder place to find. Bob knew how much was there, and it was getting nearly enough to go on a good drunk.

We knew Bob was going to start looking for it. Mim and I began to think about a better place to hide the money. Bob was good at finding secret places. Finally I said, "Put it in the pot under the bed." In the summertime, we ran outside to go. The slop jar was stored away under the bed until wintertime, and Bob would never think to look there.

Money was rolling in. We had $15. We knew Bob was quietly looking for it, but he didn't say anything. Then one night, as he was roaming through the rooms, he stopped, threw open the cupboard doors and flung things out. He went to the cupboard

Bob Ford sitting on Mim's porch.

under the stairs and slammed through the pots and pans. Things were really revving up.

Finally he came back into the living room with his hair all mussed up and his eyes looking like a wild man (which he was). "Where is that goddam money?" He grabbed Mim and pushed her against the wall. "Mary, give me that money!" Mim said, "No, you'll be mad in the morning if I do." Then Bob swore at Mimmie, and he hit her in the eye, and she went running out into the night. Bubby and I hid under the bed. We knew Mim would go stay at Aunt Dean's overnight. They would report Bob to the cops.

It was quiet in the morning. Bob went right out to work in the garden as if nothing had happened. Bubby played around the back door with his little dump truck. He stayed close to me. I swept the kitchen floor. Then I figured I better start something for lunch. I began to make biscuits.

It was about ten o'clock when Bubby hollered, "The cops are here." I rushed to the back door. Bubby was jumping up and down. His eyes looked like they were sure to pop out. Bob was flying through the pumpkins and the corn with a cop firing a gun over his head. Another cop had run around the garden and stuck a gun at him from the other direction. So there was nothing Bob could do but stick up his hands. They put handcuffs on him, and he plodded along between them back to their car. They disappeared down the old dirt road in a cloud of dust. I was so mad at them, but I went back to making the biscuits. Might as well.

Mim came home a bit later. I told her they got Bob, that they took him to jail. "Oh my God," said Mim. She went in and got the $15.46 out of the slop jar, and away she went to get Bob out of jail.

So Bob was back tromping through the rooms every night. We were right back where we started from, only there was no money. We had to start saving all over again.

All About Eggs

Mim and Bob had taken a job working on Mrs. Chester's egg farm. Bub and I could go with them and bring our old dog, Sulfur, with us.

Old Sulfur had worked bringing in the cows on Uncle Tobe's farm for a good many years. He was too old now for anything but lying around the house. As Old Sulfur was no good on the farm anymore, he would have been shot. Mim, Bub and I loved Old Sulfur too much for that, so he came to live with us. There was only one bad thing about him. Ever since he was a puppy, he let "slide-outs" frequently that smelled like rotten eggs—hence his name, "Sulfur."

Anyway, to go on with the story, we were so excited. Bob would make one dollar a day, Mim fifty cents, and we all got room and board.

We soon found out there was much more to that farm than hens. Bob had to take care of horses, cows, barns, haying and more. Mim had to do all the housework and cooking and slop the hogs. Bubby had to bring in the wood and run errands for everyone. He also had to pick vegetables out of the garden for our meals. I had to feed the hens, rake out their houses, and collect the eggs. I had to put the eggs out in the cooling room in the barn. Only Old Sulfur was lucky. As long as he stayed out of Mrs. Chester's way, he could loaf.

We worked from dawn to dusk. Mrs. Chester always spoke very sharply to me and Bubby. Now that was okay, only Mrs. Chester had three granddaughters around my age who lived with her. They were her pride and joy. They didn't have to do any-

Bubby and Old Sulfur. This was before Old Sulfur came to live with us.

thing, and boy, did they lord it over me! They said mean things about me so I could hear them and hid my egg baskets. It didn't bother me too much, except I was afraid they'd break some eggs and blame it on me, but they never thought of that.

County fair week came. That was the big event of the summer. Everyone looked forward to it, and everybody went. Mrs. Chester and the girls were going, and I thought we were too. But no, Mrs. Chester said we had to stay and look after the farm. Mim asked if we could go for a couple of hours. That amount of time wouldn't have made any difference to the farm, but Mrs. Chester said no, she couldn't spare us at all.

The girls talked about all the great things they were going to do at the fair and were laughing because I couldn't go.

The morning of the fair, we loaded all the eggs from the cooling room in the wagon. Mrs. Chester told Mim to be sure all the eggs were gathered that day and put to cool right away. She said she had to have that money to buy the girls clothes and shoes for school, which was starting in a couple of weeks.

The girls sat in the wagon and stuck their tongues out at me when Mrs. Chester wasn't looking. I thumbed my nose at them, but it was small consolation. Mrs. Chester "clucked up" the old horse, and the girls, looking very smug, were off to the fair.

I knew Mim was smarting at being treated like low-class hired help. We had worked very hard for Mrs. Chester, and she could have let us go to the fair, at least for a couple of hours.

Slowly, I picked up my basket to gather eggs. Mim said, "When you pick up the eggs, bring them here. Also, leave the hen yard door open." I was surprised. I said, "But, Mim, the hens will get out, and I'll never get them back in." She said she knew that. I did what she said.

When I got all the eggs into the kitchen, there must have been eighty to eighty-five of them. Mim started cooking. She made a big egg pudding, scrambled eggs, French toast, fried eggs, a big souffle and even deviled eggs. Some eggs, about four dozen, she hard-boiled, put in a box, and told me to put out in our truck, which I did.

Mim was a fast worker and a great cook. She had everything going at once, and soon she slapped it all on the table. I called Bob and Bubby, and we all sat down for the feast.

An egg was a very great delicacy to us. If we each had three or four eggs a month, we were lucky. So we were laughing and eating as fast as we could. We shoveled eggs of all kinds into our mouths until we couldn't stuff in another bite, and there were still some eggs left over.

Mim scraped everything into a big dish and put it on the floor for old Sulfur. He gobbled up all the eggs and licked the dish. He thought he'd died and gone to heaven. But we knew he hadn't because as he settled down on the floor, he let out one of his specials.

We cleaned up everything. Bub and I buried the eggshells down back in the swamp. Mim and Bob gathered up our few belongings and put them in the old truck. As soon as everything was slick as a whistle, we sat down in the little room off the kitchen to wait for Mrs. Chester and the girls. Hens were every-where—in the yard, over around the woods and walking up and down the road.

Finally Mrs. Chester and the girls came storming in. Mrs. Chester said, "What are all the hens doing out? What about the eggs?" Mim said the hens had gotten out before they could lay any eggs. Mrs. Chester turned purple. She didn't know what we'd done, but she was sure we were to blame for whatever had happened. She screamed, "Get your things and get out! You're fired!" Bob said, "We already have our things, and you can't fire us. We've already quit!"

We stood up, and Bob, Mim and Bubby walked slowly, with dignity, out the door. I grabbed old Sulfur by his collar and started after them.

Then old Sulfur really outdid himself. He let out the biggest, most gorgeous sulfur bomb he ever let. I walked him out real slow to leave all the smell possible in the room behind him. Hap-pily, I could hear them gagging as we stepped off the porch. But best of all, there wasn't an egg left in sight, nowhere!

Solving Problems

That July day dawned dreary, but everyone got up in a good mood, especially Bubby. He took off to stay overnight with Uncle Amacy to go fishing.

After breakfast, Bob decided he was not going to go to work. That perked Mim up because she thought she could get him to help her work at putting a porch on the house. Bob said that maybe after lunch he'd help, but first he was going to "lay idle" for a while. Mim didn't like it, but there was nothing she could do about it.

When Bob got up, he said he was going to milk the cows a little early so he could rest some more. He grabbed the milk pail and took off for the barn. I knew he had a quart of liquor stashed away in the grain storage shed, so I knew what he was up to.

Mim was so mad she went out and started sawing 2x4's and banging and nailing them against the side of the house. I could hear her muttering and raving to herself.

Then Aunt Emmie came running in the door. She was seven months pregnant with Gary D.'s baby. The only thing was, she was married to Uncle Fred. This wouldn't have happened, but Uncle Fred had been running around for a long time with Thelma R., and Aunt Emmie had gotten lonely. Anyway, every time Uncle Fred had come near Aunt Emmie for the last few months, she pleaded that she was having diarrhea. Now Uncle Fred had finally realized that no woman has diarrhea for months steadily and keeps getting fatter. He was fuming about it and getting madder and madder. He told Aunt Flo about it, and she told

Aunt Emmie. So that afternoon when Aunt Emmie saw Uncle Fred coming, storming up the front steps, she hightailed it out the back door over the hill up the back way to our house. I took her upstairs to my room to hide. She rushed in my closet and shut the door. Aunt Em was scared silly of Uncle Fred.

I looked down toward the barn to be sure Bob hadn't seen Aunt Emmie. He would have kicked her out, but he was just going in the grain storage shed, and he pulled the door shut behind him. I had to keep him from knowing Aunt Emmie was in the house.

He'd been swilling his quart for a while, so I sneaked over and put the bar across the shed door. No one could get out of that shed when the door was barred. It was made of real heavy lumber. The pigs were busy eating, the hens were locked in their coop, and the milk was in a pail sitting by the path. So I knew Bob had done all the chores before going into the shed. It made me feel good to know the animals were all taken care of for the night. I picked up the milk pail and went back to the house.

Just as I went in the front door, Uncle Fred went flying by the door in his old Ford coupe. He had his head out the window roaring, "I know you're in there, Emmie. I'm going to get you!" He turned around and went tearing back by the house, yelling and spitting out the window. He didn't dare stop because he was afraid of Bob. Every few minutes, Uncle Fred would turn around and go roaring by the house, back and forth, back and forth, yelling and tooting his horn.

Bob heard the noise, and he was trying to get out of the shed to see what the matter was, only he couldn't, being barred in. He started kicking the door, hollering, and swearing. Of course, it didn't do him any good.

Mim stayed slamming and banging, building the porch. She paid no attention to any of them—to hell with 'em.

Then Harry J. stopped in to borrow Bob's chain saw. He heard Bob roaring down in the shed. He said, "What is that?" I told him that Bob was kind of tied up down in the barn right then. He said, "Good! Then I'll take these too," and he took two axes and some rope. Harry was mad at Bob for something. They were always fighting. Harry stopped down below the barn and cut down two maple trees that he knew were Bob's favorites for tapping for syrup. All the time there was nothing Bob could do but roar, kick the door, and get drunker. I knew Bob would get even with Harry for cutting down his maples, but I couldn't worry about it.

Uncle Fred kept running back and forth in his car. Just as he was turning around down at the corner to give it another run, a tire blew, and he had no spare. He didn't know Bob was locked in the shed. Uncle Fred didn't dare walk up to the house and holler around because Bob might blow the ground right out from under him. Bob kept a loaded shotgun just inside the door, and he hated noise.

Well, with Mim completely engrossed in banging on the porch, Bob safely barred in the shed, and Aunt Emmie safe in the upstairs closet, I figured everything was under control. So I got supper and hoped for the best.

Later that night, when Bob had quieted down and I knew he was passed out drunk, I sneaked down and unbarred the shed door. When he came up to the house the next morning, he'd been so blacked out that he couldn't remember what had happened, and his head was so big he didn't care. Gary D. came and picked up Aunt Emmie, and they ran off together for parts unknown.

There was still one problem left. Mim. She got up early and was still banging, building the porch, madder than ever. I took her out a cup of tea and sat down with her while she drank it, and I admired her handiwork. Soon Mim was her old self again. A little praise took her a long way. Now everything was calmed down, and I could relax until the next performance.

Kayo, Free Spirit

Aunt Dot married Paul Nidow from Ticonderoga. They had three kids, Bobbie, Connie and little Paul, and lived in Ticonderoga where Uncle Paul had a good oil business going. He also raised beagles. As he bred more dogs, he needed more room, so he bought land on the road to Grandma and Grandpa's farm.

Aunt Dot and Uncle Paul built a nice long white house with a cellar and garage underneath. That interested me because I'd never seen a house built like that. Uncle Paul built long kennels out back. There were many cages and runways. They moved into the house, and the dogs grew and thrived in the kennels. Uncle Paul didn't want the dogs excited or bothered. They were raised strictly as hunting dogs.

There was one dog named Kayo who was different. He kept digging under the fence around his runway trying to get out. He would not eat dog food. Uncle Paul had to feed him hamburger and boiled-up chicken parts. Kayo wasn't friendly with the other dogs or people. He didn't bark, play or run and bay with the other dogs when they were taken out to chase rabbits. Kayo sat, most of the time, by the gate of his runway, waiting to escape.

Uncle Paul got sick of Kayo. No one would buy him, and who could blame them? So he gave Kayo to Mim, Bub and me. We took him up to our farm and tied him up because we were afraid he'd go back to the kennels. Uncle Paul was going to have him put to sleep if he did. After a week, we set Kayo free, and we needn't have worried. He made no move to go back to Uncle Paul's.

Kayo and Skishie sitting on Mim's porch.

Bub and I'd take Kayo with us when we'd go down in the swamp to catch frogs or up on the ledges to play. Gradually, Kayo began to chase rabbits and go baying across the ledges. After a while, he went up there by himself. He didn't wait for us anymore. We loved to hear him singing *"o-o-o-o-o-w"* as he raced across the ledges, and then he'd be out of earshot, running farther back through the mountains.

Then came the time when Kayo would be gone for five or six days. He was hunting and staying in the woods. Every week or so, he'd come back. On an evening, we'd be sitting on the porch, and he'd glide up to us like a little shadow.

I'd offer him a piece of bread with oleo on it or a little left-over meat. He always refused it, and why not? He was eating rabbits and, we were sure, an occasional deer. What would he want with leftover people food?

Kayo would sit there at our feet while the dusk settled in and the whippoorwills started calling. Suddenly he'd lift his head quickly, sniff the air, and he'd be gone, but we knew he'd be back.

We knew Kayo loved us as much as he could love any people. I think he figured we were the nearest thing to wild that any people could be, and he had a point. We lived from hand to mouth and made demands of no one, including him.

For a couple of years, Kayo slipped this way in and out of our lives. We heard him many times baying, singing his song across the cliffs and over the hills, *"o-o-o-o-o-w."*

I would have liked to go with him. I envied him roaming free over the hills, but I was happy for him too. He was where he belonged.

That fall, the last time we saw him, I noticed Kayo looked much older and thinner, but his eyes were bright and I could sense his spirit still going strong, free. I petted him a while, then he licked my cheek and he was gone. But we knew he'd be back. A few minutes later, we heard him, *"o-o-o-o-o-w,"* singing up over the cliffs.

We heard him singing over the hills for the next couple of weeks. Then school started, we were busy getting the last of the hay in for our cows for the winter, and a month passed by very fast.

We loved to hear Kayo singing *"o-o-o-o-o-w"* as he raced across the ledge.

Suddenly, we realized we hadn't heard Kayo for a while. We listened, and we called to him for a long time after that, but the hills and cliffs were silent—no more of Kayo's singing. We had to finally admit to ourselves that Kayo was gone. This time he wouldn't be back.

I knew then, and I know now, Kayo's running free somewhere, singing over the hills, in dog heaven, *"o-o-o-o-o-w."*

Rolland Rivers' Rope

The first time we saw Rolland Rivers, he was stamping up the road past our farm, headed toward Bear Pond. We had never seen him before, and we couldn't figure out from where he came.

Every few days, Rolland would go down the road headed for where? Then in the evening, he'd come up past the farm headed for Bear Pond. He was a good-looking man with real black hair. He was probably about 30 years old.

One evening, I was swinging back and forth on the barnyard gate when Rolland came by. I said hello, and he looked very surprised, but he answered. Then he asked me if I knew where he could get a pot to boil water. I said to wait a minute, and I went in the house to ask Mim. She said, "Give him one of ours." We only had three pots, but I took the biggest one out and gave it to Rolland. He said, "Now I won't have to borrow Charlie Fox's," and he went on up the road.

The next day, Charlie Fox came by, raving to Mim. "Did you see that nut who's moved in up at the pond near me? He started living in a tree right by my camp, but I made him move to a tree farther down the pond. I drew a line in the dirt near my camp and put stones in it to mark it good. I told him never to come over that line because he keeps me awake nights singing 'Bill Bailey.' If I holler at him, he stops, but soon starts up again singing 'Sweet Adeline.' I don't know which is worse."

A couple of days later, Rolland came along as I was jumping rope out in the road. I was trying to double-step backward. Rolland said, "That's wrong, let me show you. Get me a rope." I didn't have another rope, so he said to never mind, he'd use his. He reached into his pocket and made the motions of pulling out a rope, only there wasn't any there.

Rolland flung his imaginary rope behind his back and went through the motions with his arms of swinging the rope around. I never saw such footwork in my life. He twirled through the air backward and forward, doing all kinds of tricky maneuvers with his feet. Then he did a somersault, flying through the air, all with his imaginary rope. He said, "There, practice that. I'll be back tomorrow to show you some more. Right now I got to go make my applesauce. I put cloves in it, makes it better," and he went running up the trail toward Bear Pond.

I told Mim about Rolland's imaginary rope. She said, "Are you learning by watching him?" Of course I was, so she said, "Okay, then don't worry about it, just jump rope." Mim had a great sense of humor.

Rolland came most every day, and I learned the steps from him. Twirling through the air one day, I managed a wobbly somersault. It was one of the happiest days of my life.

One afternoon, Bob came home from work early. He grabbed his bottle of liquor and started drinking. Mim was out on the porch watching Rolland and me jump rope.

After a while, Bob came out, and he was really getting into his cups. He watched us a few minutes.

Rolland said to drop my real rope and use an imaginary one like his. I did, and we went backward twirling through the air, all the time swinging our imaginary ropes.

Bob watched for a minute and then he said, "What the hell are they doing?" Mim said that we were jumping rope. Now, Bob didn't see any ropes, but he was too proud to admit it. He thought instead of seeing things, he wasn't seeing things, and he blamed it on the liquor.

Just then, Rolland and I did our somersaults, flying through the air, and Mim, grinning, said to Bob, "Did you see how smoothly they cleared those ropes?" That did it! Bob shoved the cork into the bottle and threw the bottle under the corner of the porch. He didn't touch it again that evening.

A few days later, Charlie came down to the farm, complaining to Mim again. He said when he'd go hunting or over to the other side of the pond, fishing, and came home, his whole camp would be all changed around. His table would be on the left side of the room instead of on the right side. His dishes would all be over on the other side of the room from where he'd left them. His wood pile would be on the right side of his front door instead of the left. In fact, everything would be just the opposite from how he left it, but nothing was ever stolen.

Charlie said he couldn't prove it was Rolland, but who else could it be? He warned Rolland two or three times not to do it anymore, but he kept on doing it. So Charlie took his shotgun over to where Rolland was up his tree, and he shot the gun up in the air. Charlie told Rolland, "The next time I'll shoot it right up your ass if you bother my place again."

That night, Charlie thought over what he'd said, and he felt bad. The next morning, he went over to Rolland's tree to tell him he would never shoot him, but Rolland wasn't there. Now Charlie was worried about Rolland and was out looking for him. We hadn't seen him, so we couldn't help out.

A couple of nights later, Mim and I were trying to figure out what to have for supper as we didn't have much in the house to eat. Then Bob came in, bringing a bushel of potatoes that he got somewhere.

Mim had some bacon grease in a jar, so we fried a lot of potatoes in that. We made mashed potatoes and boiled some with wild leeks.

We put three big bowls of potatoes on the table, and with a big pot of hot black tea to wash it down, that was going to be our supper.

Bob, Bubby, Nelson Burroughs, By Lightnin' Cross, little Johnny Baker, Mim and I sat down to eat. We were just going to fill our plates when Rolland walked in.

He looked like death warmed over. His shirt was torn, and his eyes looked wild. He climbed up on the table and grabbed the three bowls of potatoes and started wolfing them down. He picked up the hot pot of tea and poured it right from the spout into his mouth. It was awfully hot, but it didn't seem to bother him a bit.

Rolland then stood up in the middle of the table and sang a beautiful rendition of "Oh Come, All Ye Faithful." We sat there, speechless.

Suddenly, he jumped off the table, grabbed the flashlight off the bench by the door, and went out on the back porch. He stood there, waving his arms, and shining the flashlight up in the air, yodeling.

Mim said to Bob, "We gotta do something. He's nuttier than a fruitcake." Just then, Frankie Dougal drove into the yard. He was looking very happy when he drove in, but he didn't look so happy when he drove out.

Rolland came in and sat down at the table to eat the rest of the food. Bob, Nelson and Frankie grabbed Rolland from behind and they got him loaded into the backseat of Frankie's car, but not before Nelson got a black eye and Frankie a nosebleed.

Mim said, "Take him down to Mary Stowell's. She'll know what to do." Nelson and By Lightnin' went with Frankie. They had an awful time getting Rolland down to Mary's house. He bit and kicked and screamed all the way. It was all they could do to keep him in the car.

When they got to Mary's house, she sent them on to Ticonderoga, to Dr. Cummings. He said, "Put him in jail until morning." So with the help of a trooper, they got Rolland in a cell, and Frankie, By Lightnin' and Nelson came back to the farm. The inside of the car was a mess, but they were laughing when they drove into the yard.

We never found out who Rolland was or from where he came. We wondered what they would do with him. However, no one went to Ticonderoga to find out. We were afraid they just might make us take him home.

The inside of Frankie's car was never the same again, and Charlie Fox put a ring of stones around Rolland's tree in memory of him.

I put my real jumping rope and my imaginary jumping rope away for good. Without Rolland, it wasn't fun anymore.

Silence

It was a day in mid-June. We kids were in school, and we were getting worried. We were reviewing and trying to cram for the end-of-year tests that were coming up soon. Most of our minds were blank, and we were wishing we'd listened to the teacher and had paid attention during the year.

The morning was hot and muggy. All the school windows and doors were open. Music was blaring in from across the road. The Bards lived there, and they had an old Victrola out in their yard.

Abie Bard had just been laid off from his job at the Ti mill. To console himself, he was drinking a few homebrews; in fact, many homebrews. He was sitting there with the music blaring: *"Oh, they cut down the old pine tree and they hauled it away to the mill—To make a coffin of pine for that sweetheart of mine when they cut down the old pine tree."* The song blared on and on.

We couldn't hear ourselves think, let alone study. Our teacher finally sent Jimmy G. over to ask Abie to turn off the Victrola, or at least turn it down. That was the last straw for Abie. He shook his fist and shouted that it was a free country, that no one could stop him from doing what he was doing, and he turned the music up as high as it would go.

Now we kids had found this quite amusing until we realized the music wasn't going to stop. Then it became unbearable. Shut up! Shut up! Turn that damned music off! It stopped only when Abie had to wind up the Victrola.

While Abie was doing that, a man came in the schoolhouse door. He was Jack and Jerry D.'s uncle. He called them up to him and put his arms around them. He said, loud enough so we could hear, "Boys, your mother died a little while ago giving birth to your little brother." The boys started to sob. Jack turned around as though looking for help, anything. For a second, his eyes caught mine. I mouthed the words, "I'm so sorry," before the three were gone out the door. By then, Abie had that damned music blaring again.

Now if there was any food in the house, mothers saw that you got your share. If you didn't have any clothes to wear, they made you some out of feedbags. If you had a cold, mothers rubbed Vicks VapoRub on your chest and told you you'd feel better in the morning. If you did something wrong, mothers first straightened you out and then, with a hug, told you it would be okay.

In the rough times of the '30s, the one thing you were sure of was your mother, and now our friends had gone home and their mother wasn't there.

"They built a coffin of pine . . ." blared in through the windows. Please turn off that damned music! Abruptly, it stopped. Someone had gotten to Abie.

We sat there so full of sorrow in silence. The silence pushed down from the ceiling. The silence pushed up from the floor. The silence pushed in from the windows. Oh, God, the silence!

Abie, please turn on that music again. I looked out the window. Abie was lying, dead drunk, on the ground.

Willie S. slipped out the door, went over, and turned on the Victrola again. Anything was better than the silence. While that damned music blared, we picked up our books and went home. We were very lucky, our mothers were still there.

Well, my mother wasn't exactly there. She'd been gone for about five days. Therefore, I knew she'd be back, from wherever she'd been, soon. She never stayed away more than a week at a time.

Up in the Overshot

Bob had a pulp job for the summer up in the Overshot. This was land way back in the woods over toward Crown Point. In the middle was a big pond. There were some cliffs that hung out over it. I guess that's how the place got the name, Overshot.

Bubby and I couldn't wait for school to be out. Mim, Bob and some of the lumberjacks Bob had hired were busy putting up the lumber camp buildings. They built a large kitchen/dining room building and a long low building for the lumberjacks' bunkhouse. We would sleep in a little room tacked on back of the kitchen building. Most everything was made out of logs. The windows had no glass, just cheesecloth tacked over them; otherwise no one could have stood the mosquitoes. The lumberjacks made us all peeled log bunks and made a big long table with benches for the dining hall. We didn't need a privy. After all, there were miles of woods to go in.

Mim and Bob loaded the cook stove from the farm's kitchen and all our pots and pans and dishes on the old truck, along with bedding and towels. Then Mim went to Ticonderoga and got some storekeeper to trust her for a big bunch of groceries. I like to think he got his money in time, but I don't know. Anyway, that day when school was out for the summer, we were off on a new adventure.

The lumberjacks had put spruce bows in the beds on slats for us to sleep on, and we threw our blankets and pillows on them. They weren't the softest beds in the world, but they sure smelled great.

I was ten years old that summer, ready to go to work in earnest. Mim and I struck a deal. I would get ten cents a day plus room and board. We were up every morning at 5 a.m. to get the lumberjacks off to work at daybreak, usually about 6:30. Oh, the breakfasts we made! Mim heaped pancakes, eggs, sausages, etc., etc. in big dishes, and there was plenty of strong hot coffee. Lumberjacks had to eat a lot because they had to work so very hard for long hours.

I set the big table, washed dishes, put up lunches, swept the floors, and made up the bunks the best I could. Bub and I lugged water from the brook down back. We had a big empty tin oil barrel where we dumped the water. We kept a wood fire going under it, so we usually had all the warm water we needed for dishes.

I never got my ten cents a day, but that summer I ate the best of my life up to that time, and a long time afterward too. That made up for it a lot. Besides, Mim asked, where would I spend my money anyway? We were three miles from nowhere back in the woods.

When we had a few minutes of free time, Bub and I used to go exploring around. In the swamp and lowland around the pond, we saw the biggest turtles I ever saw in the mountains. Some of them had shells one and a half feet to two feet across. We found a lot of big shells that were turned upside down. We wondered why they were that way, and the lumberjacks told us the big male turtles would fight until one would be turned over. Then the winner would go on his way, and the other turtle would just stay there and die as he couldn't turn himself right side up again.

Things went busily along, and when you work eleven to twelve hours a day, you need at least eight hours' sleep. We only had a couple of old kerosene lamps, so when darkness closed in, everyone hit the bunks. There was nothing else to do anyway.

One day, a boy about twelve walked into camp and asked for work. It surprised us because he seemed to come out of nowhere. He said he had come through the woods from up Malone way. His name was Buck Malarney. He was thin and starved-looking. He said he had no parents and had run away from his foster parents' home because they were so mean to him. Of course,

Mim believed him and took him in and gave him a good meal. Bob said he could stay and work. Buck didn't know much about lumbering, but the lumberjacks helped him and taught him to peel pulp and drive the big team of horses, skidding the pulp to the trail. There, our big old truck could be loaded and the pulp taken to Ticonderoga Pulp Mill.

Buck ate like a horse, and he started filling out and developed muscles from the hard work he was doing. I liked him a lot. He seemed just like a big brother to me. He helped me and Bub carry water from the brook. Sometimes he even helped me peel potatoes when it was too rainy to work in the woods.

Now the lumberjacks all got a big kick out of Buck and were very good to him. He thought he was right up there with any of them, and so when they asked him to go into town with them on one of their Saturday night excursions, he was right there raring to go, with his face washed and hair all splatted down. Mim didn't think he should go, but the lumberjacks laughed and said he would be fine, and away they went. Bob let them use the old lumber truck.

Buck got drunk with the lumberjacks and got in with some "wild" women. The lumberjacks thought it was hilarious, and Buck was proving he was one of the boys, and of course, having all been Buck's age once and in the same boat, they were all for it.

Monday morning they were one hung-over bunch, but back at work. Buck looked a little green around the gills, but he covered up and kept on going. He was still proving he was one of the boys.

A few days later, Buck came from work late in the morning and told Mim he didn't feel well. She felt his forehead, and it was hot as fire. She put him to bed in his bunk, and he stayed there until the next day. The following morning, he was moaning and shaking with chills. Mim was scared and said he had to go out to see Dr. Cummings. The lumberjacks were laughing and said Buck would just have to suffer it out, that the salve Dr. Cummings would give him wouldn't do any good. But Mim insisted, so a couple of them said they'd do it, and they took Buck in the old truck to see the doctor.

When they came back, Buck was carrying a big can of salve. The odor about him was terrible, and he seemed in great pain, especially when he tried to walk. The lumberjacks said, "Told you so. He just has to suffer it out," and they laughingly put Buck to bed out in the hay pile beside the horses' shed. They said they couldn't stand the smell in the bunkhouse, and that's where Buck stayed for the next two weeks.

At that time, Mim decided to go on one of her disappearances again, I don't know to where. She left Joe Pereau (one of the oldest lumberjacks) and me to cook for the men. We didn't have many supplies. Joe shot a deer for meat, which helped a lot. I didn't know what was wrong with Buck, and I was scared because he was so sick. I asked Joe what Buck had, and he hemmed and hawed and finally said, "He's got the clap." I said, "What's that?" Joe answered, "Never mind, but stay away from him or you might get it."

Of course, that made me more scared than ever, but I could hear Buck moaning and asking for water. It was a terribly hot day, and no one was around, so I took a pail of water with a dipper in it, and holding my nose, I went and set it beside him. I got him some gravy on bread and tea. Then I got brave and got a cloth to wash off his face because he looked so sweaty and sick. But he wouldn't let me. He kept saying, "Yada, keep away, just leave things where I can reach them."

Buck stayed sick for four or five days before he seemed a little better. The lumberjacks still thought it was funny and said he'd live, ha! ha! ha! I did all I could for him, but he couldn't get to the brook to wash up and he was getting stinkier and stinkier. I did all I could, but I couldn't give him a bath. He was too big, and I was too small.

Finally Mim came back from wherever she had gone, and she checked on Buck. She had me get the big tub, and we filled it with hot water. She was bigger than Buck. She stripped off his clothes and put him in the tub. He couldn't stop her. Buck got the scrubbing of his life. Then we put him to bed in his own bunk. Mim told the lumberjacks they were to blame for Buck's condition, and if anyone tried to get him out of that bunk, they'd answer to her. No one tried.

Buck slowly recovered, but he wasn't able to work in the woods anymore. He did chores for Mim and took care of the horses as he slowly got back his health.

Late in the summer, the pulp job was over, so we gathered the stove, pots and pans and our bedding, and headed back for the farm. Bob had taken the horses back the day before. All the lumberjacks had left, walking out heading for other jobs, and we waved as we passed them in our loaded truck. Then we came alongside of Buck. He just stood there beside the road looking at us so forlorn and lost. Bub and I felt so sad looking at him. Mim said, "Bob, stop the truck." He did. Then Mim said, "Come on, Buck," and with a big grin, Buck hopped up on the back of the truck with Bub and me, and we took off for the farm again.

Buck stayed with us for quite a few years. He even moved to Maine with us and lived there for the two years or so that we were there.

Anyway, Buck became like a big brother to me. He got in and out of trouble a lot, but I don't know how he did as good as he did from the way he'd been kicked around all his life. Mim always got him straightened out, and he'd go merrily on his way to the next deal he'd get into.

When we moved to Newcomb, Buck didn't go with us. Soon after that move, World War II started, and we all went in different directions. I lost track of a lot of people, including Buck. I hope he made it okay.

In Every Garden There's a Serpent

W^e vaguely knew that Mrs. Riley was an invalid. She hadn't been out of bed in years. She and her daughter, Cathy, lived halfway up a small hill in a big old cottage covered with vines. There was a small, but very lush, rose garden around it.

It was a very hot moist summer. The roses were gorgeous. Whenever I wanted to go up to my friend Joan's house to play, I went by the Rileys' house. I would slow way down and look and look. Sometimes I would stand in the road and pretend it was my home.

Every time I stopped, there was always an open upstairs window. Usually, a pale pudgy hand would come out of it and flutter back and forth. I always waved back as I went on up the hill.

One day as I was looking at the garden, Cathy came around the edge of the house. She was busy choosing roses to cut and put in the open basket she carried. As I started to move on up the hill, she spied me and called, "Hello, little girl, would you like to come in and see the flowers?" Would I! Soon I was sticking my nose in roses, and she was telling me names and pointing out bigger and bigger blossoms.

The air smelled like perfume, and bees were slowly wandering from one rose to another, gathering pollen. The pollen looked like little yellow boots on their hind legs. Birds were flitting here and there. Occasionally one would sing out joyously. The clouds of color around me made me feel like I was in flower heaven. It was beautiful, so beautiful.

241

Suddenly I noticed the pale pudgy hand fluttering from the usual upstairs window. As I was looking up, Cathy noticed it too. "Oh, that's mother. Would you like to meet her?" I answered that I would, but most of all, I wanted to see the inside of my dream home.

It was cool as we went into the hallway. I noticed that the ceilings were very high and the windows sparkled. There were white fluffy ruffled curtains on them.

There was a fireplace on one wall with lots of knickknacks on the mantel. Two china dogs about 18 inches high stared down at me. I thought, "They are twins, just like some people." The furniture was beautifully upholstered without a stain or tear anywhere.

But the wood in that room! It was shiny and dark, like black glass. Then I noticed the stairway. We started up it. You could see your face in the steps. I instinctively took hold of the handrail. It felt smooth and soft. All the wood was shiny like glass. I knew you could fall and break your neck on stairs like that, but how beautiful!

We reached the hall and went in the first door on the left. It had the same woodwork and windows and curtains as were downstairs. There was a big, wide bed in the middle of the room, but the woman in the bed was what you saw most. She was so big that she loped over both sides of the bed. Flab hung everywhere. Two eyes pushed out of rolls of fat and stared up at me as I stood beside the bed.

Cathy said, "This is Gloria, Mim's little girl." A big hand darted and circled my arm. "Oh, yes, Mim's little girl." And the hand gently kneaded my arm. The hand felt very hot, flabby and soft. I didn't like it, but I didn't think it would be polite to move away. Then Mrs. Riley said, "Cathy, why don't you go get us some sugar cookies and make some lemonade to go with them?" Cathy said, "Yes, mother," and went downstairs.

Mrs. Riley kept stroking my arm. "Oh, yes, Mim's little girl." Then the hand started stroking and kneading my chest. The other hand came up and clung on to my back. Then it started massaging too. It went on and on until finally the hands were working around my waist. Mrs. Riley's eyes looked funny and her breathing sounded labored. I felt like I was caught in a vise. I felt like I was suffocating.

Then those horrible hands went down my thighs, massaging, massaging. I knocked those terrible hands away and bolted out the door.

Mrs. Riley kept gasping, "Come back here! You come back here!" as I bounded for the stairs.

I stumbled down those beautiful shiny, slippery stairs. I knocked Cathy around as I stumbled on down. The lemonade set rattled on its tray. "What is wrong, little girl?" Cathy exclaimed. What could I tell her? I rushed out the door.

Many times after that I met Cathy in the post office, at church, or on the road. She always told me "Mother" kept asking for me and wanted me to come visit again. I made up excuses that I'd come next week, or later, but no way was I going near that house. Wild horses couldn't drag me there.

I still wanted to go up to Joan's house to play, but I wasn't going by Mrs. Riley's house. Every time at the bottom of the hill, I cut kitty-corner across the field, along the brook, swung around, and came out on top of the hill above the Riley house.

Later in the summer, Mrs. Riley died. People wondered, "Did Mrs. Riley leave her money to Cathy? Did Mrs. Riley leave any money to the church?" I only wondered, "Are her hands still now?"

Always after that, whenever I went up to Joan's house, as I reached Mrs. Riley's hill, I continued to go kitty-corner over the field, along the brook, swing around, and come out on top of the hill. I still wasn't sure that pale pudgy hand wouldn't flutter from the upstairs window.

Playing With Fire

"Noo-Noo" Carnel looked just like a man but, believe me, she was all woman. She worked with her brother-in-law, Otis Million, who was Chilson's road superintendent at the time.

Women weren't allowed to work on the state road in those days, but Noo-Noo got away with it because her real name was Marion. Now, Marion can be a man or woman's name. So the state road powers-that-be in Ticonderoga, the ones who made out the paychecks and sent them to Chilson, weren't aware that this Marion wasn't a man.

Otis was married to Noo-Noo's sister, Margery, who was away at Lake Placid Sanitarium most of the time because she had tuberculosis. Otis and Noo-Noo had a long-time affair going.

Margery came home occasionally for a few days' visit. That didn't interfere with Otis and Noo-Noo's love life, though. They'd just quit work a little early and sneak out in the barn before they went home for supper.

Margery began to get wise, so she went out to the back of the barn one afternoon and peeked through a crack in the barn wall. She caught Otis and Noo-Noo. Margery didn't say anything to them, but she reported the fact that Marion, the road worker, was a woman, not a man, to the state road powers-that-be.

Then Margery told Effie Oscier what she had done. She might as well have put it in a newspaper. Effie never told who snitched on them, but Otis and Noo-Noo were forewarned. A few days later, when they saw the state car coming across the flats at the top of Chilson Hill, Noo-Noo ducked down in the ditch by the road and crawled into a culvert and out of sight.

The state road bosses reamed Otis out good. They wanted to see Marion, but Otis told them "he" was home sick that day. They told Otis not to let Marion work anymore or he, Otis, would be fired. Otis said he'd fire Marion even though he stuck to his guns and insisted that Marion was a man. That way there wouldn't be any more trouble, and the state road bosses went back to Ticonderoga satisfied. Noo-Noo crawled out of the culvert and went right on working.

When payday came, Otis sent Noo-Noo's name to be paid as "M" instead of Marion Carnel, and they paid it and there was no question about it. However, Noo-Noo quickly lay down in the ditch every time she saw a strange car coming over the flats, just to be sure. As there were hardly any cars through Chilson at the time, let alone strange ones, she didn't have to hit the dirt too often.

Now Margery was mad that Otis and Noo-Noo got away with this, but she didn't want Otis to get fired as jobs were scarce and they needed the money. She didn't report them again. She cooked up another way to get them. I heard Mim and Dean talking about this and wondering what Margery would do next. Something was going to happen.

A couple of days later, Margery sent word to Mim that she needed a couple of pints of Canadian stock, the good stuff. I brought it over to Margery's house and collected the money.

Margery showed Dodger and Sny the liquor and told them they could have it as soon as they did a favor for her. Late in the afternoon, she had them put Adeline, a cow, into a stall in the barn and lock the door so she couldn't get out. Adeline was what we called bulling. She was ready to be bred and looking for a bull.

Otis and Noo-Noo came into the barn at their usual time and climbed up into the haymow. They didn't pay any attention to Adeline locked up in the stall. They were too intent on going about their daily get-together.

Next, Dodger and Sny brought Brute, a big black bull who lived in a pen over in the field, to the barn. They led him on a lead attached to an iron ring in his nose. They quietly put him in the barn and quickly bolted the door behind him. In a minute,

Brute discovered Adeline, but he couldn't get to her. He was mad at the world and was roaring and kicking and butting the side of Adeline's stall.

Otis and Noo-Noo couldn't come down out of the haymow because Brute was on the floor beneath them blocking their way. He would have gored them with his horns for sure.

You could hear Adeline mooing and Brute roaring and thrashing around the barn halfway down Chilson Hill. Noo-Noo's father came running in from the hayfield and, not knowing what was going on, started ringing the big dinner bell by the back porch for people to come and help. Add Noo-Noo's screaming, "Help, help, help," and Otis hollering, "Shut up, shut up, shut up!" over and over again, and it was a mind-boggling, noisy uproar.

No one knew what was happening, but people came running from all around, including Mim, Bub and me. In the crowd, I saw Dodger and Sny tipping up their pints, having a great time. And I saw Margery looking out from her bedroom window with one of the most self-satisfied smirks on a face that I have ever seen.

Finally, someone peeked through a crack in the barn wall and saw what was going on. A couple of men opened the door that led from Adeline's stall to the outdoors. Adeline had had enough of the noise and performance and went running out into the field. The men then went in and opened the front door of the stall, staying way in back of the door. Brute tore through the stall and outdoors. He was only interested in Adeline and went slamming through the field after her as she disappeared over the hill.

Everyone crowded into the barn and stood looking up at the haymow where two very embarrassed faces were peering down at them. People were laughing and patting each other on the back. Someone pulled out a harmonica and everyone was dancing and hooting. Otis and Noo-Noo just stayed up in the haymow, looking mortified.

I asked Mim, "Why are Otis and Noo-Noo's faces so red?"

Mim said, "When you play with fire, you get burned with fire."

I looked around and I didn't see any fire, but I let it go at that. Besides, my feet were busy jogging to the music.

My One and Only

I'd stayed overnight at Marion's house, and I was on my way home. I was skipping along, going by the old store, and someone said, "Hi, Yada." It was Cowboy. He was standing by Owney Flanigan's car, waiting for Owney. Cowboy rarely drank, while Owney was always three sheets to the wind. Different as they were, Cowboy and Owney were best friends and spent a lot of time together.

I was so glad to see Cowboy, and after a few minutes, I got my nerve up to say, "Cowboy, will you come back and live with us?" I didn't see why he couldn't even if Bob was there. He realized I didn't understand, so he didn't laugh at me. He hugged me, saying, "I can't, Yada, but you're still my little girl, always." He gave me a pack of gum and a nickel.

Owney came out of the store and was feeling no pain. He had a pint of booze stuck in each of his back pockets. He was already half-luked.

Owney said, "Hi, Yada. The deer are going to catch hell today. Come on, Cowboy." They climbed in Owney's old car, going off hunting. I skipped on home.

That was Monday. Everything was going along pretty quiet until Thursday morning, when Deannie drove fast into the driveway. She ran in the house hollering for Mim. I heard Mim scream, and I went running in. Mim was crying. Deannie said, "Cowboy's dead. Owney shot him. He thought Cowboy was a deer. Cowboy's dead. The funeral's this afternoon."

News traveled slowly in those days. It had happened in the woods, quite a ways from us. That's why it took us a few days to hear it. Cowboy was at his parents' home in Hague. That's where the funeral would be. Deannie had stopped to pick up Mim to go there. They could make it if they moved right along. Mim had a skirt she could wear, but no blouse.

Bob was there, and he was mad. He couldn't keep Mim from going to the funeral. Wild horses couldn't keep her from going, if she had something to wear. Bob might not be able to keep her from going, but he certainly wouldn't give her any money for a blouse.

Mim had no money. She had a puff-sleeved dress on lay-away for me in Pearl's Department Store in Ticonderoga. She paid $1.50 to hold it and still owed $1. I was living for the day we could pay it off and bring that dress home.

Mim looked at me and I at her. I said to take the dress off layaway, and get the money back. In those days $1.50 would buy a nice blouse. Oh, the look of thank you in her eyes! I didn't care about the dress anymore.

Mim loaded Bubby into the car. He wanted to go stay with Deannie's kids at Aunt Dot's until Mim got back. They could stop at Pearl's on their way to Hague and grab a blouse. Off they went, like a shot, out of the driveway.

Bob was swearing around the kitchen. I knew we'd catch it later when Mim got home, but I didn't have to listen to him now. I sneaked out the back door and headed down toward the swamp.

I went over to the side of the swamp where big vicious water snakes lived. It was a scary place where we never went. That's why I went there. If Bob bothered to look for me, he'd never look there.

I walked into the swamp until I came to a big rock. I climbed up on it and sat down. A snake glided by in the water, but it didn't pay any attention to me.

I sat there with my thoughts whirling around. My feelings were all mixed up. I kept whispering, "Cowboy, Cowboy, Cowboy," trying to relieve the pain within me, but the tears wouldn't come.

I thought about my biological father, who was off leading the good life somewhere. He didn't care if we lived or died.

I thought about my stepfather. He was mean to us most of the time. I was always trying to keep out of his way.

I thought about Cowboy and how good he was to us. I thought about the fun times we had together. I thought about the way he made us laugh, and a warm feeling went through me. Then I heard him say again, "You're still my little girl, always."

It was like a dam broke loose within me. The tears poured down and down because I realized I was saying goodbye to my one and only father that day.

Henry Galusha's Bananas

Henry Galusha came through Chilson once a week with his old truck loaded with goodies. You stepped up into the truck and walked around to pick out what you wanted. He had so much. It made our mouths water, but we never had any money to buy anything. Mim did buy us some walnuts once, four for a penny. We went over in the woods and ate them so Bob wouldn't find the shells.

Now Bob was awfully jealous. When he came home from working in the woods, he always went round and round the house looking for men's foot tracks. Sometimes he even got down on his hands and knees to look when he thought he saw something suspicious.

Mim and Henry had been good friends since they were kids together. He liked Mim more than she liked him. He said he was going to take Mim away from Bob. She said no and that he better stay away from our farm as Bob was threatening to beat him up. Henry said that he wasn't scared, that he was bigger than Bob, and he kept coming.

Henry Galusha always had a big bunch of bananas, usually very ripe, hanging on the side of the truck. We could never afford one as they cost one penny apiece. But if you stood in back of the truck, the breeze always blew off the hill just right, and oh, the smell that drifted out from those bananas! Delicious! Whenever Henry Galusha came, you always found me in back of his truck, sniffing.

Bob couldn't catch Henry, and he was getting madder and madder. He put a gun in the car and said he was going to shoot Henry Galusha first time he found him on our farm road.

Things were not looking good. Henry had to be warned. The next afternoon, when Bob was gone, Bubby went up over the back hill to George Putnam's house to play cowboys and Indians. Mim went hurrying down to the end of the road to warn Henry. Of course, I was trotting right by her side.

Mim and I hid in the bushes to wait for Henry. We didn't dare wait in the road 'cause Bob might show up. He wasn't due home until dark, but you never knew.

At last, Henry Galusha came across the flats and turned onto our road. Mim and I stepped out of the bushes and flagged him down. He looked surprised but, as usual, glad to see Mim.

Mim told him about the gun and said, "Don't come up to the farm anymore." He looked sad, but mostly scared. No matter how big you are, it makes no difference to a gun. He kissed Mim on the cheek, said goodbye, and got out of there. Mim and I went home, relieved that Bob hadn't caught us.

Henry Galusha didn't come to our farm anymore. I missed him, but most of all, I missed standing in the wind, smelling those bananas.

Our Maine Adventure 1937

Bob cleaned up his lumbering job that spring, and no new jobs were being given out. The pulp mill in Ticonderoga was glutted with more pulp than it could use.

Bob had come to Chilson from Maine. Mim decided we should go with him to live on the small farm he had there. Bob had been married before, to a lady much older than him. He said she had died and left the farm to him. He said we could grow crops like peas and string beans and make a good living. Buck Malarney, the young guy who Mim let live with us, came along.

Jack Ford, Bob's older brother, had come down from Canada where he had been panning for gold. He said he was sick of that and came to Chilson to see what Bob was doing. Jack was a big man, six feet, four inches, taller by two inches than Bob. Jack was just as bad an alcoholic as Bob but did not have the violent, cruel nature when drunk. Jack could be mean, but nothing like Bob.

One morning I heard Jack tell Mim that we shouldn't go with Bob to Maine. Bob came in while they were talking. He got mad at Jack for what he was saying. He told Jack to take off and not come back. Jack left in a huff down the road. He hadn't had time to tell Mim why we shouldn't go away with Bob.

Years later, Jack told me that up on the Maine farm, Bob had beat up his wife and knocked her down the cellar stairs. Then he took off, and his wife lay at the bottom of the stairs until Jack found her three days later. She was very badly hurt—both her back and internally.

Jack carried her upstairs to bed, but she wouldn't let him call a doctor or the sheriff. She made Jack swear not to tell anyone what happened. She died a few days later.

Bob was long gone. No one tried to find him, so he got away with murder. It was our luck he had ended up in Chilson and in our lives. I know Mim would not have taken off with Bob if she had known. A few years later, Bob tried to kill Mim, but that's another story. In the meanwhile, we were off for Palmyra, Maine, to Bob's farm.

It was a nice old house connected to the woodshed, and then the woodshed connected to the barn. That way, you never had to go outdoors to get to the animals to do the chores in the harsh Maine winters. A lot of the farms around there were built like that.

The land was very flat, and I missed the hill sides and mountains of Chilson. Otherwise it was pretty. It was May, and wild cherry trees were in blossom all around the farm. A little brook ran along the edge of the field out back of the barn.

That field was enormous. Bob said we'd plant half of it to string beans and the other half to peas. The only thing was the field had not been planted for a few years, so it had grown to thick hay. Bob said the field would have to be burned off.

One bright dry morning, Bob and Mim told Bub and me to set fire to the field. Then Mim and Bob went back to bed. Bubby couldn't wait to get the fire going, but I was scared. But hadn't Mim said to do it? So finally, we took matches from the kitchen and lit one end of the field. It caught and burned wildly and quickly down to the brook. We were lucky that the fire stopped there and didn't go over into the woods. From there, Lord knows where it would've ended up.

If the fire had gone into the woods, Mim and Bob were going to say we kids had been playing with matches, and they knew nothing about it, thus they couldn't be blamed, and what could anyone do to two little kids? I heard them laughing about it later.

Well, anyway, the field was burned off, and it had to be plowed. Bob got a farmer from up the road to plow the field. The man had an old tractor and it took him two days. Bob was supposed to pay him, but I don't think he ever did. For a week, Bob and Mim planted the string beans and peas from early morning to night. Bub and I had to stay out of their way. In a couple of weeks, things started to grow. We kids had to help keep the weeds down by chopping them with a hoe. We never could keep ahead of them because the field was so big, but the string beans and peas grew and thrived.

We had to wait each morning until 10 a.m. to pick string beans because the dew had to be dried off them or they would form rust when you touched them. We picked and picked, but we couldn't make a dent in the string beans. Many of them rotted on the vines, although Mim canned a lot of them for winter. She found canning jars in the cellar. I hated the job of snapping beans and the hot kitchen from all the steaming of the jars. The string beans we managed to harvest and did not can, Bob sold to a factory in Bangor.

The peas we harvested by mowing them down like hay. We'd pitch a big load of them on to the back of the truck and take them into the factory. Bub and I rode on top of the peas. You could deliver to the factory anytime. We always went late in the evening when there was less chance of meeting troopers. We didn't have any license on the truck.

It was early August, and the trips coming back from the factory were beautiful. Bubby and I would lie on our backs in the rear of the empty truck and gaze up at the clear black sky. Shooting stars would be falling all over the place. It is one of my favorite memories, Bub and me riding on the truck watching the stars fall in all directions.

In Chilson, we never had a phone, but in the living room in Maine, there was an old box telephone hanging on the wall. It was a leftover from when Bob's first wife had lived there. It only cost fifty cents a month to use, so Mim had it turned on. That telephone turned out to be a great source of information for me. Who needed a radio or newspaper?

Our ring was three shorts, but everyone's ring came in. There were no private lines. Everyone was on what was called the party line. You put your hand over the mouthpiece and carefully picked up the earpiece, and you could listen in to everything said.

Everyone did this. Sometimes there would be eight or ten people listening in. You could hear breathing and noises in the background when people didn't cover their mouthpiece well. Sure, everyone listened in, but no one ever admitted it.

Sometimes, someone talking would say, "Get the hell off the line!" Then you'd hear some clicks as people hung up, but they'd pick right up again. I was careful not to let Mim catch me, or she'd ream me out good. She said it was impolite.

But I managed to get in my share of listening. I knew who had a new calf, or whose wife was cheating on whom, or whose mother was sick, or who couldn't pay their bills.

Every once in a while during his noon hour, a hired hand called his girlfriend at a nearby farm. They'd whisper and giggle about what they'd done the night before. Oh, I picked up many a juicy tidbit listening in on the party line.

A little dog wandered on to the farm one day. Of course, no one wanted it around but me. I named her Flossie, and she went everywhere with me.

Something was wrong with animals around there. A lot were having "fits." We thought it was because it was so hot that August, just "dog days fever."

One day, Flossie and I were way up the road, busy picking blackberries. We started to go back toward the farm when, all of a sudden, a moose appeared right in front of us out of nowhere. It acted funny. Its eyes looked glazed and it staggered around. Flossie got between me and the moose and barked and yapped at it till it wandered back away from me, but not before it nipped Flossie a little on her hind leg. Flossie and I ran for our farm.

Flossie licked the wound clean, and as it didn't look like much, I paid no more attention to it. I told Mim about the moose, and she said the farmers around had been saying they had seen a moose in the fields that acted oddly. But no one seemed worried or concerned. The animals just continued having their "fits."

A couple of weeks later, Flossie and I were down by the brook playing. She didn't act like her usual self. She didn't jump at the frogs or run in and out of the water as she usually did. She restlessly wandered around and kept looking at me with her big eyes. I thought she was sick, so we went back to the farm. Maybe she'd take a nap and wake up feeling better.

We went into the kitchen. Mim was there, and suddenly Flossie sort of howled and dove at her. Mim jumped up on the countertop and Flossie kept trying to jump up and get her. The broom was beside the counter, and Mim grabbed it. She kept pushing Flossie back with it. Mim screamed at me to get out and close the door.

After a few minutes, Flossie quieted down. I opened the door a little, and she staggered out. Her mouth was all foam, and I could see she was blind as she kept running into things. Mim was still up on the counter. She was white as a sheet, and she told me to go find Bob. He was in the barn.

Bob looked at Flossie and went in for his gun. I walked toward her. I wanted to do something for her because I loved her so much. Mim screamed, "Get away from her!"

I quickly climbed the cherry tree by the side of the house and called to Flossie. She came over and stood under the tree. I talked to her and she lay down. Terribly ill as she was, she knew I was there. I calmed her down.

Bob came out and shot Flossie in the head. I knew she was suffering and it had to be done, but it really shook me up. I stayed in the tree a long time, crying.

I don't know why Bob didn't bury Flossie that night, but he didn't. So the next morning, Bubby and I dragged her way down in the field. The dirt was so hard that we couldn't dig a grave for her. Instead, over on one side in a ditch by the brook, there was a big old beat-up galvanized tin tub. We put that over her and sadly went back to the house.

I never went where Flossie was again, though I looked down that way often. On a nice day, you could just see a little bit of that tin tub shining in the sun. I hoped Flossie knew I'd always love her.

And that's how it was. Animals kept having fits. And no one ever said the word "rabies." It was just "fits."

One day, Bub and I were up at Fays' farm. Pat Fay and her brothers, Tom and Dick, were playmates of ours. We liked to go up to their farm because they had Little Big Books. These books cost ten cents each. An unheard-of luxury for Bub and me, but the Fays had a lot of those books, and they let us read them.

After reading for a while, we all went out in their back field to slide down the haystacks piled up there. All of a sudden, Gee's dog, Blacky, started running in circles and growling and barking.

We kids all dove for a haystack and climbed up. All except Tommy. He was fatter and slower and didn't make it before Blacky was after him. He was hollering, "Help me! Help me!" We thought it was funny, and we let Blacky chase him around the haystack a couple of times before we reached down and pulled him to safety. Thank God, Blacky never caught up with Tommy to bite him. At last Blacky wandered off, and we climbed down from the haystack and went in the house to read some more Little Big Books.

Our peas were gone and we didn't have any money coming in. One day, Mim took Bub and me to hire out to pick string beans. An old bus took us with other people to a big field about five miles from our farm.

A gruff-acting man gave us each a big basket and told us to get started picking. We would be paid a half-cent for each pound we picked. Someone whispered we were supposed to be getting a penny a pound, but the overseer was keeping half for himself. No one dared to say anything to him or to complain about it. He didn't have a whip in his hand, but I was sure he had one right there handy.

Everyone rushed to get to work except Bubby. It was terribly hot, and he pooped out right away. Bob had kept us awake most of the night before, roaring in one of his tantrums all around the house, so Bub had had it. He just lay down in a row of string beans and went to sleep.

I halfheartedly went down a row and then sneaked over into a big patch of tame raspberries. I ate a lot of them and then jumped in a spring pond that was there to cool off. No one saw me or paid any attention.

Mim picked quite steadily for the hours we were there. I think she made sixty-one cents, I made three cents, and Bubby made nothing. We got on the bus and went back to our farm. I was afraid Mim was going to make us go back the next day, but she didn't say anything about it. So luckily, that deal was over.

We became friends with the Ralph Bray family because Bob was good friends with Ralph. The Brays lived about a mile away from us on the back of the Aroostook River. They were of pure Indian descent on Ralph's side. I don't know about Mrs. Bray. She was a very blond little woman. She was in a mental institution most of the time we lived there. She came home for a visit once but only stayed a week or so, then cracked up and went back to the institution.

Isabel told me that her mother wouldn't stay home because Ralph was always after her and she kept falling out of bed to keep away from him. When enough was enough, Mrs. Bray would throw a tantrum, and away she'd go again.

Isabel was dark like her father. Ina was blond like her mother. I liked them a lot. They were the smartest kids I ever knew. In school, they got highest marks in everything. No one could touch them.

Ralph had big iron tubs down by the river that he fired up every Sunday full of food. Many people came to eat, us included. Everyone brought something to throw in the pots with the raccoon and rabbit Ralph had cooking there. Sometimes he even had a deer. What did we bring? You guessed it—string beans and peas!

The kids would go swimming in the river, all except me. There were great big black bloodsuckers in the water with bright red bellies. The kids had a contest going to see who could come out of the water with the most bloodsuckers on them. The record was seven. This was too gross for me, and I wouldn't go near the water.

The kids laughed at me, calling me "fraidy cat" and "scaredy cat" and worse than that, but nothing bothered me or budged me to get in that river. While the kids were in the water, I'd walk along the bank and dig for turtle eggs. I also saw where a lot of bloodsuckers gathered by an old log.

One Sunday was the end. The kids called me every name they could think of. Finally someone called me "Chilson chicken." That did it. I saw red and went over, climbed down off the log, and stood there in the water, grossed right out. When I came out of the water, the kids pulled fourteen big bloodsuckers off me. I was now the champion, and no one ever called me "Chilson chicken" again.

Bob got some odd jobs working around the farms, and so did Buck. We had barely enough to eat, and it was a long hard winter. Mim decided the school in Palmyra was too tough for me. The boys there swore and talked dirty to the girls. She was afraid that wasn't all they'd do. I don't know how, but somewhere she got the money ($9 per semester) for tuition, and I went into Bangor on the bus to school. I went, but I don't remember much about the school as it was a quiet place. However, I felt a little uppity going in to the big school in Bangor, and all my friends had to go to the little school in Palmyra. Bubby stayed there too as Mim considered it safe for him as he was a boy.

Came spring, and May flowers! Up there they hung May baskets. You made a little basket and put flowers in it. All through May, you never knew when kids would hang the May basket on your door and holler, "May basket! May basket!" You had to go out and chase the kids down. Then they all came in the house and had cookies and cocoa or some treat like that.

Came the night the May basket was hung on our door. Bub and I rushed out into the dark to catch the kids. I found Pat and Ina. Ina was looking for her older sister, Isabel, who some of the big boys had picked off her feet and, laughing, ran away with.

We told Ina to stay with the other kids, and Pat and I went to find Isabel. We rushed down through the path in the woods. It was very dark. We heard something ahead of us and we cautiously stopped, staying quiet. Isabel was saying, "Stop, that's enough, leave me alone." There were a lot of weird noises, and the boys were laughing. Pat started to rush up where they were, but I grabbed her and put my hand over her mouth. I was awfully scared and knew we couldn't do anything. We had to get out of there and get help, but just then Isabel ran by us, crying. The boys came along, laughing down the path, and one said, "Let's go get another bitch." Pat wilted to the ground. We lucked out. They didn't see or hear us in the dark.

The next day I saw Isabel. Her face was swollen and she couldn't walk very well. I asked her if she was okay. She said,

"Yes, why shouldn't I be?" Being only twelve years old to Isabel's fifteen, what could I say or what could I do? No one would believe me if Isabel denied it. Pat tried, but Isabel wouldn't talk to her, either.

Mim had been right about those boys, and Pat and I didn't hang any more May baskets, even though invited.

Bob went to work in the woods, peeling pulp, so he could make more money. He didn't like taking orders from anyone, and he got in a fight and beat up his boss. That was the end of that job. There was nothing to do but pack up our old truck and head for Chilson.

In the meantime, Buck had gotten a neighbor farm girl pregnant. He didn't want any part of that, so he took off for Chilson in his old car ahead of us.

Someone had given us a puppy. But it didn't act right and was very quiet riding on the back of the truck with Bub and me and the horses. We made a pee stop somewhere in the Green Mountains of Vermont, and the puppy ran off, having a fit, into the woods. Luckily, we couldn't find it. Poor little thing. I'm sure it died soon. How lucky that we hadn't brought it back to Chilson. He could have spread the rabies there. The way those rabid animals lived in with everyone up there in Maine that year, how no person got it, I'll never know, but they didn't that I know of.

We arrived back in Chilson on our old farm. We had no money, no food, no job, poorer than ever, but it was sure good to be home. And the whole summer was ahead. There was no way to go but up.

Learning About Sex and Musterole

Mrs. Monty lived on land that she had farmed all of her life. Her husband had died that winter. She never had any children. Most older widows on farms who had no sons to help them would cut back on their animals and activities. They would live quietly in the house, waiting to "pass on." Not Mrs. Monty. She decided to keep her farm going. She hired two men to help her. One was a guy named Tex from up Mineville way, and the other was my Uncle Riley, Mim's stepbrother.

Mrs. Monty loved all kids. But she especially liked my cousin Jimmy and me. We were young enough to make her laugh, but old enough so that she didn't have to watch us every minute, or so she thought. Sometimes we stayed with her for a few days.

Mrs. Monty made donuts most every morning in a big pan of sizzling hot fat. When we came downstairs for breakfast, she would hand them over to us on the end of a long frying fork. With big glasses of cold creamy milk, they were scrumptious. Other mornings, she fried homemade bread and poured lots of homemade maple syrup over it. That, with scrambled eggs, and apple, rhubarb and venison pies to pick from, we could hardly walk when we left the table. Now at home most mornings, breakfast was "skips." No wonder we loved to visit Mrs. Monty.

On one visit, we were out in the barn petting the sheep when Tex and Uncle Riley came in. They went over to clean out the horse stalls, and they were talking about going to Bovine's Dance Hall that evening. Bovine's was run by Mim's sister, Aunt Ethel, and her husband, Joe Bovine. People came from all over on Saturday nights to go there. I knew they square danced, and I didn't know what else, but I was willing to find out. Jim was game for anything, so we decided to follow Tex and Uncle Riley to Bovine's that night. We let them get ahead of us a little ways. They were going crosscut through the woods, so they didn't see us following them because of the trees, and the growing darkness.

Finally, Bovine's was in front of us. Tex and Uncle Riley went over and into the doorway. Jim and I stayed on the edge of the woods, out of sight. The woods were only fifty feet or so away from the dance hall. The music (piano, drum and fiddle) blared out the door. We could see dancers going right to town through the windows. Some men, and a few women, were standing around outside. They were drinking whiskey out of pint bottles. When they finished a bottle, they would just throw it on the ground. Aunt Ethel wouldn't let them drink inside because she didn't have a liquor license, so it was against the law to have liquor anywhere on the premises. However, Joe Bovine was selling the stuff as fast as he could out back of the dance hall. They didn't have a license for out there, either.

On some of the bushes around the dance hall there were these white things hanging down. They looked like they had

Bovine's Tavern, circa 1938.

been flung there. I asked Jim what they were, and he said they were "safes." He gave me some more details about them and concluded with, "You gotta use one if you don't want to get a girl 'knocked up.'" I don't know how Jim knew all this fascinating stuff, but it was all new to me.

I knew I'd have to think all this over, but I pushed it back in my mind so I could settle down and listen to the music and watch the performance going on. Every little while, a guy and girl would stagger out of Bovine's and head for the bushes. Tex was in and out a couple of times. Then, here came Uncle Riley with a girl named Sadie, who we knew.

Uncle Riley.

Uncle Riley had his arms around Sadie, and they were headed right for us. We decided we better not press our luck any further, and we scurried off back to Mrs. Monty's.

Jim, who I now considered to be an authority on such things, said, "Do you want to find out what happened with Uncle Riley and Sadie?" You bet I did! So when we heard Tex and Uncle Riley come into the house, we rushed up to their room and hid under one of the beds.

I looked the room over. There were a couple of jackets hanging on pegs along the walls and piles of underwear thrown here and there on the floor.

On the windowsill, all in a row, were their medicines. There was iodine for cuts, VapoRub for sore throats, Vaseline to sooth chapped skin and burns, and Musterole for coughs. If you had a cold, you rubbed Musterole on your chest to help break up the congestion. It was awfully strong. It could burn and blister your skin very easily.

Tex and Uncle Riley came in and sat on the beds. They started taking off their shoes and pants. They were half-loaded, and Tex was kidding Uncle Riley. Tex was laughing and saying that he knew Uncle Riley hadn't gotten anywhere with Sadie. Uncle Riley said, "To hell, I didn't!" Tex said, "What did you do, tickle her neck? Ha-ha-ha." At this, Uncle Riley got real mad. He said, "I'll show you what I did to her." He reached for the Vaseline, but he was so mad that he didn't notice he grabbed the Musterole instead. He stuck his penis right to the hilt in the Musterole jar. For a second, he just sat there. Then he exploded. He let out the most god-awful scream and went tearing down the stairs and out the door. He flew, with bare behind, across the yard and jumped feet first into the horses' watering trough. Tex rushed out after him and stood by the trough, doubled up, laughing. Mrs. Monty came running out, and she was mad because Uncle Riley was polluting the horses' water. Jim and I sneaked off to our beds.

As I lay there falling asleep, I wasn't too sure what I had learned that evening, except what not to do with Musterole.

Davey vs. Old Faithful

Kerosene lamps can sometimes go a week or more without needing their chimneys washed. However, we had one that was a real oddball. No matter what we did to it, every night at some time, early or late, its flame would suddenly streak up and shoot black smoke and soot out of the top of its chimney. It would erupt like that for one minute or so before it would calm down again. Because of this, we called that lamp Old Faithful.

We kept Old Faithful on an orange crate by the front window. I had to clean Old Faithful every day. I hated that job and resented it more all the time, but there was no getting around it. It was my job, and I had to do it.

One night around dark, Bubby came running into the kitchen. He was all sweaty and gasping for breath. It took Mim a few minutes to quiet him down and find out what was wrong. Bubby said that no matter how fast he had run, something up on the cliff had kept pace with him and screamed beside him all the way home. Bub had dropped his bicycle down the road a ways because, on the sandy road, it was quicker to run than to ride the bike.

Bob took a lantern and went to get Bub's bike. When he came back, he said it was a wildcat up on the cliff screaming and that it probably wouldn't bother anyone. Probably wouldn't bother anyone? Bub and I weren't too sure. So when we got off our school bus down at the corners, we'd run all the way up our road to get home before dark. We did this for a few days, and as we didn't hear anything up on the cliff, we decided if we weren't on the road after dark, we would be safe.

Down at the corners, when a group of us kids got off the bus, we would sometimes hang around and play poker or hopscotch. If you didn't have any pennies to play poker, you had to play hopscotch. As I hardly ever had any pennies, it was my luck to have to play hopscotch while I enviously watched the kids sitting in the grass playing poker. However, whenever we stayed at the corners, Bub and I kept it always in mind to go running up our road at the first slight hint of darkness.

One Friday night, we were at the corners and I was flying high because I had three pennies to play poker. We played a few hands, and I was winning. I'd lose a penny or two, then win them back. I was having so much fun and was so interested in my gambling that when Bubby said, "Come on, Yada, it's getting too near dark, let's get for home," I said, "Go ahead, I'll catch you in a minute." Bubby took off, and I forgot everything but the fun of that game. Suddenly, I realized it was late and I'd never make it home before it was really dark.

I said to my friend Anna, "I'm scared. How am I ever going to get up that road home?" Davey F. heard me and said he'd give me a ride. He had an old car, and I jumped at the chance for a ride. I thought it was awfully nice for him to offer.

Davey was a nice looking blond boy, about four years older than me. Once, when I was in the fourth grade, he visited our school. He was very friendly and talked to all the kids. I was bashful and slumped down in my seat, hoping not to be noticed. Davey caught my eye and said hello. I sunk lower into my seat, and he laughed. Davey had such a nice, happy laugh. It made you feel good—as if you were someone special.

A couple of winters later, Davey was sliding on the main road. Somehow he ended up under a car that was coming up the road. He suffered a severe head injury. They got him to Dr. Cummings in Ticonderoga quickly. Rumor went around that some of Davey's brain was found in his cap. Bub and I were horrified by that. We said a prayer for Davey every night.

Davey was in the hospital a long time. When he came home, one arm was a little stiff, one leg shuffled along, and his face was drawn a little to one side. We heard that he couldn't remember anything for long, and that it was hard for him to learn, but he kept right on trying. I liked him and thought he had a lot of guts. Only thing though, I noticed that his happy special laugh was now a very weird-sounding one.

Davey had his old car wired so that if you took hold of the door, he could reach under his dash, push something, and give you an electric shock. He got me to take hold of his door once, and I couldn't move while he shocked me. Then he laughed his weird laugh.

He also would holler at people for no apparent reason, but everyone thought, "Oh, that's just Davey," and that he was harmless. He had to have some fun, didn't he?

Anyway, to get back to my story, I got in the car with Davey, and we went up the road toward my house. He stopped the car a little ways down the road from the house. He was laughing his weird laugh, and then he grabbed me. He said he was going to kiss me and then do some "awful things" to me. It was very dark. The only light was Old Faithful shining from our front window. Davey was so strong that I couldn't move, and I was petrified. I knew he meant what he was saying and more, and it made it worse that he was laughing his weird laugh.

Suddenly, Old Faithful erupted in the window. It never did a better job of shooting flames and smoke into the air. Davey was startled and he loosened his grip on me. I jerked free, out of the car, up the road, up the steps onto the front porch. I slumped down on the floor in relief as I listened to his weird laugh going down the road and into the distance.

I kept a wide berth from Davey after that, and I never again resented having to clean Old Faithful.

P.S. Now, kids, even after this happened, I have to admit that the lure of the poker game occasionally got the best of me and I stayed too long at the corners. It would be dark, and sometimes Davey, again with his weird laugh, would offer me a ride home. Boy, I'd take off like a shot up our dirt road. Of course it was scary running alone in the dark when that old wildcat started screaming from the cliff, but I had no one to blame but myself.

Crown Point Bay

There was one place on Eagle Lake that we kids loved to go. That was Crown Point Bay. It was a long strip of beautiful sand that was far away from the road, so there were no adults anywhere nearby. No one to tell us to be quiet, stop making so much noise, or to shut up. There were about fourteen of us, ranging in age from nine to twelve. We were happy to be alive and full of good health and vinegar. World War II was not yet looming on the horizon, and we had absolutely no idea of what was ahead of us. So all we thought about was the present and having a laughing good time. We had a couple of dented up pots to cook in, and a log raft tied together with rope hidden in the bushes. Everything else was wild and pristine.

Once or twice a month on a Saturday, we'd meet on Crown Point Bay. All we took off was our shoes. We went swimming in our clothes and pushed each other off the raft. No matter what we did, we were laughing, laughing, laughing.

We watched baby bullheads swirling around together in circles. We would bet which group would scatter the quickest when we splashed water at them, maybe because we believed their mothers were nearby with their big horns to frighten us. They made us laugh as they swirled on their way.

The water along the shore was very warm for about three feet into the lake from the sun beating down on it. Warm water was a luxury to us. If we had any at home, the water had to be heated on the stove. So we sat in that lovely warm water at the lake's edge and rolled around in it. The boys wrassled in it and the girls splashed each other. We laughed all the while for the sheer joy of having that warm water. We were so happy on Crown Point Bay.

We ran up and down the beach, playing tag and gathering freshwater clams to put in our stews. Some kids brought potatoes or onions when their fathers let them have the vegetables from their gardens. If they didn't, the kids would snatch the vegetables anyway. I always brought tomatoes—the only thing I could take from the garden without getting caught. When our stew was ready, we had to eat it with our fingers as we had no cutlery. We really smeared our faces and, of course, got a big laugh out of who looked the worst.

I can't remember all that happened down on Crown Point Bay, but I do remember the laughing—all the time.

A couple of years ago, I was on my way to Chilson to visit Aunt Dean. As I was going by Eagle Lake, I pulled off the road, got out of the car, and stood there looking down the lake toward Crown Point Bay. The strip of sand was silent in the warm sun. Nothing moved or stirred down on Crown Point Bay. It had been seventy years since I'd been there, but I knew it was still waiting for us kids to come again.

Then as I sadly turned away, I heard it. I clearly heard the laughter down on Crown Point Bay.

Kitchen Hops, "Staying Good," and Swearing Off Men

From the time I was in third grade, Alan L. was my secret love. I worshipped him from afar. He was two grades ahead of me, so he hardly knew I existed. He was tall for his age, and he had a flashing grin. It didn't matter that he was cross-eyed. To me, he was handsome.

I watched Alan flirt with other girls up through the seventh and eighth grades. Girls liked him a lot. He would flash his grin and speak to me occasionally. Then I would melt and be tongue-tied. I watched him go out with many different girls. That's all I could do, watch, because back then a "nice" girl didn't try to get attention from a guy. He had to approach you. Only "available" girls chased guys.

That fall, Mim was away working, and I needed advice. The only one I could ask was Gram. I figured she ought to know something. She had gotten married at fifteen to Grandpa Hammond.

One day, Gram and I were sorting apples up in the doggery (a big dry room used for storage upstairs in the farmhouse). I hesitatingly told her how much I liked Alan, and maybe I should not be one of the nice girls and should be known as being available. Then Alan might be more interested in me. Besides, the available girls had much more fun than us nice girls—at least that's the way I saw it.

Gram didn't change her expression and kept right on sorting apples. She said, "Gloria,"—she called me Gloria instead of Yada, so I knew she was really hearing me—"don't you ever change from being a nice girl. You have a long way to go, and you're going to have some life of your own before you get married."

I answered, "But you got married young. You had Aunt Etta when you were sixteen." She said, "Yes, but you let your babies sleep under your heart for a lot of years yet. I want you to have some life of your own before you have babies to care for."

"It hurts not being able to get Alan," I said. She told me, "He'll be there, but I bet when you can have him, you won't want him." Then she looked me right in the eye and said, "Gloria, I can't make you behave yourself, but remember this: If you burn your ass, you'll have to sit on the blister."

I nearly fell over, and I dropped the apples in my hands. My very ladylike grandma, who I had never heard say anything off-color, cared enough about me to say something like that. It shook me good, and I gave up the idea of being anything but a nice girl, even though it was boring.

One of the things we had for entertainment was the "kitchen hop" square dance. Most farmhouses had a big kitchen where the dance was held. Gram had a really huge kitchen.

Gram decided to have a hop. Now, everything had to be "lye soap clean" at a kitchen hop. All the other ladies would check out the hostess's housekeeping, and they never missed a trick. If her privy wasn't limed just right, or there was a cobweb anywhere in the bedroom where you put your coat during the hop, God help the hop hostess at the next "teatime get-together." If she wasn't there, her housekeeping got torn to shreds. With that as incentive, we got most of the house scrubbed and slicked up on the day before the hop. The next morning we were up early to set the kitchen right. We started with cleaning the ceiling. Everything was wiped down. The windows were washed, and new curtains that Gram had made were put up. She scoured the old soft pine floor until it looked like cream. We put the big kitchen table in the back shed. What chairs we had, we put along the walls. Every dish and pan was out of sight.

That night, Grandpa had to eat a cold supper, standing at the table in the shed. He was fussing and mumbling about it to himself, but Gram paid no attention. She was busy blacking the old wood cook stove, the one thing we couldn't move out of the kitchen. Grandpa finished eating and had to go out the shed door and walk way around the house to get to the barn. He couldn't cut through the kitchen as no one was allowed to walk on the clean floor. "Damn foolishness," he said, but he didn't take any chances to rile up Gram by going through there.

Well, after the cleaning and clearing, we put the kerosene lamps around, waiting to be lit, on the wide windowsills, and the kitchen was ready. It was just starting to get dusk. All we had to do was gussy ourselves up and wait.

Now, my friend Mary had told me a week before, that Alan had told her he had something to tell me. He was going to tell me at the kitchen hop. I daydreamed about the lovely something he was going to say to me. I was blushing when I thought about it, but so "goose-pimply" excited. I nearly told Gram, but I didn't.

Right after dark, people started arriving. Joe, the fiddler, and Bill, the square dance caller, arrived. Gramp helped roll in the piano off Uncle Amacy's wagon. They set it back by the kitchen stove. Not many people had a piano, but Aunt Sadie did. Very few could afford one. Uncle Amacy had gone and got Aunt Sadie and her piano for us. There was only one thing though—Aunt Sadie insisted on playing the piano.

We had better piano players, but Aunt Sadie wouldn't bring her piano unless she could play. She missed some notes now and then because she was always reaching up to pull out her gum that got caught in one of her crooked teeth. But most of the time she tinkled out a pretty good tune. It really didn't matter. There was so much noise, and the fiddler and the caller covered up her mistakes.

Many people came to kitchen hops. Single folks, men and their wives, kids of all ages, and old ladies to hold babies while sitting in chairs along the walls. Oh, the gossiping that went on in those chairs along the walls. The old ladies caught up on all the news, the more rancorous, the better. A kitchen hop was really a family affair. Even the tiniest babies were brought. How they slept through the whole thing, I don't know, but they did.

No drinking ever went on inside the kitchen at a hop. The women did not drink, that I ever saw at these affairs, but the men would be tipping up their jugs and slugging it down outside. Of course the men were sneaking it on the women, or so they thought, but everybody knew.

At Gram's hop, the music started slow and steady as the fiddler and Aunt Sadie and the caller warmed up. The square dances were correct and gracefully done, at first. After each set of square dances, the musicians would disappear outdoors for a few minutes. Each time they came in and started playing again, the music got a little more spirited, and the dances got faster.

After a few more visits outside, the caller was shouting the dance calls so fast it took your breath away, and the fiddler was jigging as he fiddled up a storm. All the men loosened up the more slugs they took, and weren't so shy about letting their feet fly and weren't so timid about putting their arms around the women's waists to swirl them around.

Being twelve, I was now considered "of dating age," and I was right in there with the best of them. I got asked to dance every dance. My feet hardly touched the floor. It got better and better as it went along. I loved every minute of it.

That evening, there was a fiddling contest about halfway through the dance. The caller cleared the floor, and the fiddler started playing a fast jig, a challenge to any other fiddler who was in the room.

Of course, there were other good fiddlers there, and they were waiting. They grabbed their fiddles from the corners where they'd stuck them, and the contest began. You never heard such music as each tried to outdo the other. We were all jigging and clogging as the yodelers started in. Yodeling Pin D. was the best, but many could yodel. The notes they hit, and the sounds that came out of their mouths are not often heard!

Even the old ladies got into the act. They never left their chairs. They lifted their feet about one inch off the floor, and a wilder clogging you never saw! No other part of their bodies moved, just their clogging feet, and the babies in their arms slept on.

Someone shoved a couple of chairs onto the floor. Our bone, or spoon, players sat themselves down, and with their feet doing a wild "heel and toe" on the floor, tapped those bones on their knees. You couldn't even see their fingers moving, they were so fast.

All these contests went so fast and furious, from one to another, that no one ever knew who won what, which was good. That way there were no hard feelings, thus no fights, and the dance went merrily on its way.

Of course, that kitchen hop night, in the back of my mind, was Alan. I couldn't wait to know what he had to tell me. I'd seen him come in, and I didn't miss who he talked to or danced with. I saw him look my way once or twice, but he never came near me.

In the short lull before the dancing began again, after the bone players' performance, Mary and I went out to the privy. When we came back, another square dance was in full swing. We stood in the doorway, watching.

Suddenly, Alan was standing beside me. His crossed eyes looked intently into mine, I think. I thought, "This is it! My beautiful moment is here!"

Alan said, "Gloria, always brush your teeth at least once a week. Don't use baking soda. Use salt—it works better." Then he walked away. At that moment, I swore off men, I thought, forever. My swear-off lasted for six months until my 13th birthday party.

Finally Getting To Be Thirteen

Thirteen was coming of age, mountain style. Most everyone was given a party then, at least a kitchen hop. But Mim was away working, and old By Lightnin' Weston Cross was staying with Bubby and me up on the farm. There was no one to give me a party. I knew I'd give one to myself!

In school, I spent all afternoon planning. I sent Bubby, when we got off the school bus, over to stay the night at Gram Granger's. He was glad to go. When he stayed overnight there, he was sure to get breakfast in the morning, something we very often went without at home.

I asked Carl Covell, Clarence Wright, Marie B., Dennis M., Millie S. and Frankie Dougal to my party. I had no money, but I'd make popcorn. For drinks, I called on Frankie and Clarence to help. We knew who had the best hard cider in Chilson— Tweedle Armstrong. His cider would "sear your teeth right off," and that's what we wanted. But he was so "ramrod," we knew he'd never give us any. We knew we'd have to "borrow" it to get it.

Early that evening, Frankie, Clarence and I parked Frankie's dad's old car back down the road in a cedar grove and sneaked up to Tweedle's house. Tweedle was across the road in the barn, milking his cows.

Old Pal came around the house with a growl, but he saw me and choked off his bark. That dog and I had spent many a time fishing in the brook or picking cowslips in the swamp.

So we were safe from the dog that Tweedle had to protect his property, and we sneaked around the other side of the house.

Frankie took the little window out of the cellar wall. He climbed in, and Clarence handed him the three jugs and tubing that we had taken from the car's trunk. Then Clarence ran back into the woods. That left me to stand guard.

Frankie seemed to take a long time in the cellar. Later he told me he had to find a barrel he could get the bung out of. Finally, he handed me a jug, and another, and another, and the tubing. Then he crawled out.

We put the window back, scooched over, and started around the house. Just then, Tweedle came around the corner. He caught sight of us and dropped his milk pails. Hollering and swearing, he dove onto the porch for his shotgun.

Our feet flew over the dirt road. Clarence was long gone. Finally, *boom* went the shotgun as we turned the corner toward the cedar grove and Frankie's car. We threw the jugs in the backseat and we were out of there!

Tweedle always shot up in the air when he shot at us for picking on him, but we weren't sure he would keep it that way. After all, everyone has his "enough is enough" breaking point.

We looked along the road for Clarence, but he had scuttled up over the cliff and through the woods, home. Never mind, Frankie would pick him up for the party that night.

When I got home, Weston was down in the barn feeding the pigs. I made some pancakes for his supper. Then I made the popcorn. The old cook stove wouldn't heat up right 'cause all the wood I had for it was wet and punkie, so the popcorn was tough. It was all I had, so it had to do.

I swept the kitchen floor, brought in a pail of water from the well, "spatted down" my hair, and waited for my guests to arrive.

Frankie's old car chugged into the yard. First to come in was Carl. He had bright red hair, light blue eyes and one thumb three times as long as the other one. The thumb was stiff to the last joint on the end, which he could crook in any direction. He used to entertain us showing how fast he could move that joint. Anyway, he had his comb and his pickin' mandolin with him, so we would have music.

Carl Covell.

Marie and Clarence came in. They were mad at each other for something. They stood, on each side of the table, glaring at one another.

Millie and Dennis were next, walking hand in hand. They were boyfriend/girlfriend since kindergarten days. Millie had been on the verge of "giving in" to Dennis for a long time, but she hadn't yet.

Then came Frankie with the cider. Weston didn't look too happy as the kids piled into the house until he saw the three big jugs of cider. Then he perked up.

No one wanted any popcorn, so I got out the jelly glasses, and Frankie glugged them full. Everyone drank one glass, two glasses, then three or four. No one talked much. Suddenly, things began to happen.

Carl started playing his comb. Then he put that down and picked the mandolin. Song after song—the old kitchen just jumped with pickin' music.

Marie stood up abruptly and went over near the pantry and started clogging and singing at the top of her lungs: *"She'll be comin' round the mountain when she comes,"* over and over again. It didn't matter what song Carl was playing, she screeched, *"She'll be comin' round the mountain when she comes."* But no one cared; she was having a good time.

Dennis and Millie had walked into the bedroom. I kept calling to them and going in to pretend I was getting something out of the dresser. I didn't want Millie giving in at my party.

Old By Lightnin' sat by the table swilling the last jug of cider. Finally he said, "By lightning, I hate to complain, boys, but this cider tastes just like kerosene." Frankie smelled the jug, and he was laughing. He had filled his father's kerosene jug by mistake. He told Weston, who said, "I don't give a Continental," and he swallowed down another glassful.

In the meantime, we were swirling and dancing to Carl's music. Finally, By Lightnin' wet his pants. It poured across the floor. But no one paid any attention. We just hopped over and across the puddle as we danced.

I sneaked in the bedroom and checked out Dennis and Millie. So far, so good. They had only gotten as far as sitting on the bed.

I came out into the hall, and Frankie was standing there. He took my hand. He bent down and kissed me. We walked hand in hand out to the kitchen, and we danced and we danced.

All of a sudden, Millie came running out of the bedroom and said she had to go. Her father would be mad if she was too late getting home. They said goodnight, and the old car chugged down the road.

There were many things to be thankful for. Millie still hadn't given in to Dennis. Marie had made it outdoors to vomit instead of on the kitchen floor, and I had a boyfriend.

I looked at By Lightnin'. It would be morning before he moved from that chair. He started wetting again. This time the puddle was forming in the other direction. Oh, well, I'd clean it up in the morning. In the meantime, he was still cheerfully singing his songs.

I picked up the kerosene lamp and slowly climbed the stairs to my room. As I closed the door, By Lightnin' was into his favorite song: *"And he buried his knife in her lily-white breast!"*

I crawled happily into bed. It had been a good party, and I was officially thirteen!

Courtship

Whenever Frankie and I were going somewhere, we always wanted someone to go with us. With another couple along, we seemed to have more fun. We always asked Clarence and Marie. They were "going together." Carl Covell always went with us too.

There was one thing, though. We would be riding along, and Clarence and Marie would start arguing in the backseat.

Suddenly Clarence would say, "Stop this car." Frankie would drive along a little farther and Clarence would hit the back of the front seat and yell, "Frankie, I said stop this car." There was nothing Frankie could do but pull over and stop.

Clarence and Marie would get out and stand yelling at each other. Suddenly, they'd start swinging at each other while calling

Frankie Dougal, 1941.

Gloria Stubing (me), 1941.

each other names. Then they'd knock each other down, kicking and hitting each other as they rolled around the ground.

I'd get sort of scared, and I'd say to Frankie, "What are they doing?"

He'd grin and say, "They are having their courtship."

Courtship? That's what courtship was all about? Forget it. I was never gonna court with anyone, never.

After three to four minutes, Clarence and Marie would pull each other up off the ground, brush each other off, and climb back in the car, and we'd go on our way.

Clarence Wright, 1941.

Marie Maye (my good friend), 1941.

I'd glance in the rearview mirror and they'd be sitting there with Clarence's arm around Marie's shoulders, and they'd be billing and cooing away as if nothing had ever happened. That was courtship? Forget it!

There's Always One

Sometime in most every girl's life there's a "Ralph."
Ruth (Ralph's sister) and I were very good friends. We used to walk to the school bus together most mornings of the week. I'd go up to Ruth's—she lived in the old Moore house up on the hill—and pick her up. Only Wednesday mornings she wouldn't let me come up. She'd always meet me at the bottom of the hill.

I had strict orders from her, if she wasn't there, to wait, but never come up to her house on Wednesday mornings! That just whetted my appetite, and I knew I was going up that hill the first Wednesday morning I could. So the first Wednesday morning when she wasn't there, I walked as fast as I could up the hill to her back door and knocked.

Ruth opened the door and looked mad. Before she could say, "What are you doing here?" her brother, Ralph, was beside her. Ralph was always after me. The more I tried to stay away from him, the harder he chased me and tried to hug me.

Ralph said, "I want to talk to you." I knew Ruth was mad, so she wouldn't help me. I had outsmarted myself, and now was in for more than I'd bargained for.

Ralph grabbed my arm and propelled me into the front room right in front of the bay window. To appear nonchalant and not bothered by him, I looked out the window at the biggest iron kettle I had ever seen. There was a fire burning under it. In the kettle were many diapers bubbling about in the boiling hot water. On top of the water was—what was it swirling around?

284

Oh, no! Why didn't they empty out the messes before they put the diapers in to boil?

That's why Ruth didn't ever want me up there Wednesday mornings. It was wash day, and she was embarrassed about the boiling diapers. She needn't have worried. I would never let on I saw anything. I had secrets, too!

I felt disgusted, so I took my eyes from the boiling diapers and looked at Ralph.

He was going strong, gabbing on and on. "You won't let me touch you or kiss you. You think you're too good for me. Now you are going to be sorry as I've found another girl."

I said, "Where, under a rock?"

Ralph had a little short neck, and it was starting to turn purple. Ugh! I willingly turned my eyes back to the boiling diapers. Ruth's mother was there stirring the contents of the kettle round and round with a long stick.

Ralph was really enjoying himself and said, "You really think you are something. Well, Bertha is my girl now. She's nicer than you (could be). She's smarter than you (no way). She's prettier than you (ha! ha!), and she has nicer clothes than you (true, but a low blow)."

Ralph looked at me smugly and said, "Now what have you to say to that?"

I wanted to say, "You're full of crap"—below my dignity. So I said, "I hope you wipe yourself good!" as I started from the room. I glanced back at Ralph. He was staring at me with his chin hanging on his chest.

He hollered, "You witch!"

I screamed back, "Go jump in that kettle and bob around with your friends!"

He started toward me, and I took off like a streak of lightning. I knew walking murder when I saw it! Ralph never spoke to me again. That always made me feel a little sad. He wasn't such a bad guy.

Jencie and the Best Day Ever

Jencie was one of our gang. She was so vivacious and busy. She was everybody's best friend. She didn't walk, she didn't run, she flew around. Her feet never seemed to touch the ground.

We had two baseball teams, boys against the girls. We girls won many games, to the boys' chagrin. It was all because of Jencie. She was the best slugger on either team. She whacked that ball every time and kept us fighting every minute. I can still hear us screaming as she flew around the bases, "Go, Jencie, go! Go, Jencie, go!"

Then something happened. Jencie began to slow down. She couldn't run fast anymore. She didn't smile as much, and she looked tired all the time.

Jencie grew thinner and thinner, and would fall asleep in the middle of things. Finally, she couldn't eat because of constant nausea. So her mother took her to see Dr. Cummings. He did some tests and said that she had leukemia. He said there was nothing he could do. There was no treatment or hope for leukemia in those days. So Jencie came home.

When we heard that Jencie had leukemia, we didn't know what that meant. We had never heard that word before. But when Gram told us it was "the bad blood disease," we knew what that meant. Jencie was going to die, and soon.

Jencie's mother was devastated. She kept her in a bedroom she fixed up for her downstairs. Jencie wasn't allowed outdoors and had to rest all the time. Her mom was trying to save her strength, trying to stave off the inevitable. So all we saw of

Jencie for the next couple of months was a sad little face that we waved to through the window.

Then Jencie's mom got word that her father was terribly ill down in Whitehall, and he was calling for her to come. She would have to go. She wanted to leave the next day and come back the following night.

Mim, as usual, to the rescue. She said I could stay with Jencie during the day, and she would be with her at night.

I went over to Jencie's house the next day, and her mom gave me strict orders. Don't excite Jencie, and keep her quiet in her room, and get Mim immediately in an emergency. Then about 1 p.m., Jencie's mom and dad took off for Whitehall.

Now, we kids had a ballgame planned for three o'clock. I figured I would miss it, but no sooner was Jencie's mom out of sight down the road than Jencie motioned me over to the bed.

Jencie looked so tiny lying there. Her arms were all black and blue spots. Her eyes were black, too, and her gums were bleeding a little bit. It tired her to talk loud, so she whispered, "I want to go to the ballgame." For a minute I panicked, and then I knew we'd do it. I said, "If you will drink a glass of orange juice, and we can stop your gums from bleeding, we'll go." Jencie nodded, and for a moment I saw a glimpse of the Jencie I knew so well. I went out to the ice house and chipped some slivers off a block of ice that was covered way down in the sawdust. I held the ice to Jencie's gums, and I couldn't believe it. After a while the bleeding stopped and didn't start up again.

I went out and got Jencie's wagon from the shed. I put a blanket and pillow in it and pulled it up to the door. She used what strength she had, and by me half-carrying her and lifting, we got her down the steps and into the wagon. Jencie said she was okay, so over the road we went to the ballfield.

The kids were there. They tried to look nonchalant when they saw us, but you could see they couldn't believe their eyes. I left Jencie by the sideline for a minute to go get a drink from the dipper in the drinking pail. A couple of kids came over and said, "What'll we do? What do we say to her?" I answered, "Treat her as you always have. That's what she wants." And that's what

287

we did. It would be awkward when it came time for Jencie to bat, so to save her from feeling bad, Elmer Pelrin had a good idea. He hollered out, "Jencie is the umpire." She was moved around back of the catcher. She couldn't call out loud enough for them to hear, so I stood by her side. As she whispered her call, I would yell out "Strike!" or "Ball!" or "You're out!" What a game we had! When they were mad at one of her calls, they would roar and yell at Jencie: "Throw her out!" "You stink!" "Get some glasses!" The game was its usual roughneck performance, and Jencie loved every minute of it. She was with the gang again.

The boys won, 6-5. We girls argued it was because Jencie wasn't slugging. We told her she couldn't umpire anymore. Next time, she had to play, and we'd slaughter those guys. We told her we had to be able to yell, "Go, Jencie, go! Go, Jencie, go!" I knew she was tired, but you could tell she was very happy.

We had only played a five-inning game because we also had a rotten egg contest planned for that afternoon. We had two teams, again, boys versus girls. For weeks we searched out abandoned chicken nests under the haymows, and we'd keep the eggs until we had a big pile of them. Every kid saved them, and I'm afraid some good eggs got snuck into the pile, too, but the longer they stayed in the hot sun, the riper they got, which was the whole idea. When we had about two hundred saved, we'd have a rotten egg fight. We'd divide the eggs.

The boys lined up on one side of the field, and the girls on the other, with about fifteen feet between us. Someone yelled "Go!" and we threw the eggs as fast as we could at each other, hitting everyone we could.

When the eggs broke and smelled, the mess would gag you. The awful smell was so bad, it hurt to breathe. The idea was to whack the other team the fastest with the most eggs to make them get out of there. Of course, these rotten egg fights were a no-no to parents, so we had to sneak way out back of the sugar grove to have one.

Jencie heard the kids talking about the fight. I was about to roll her home when she whispered, "I'm going to the fight." I couldn't believe it, but that's what she wanted to do, so we scooted right along with the kids out back of the sugar grove.

We divided the eggs and lined up. God, what a rotten egg fight we had! Jencie was right in there with us. We girls protected her what we could, and no boy took direct aim at her, but she took a couple of smacks on her dress.

The stench was awful. We had yellow rotten eggs all over us, and still we fought. Then the eggs were all gone, and neither line had broken. Someone yelled out, "Who won, Jencie?" She managed to say loudly, "It's a draw!" Everyone yelled, "Jencie's right! Jencie's right!" and holding their noses, they started toward the brook to clean up. We all looked ready to vomit, but Jencie was still smiling.

I grabbed the wagon handle to take after the kids for the brook. Jencie shook her head no and pointed toward the pond. That was what she wanted, so I trotted over the path toward the pond. Jencie dozed in the wagon behind me.

The pond water was lukewarm, and I pulled Jencie in the wagon out into it. I washed off her dress. I had a clean handkerchief and I used it to gently wash her face and arms. Next, I scrubbed myself up.

Then we stayed, looking at the beauty around us. The pond lilies were gorgeous. I picked a couple and put them in Jencie's lap. Some different smell from the rotten eggs! Over on the far shore, some deer came out for a drink. Three or four big fish jumped into the air for insects. The sun was down when we left there. We went quickly over the path in the growing dusk.

As we came to the top of Big Rock Hill, the moon was just coming up into the sky. A full Chilson moon rising out of the valley from behind Lake Champlain is a sight to behold. On that bittersweet night it was big as a saucer and an orange-red color. It looked like you could reach out and pluck it from the sky. Jencie whispered, "Soon, I'll be flying way out past that moon." I held her hand tightly and said, "Oh, no, Jencie. We'll come up here again, and we'll go over to the pond." But in our hearts, we knew differently.

We went on over the path, home. I was worried how I'd get Jencie out of the wagon. I knew I couldn't carry her, but somehow, I'd do it. When we got to the house, Frankie was there. He and I had planned to go to the movie in Ticonderoga that night. He had gone to the farm looking for me, and Mim had sent him over.

So Frankie picked Jencie up and put her on her bed. I had him put the wagon away. Jencie's gums were bleeding again, so I gave Frankie a bowl to go get some more slivers of ice from the ice house.

I put Jencie's nightgown on her. She wouldn't eat anything. But she did take a few sips of cool water. Mim came in and sat by the bed. I leaned over Jencie and whispered in her ear, "See you tomorrow. We'll go out and have some more fun." Her eyes were closed, but she was smiling.

Jencie died late that night. When Mim came home, she said she didn't know what we kids had done that day, but just before she died, Jencie whispered, "I had the best day, ever." And she was smiling. Then she just stopped breathing and was gone.

I knew where she was. Jencie was now way, way beyond the moon, flying in the stars. "Go, Jencie, go!"

Not to Worry

We had odds and ends of relatives living all around the countryside. One bunch, Aunt Margie, Aunt Arabella, Aunt Liz and Cousin Alicia, lived together. No one talked about it, but it was subtly known that they were "ladies of the night."

Alicia was on the verge of changing her ways as her mother was always after her to come on back to Chilson and start over. Alicia approached Mim to see if she could come to Chilson to live with us. She told Mim she wanted to start over and that she wanted her mother not to worry. Mim, as usual, a soft touch, told Alicia okay, and she came up on the farm to live with us.

Alicia was a dumpy little woman in her early thirties. Mim and I watched her get restless with no nightlife on the farm. She told us she was going to get a man and settle down. Besides, she wanted her mother not to worry.

The snow was very deep, and we couldn't drag dead trees down off the side hill to burn. So Mim bought a cord of stove wood for fifty cents from Short Cord Andy to keep us going until the snow melted lower on the side hill.

When Short Cord came in our yard with the load of wood, Mim went out to inspect it. Satisfied that it was a full cord, Mim invited him in for a cup of tea after he had unloaded the wood. When he finished and went into the kitchen, Bub and I hurried out and threw the rest of the wood off the truck that Short Cord hadn't unloaded. He always thought he could sneak away with some wood—it amounted to quite a few pieces—and if you didn't go out and finish unloading the wood, you got a real short cord. Everyone knew Andy would do this, hence his nickname.

ever hear of getting wood up for the winter? in the Fall?

Alicia was in the kitchen when Short Cord came in. She sized him up, and we could tell she was impressed. She talked to him and told him how strong he must be to always be throwing big sticks of wood around. No one ever before had made a play for Short Cord. He was beaming. Alicia happened to mention there was a dance that night, and Short Cord got up his nerve and asked her to go. She jumped at the chance and told him she knew he was a gentleman, and she knew her mother would not have to worry about her going out with him. Short Cord left the farm looking six feet tall instead of his five feet, four inches.

Short Cord was going to pick Alicia up at 7 p.m. It was five o'clock, so she started getting ready. She heated water on the stove and lugged it upstairs to put in the big washtub she'd taken up to her room. She called down to Mim, "Where's some soap?" Mim hollered, "Up in the closet in the back room." We heard her go in and get some soap, then all was quiet.

Suddenly we heard a loud scream and Alicia yelling, "Help, help, help." We rushed up, and she was hopping around the room, holding on to her private parts. Mim got her hands away, and we checked her over. Her privates were all red and scalded-looking. Alicia had made a mistake, and instead of taking a bar of Ivory soap, she had grabbed a bar of Mim's homemade lye soap that she used only to scour out her homebrew crocks and the hog-scalding kettle. Alicia had really scrubbed herself good with that soap.

Alicia was beside herself. The inside of her groin looked like it was going to blister. No matter, she was going on her date with Short Cord. It hurt her so much to walk, and then I had an idea. We made a pad out of an old piece of cloth. We put Cloverine salve on it, and Alicia put it in her bloomers between her legs. It helped some.

She finished dressing. We helped her downstairs and went into the parlor. Mim turned the kerosene lamp real low so Short Cord wouldn't get a good view of how Alicia was walking, really shuffling along. Alicia stood by the doorway so she wouldn't have to walk so far in front of Short Cord. She said not to tell anyone about this because she didn't want her mother to worry.

I was going to the dance with Frankie Dougal. Frankie and Short Cord drove into the yard at the same time. They stopped to talk to each other for a few minutes. Short Cord was talking a blue streak to Frankie, and Frankie was laughing.

They came in the house. Alicia did the best she could getting into the car. Short Cord was so excited and important that he didn't notice Alicia was sort of hobbling along. With a flurry of hands waving goodbye, they were away.

Frankie and I went into the kitchen. We stood there talking. He told me Short Cord was all excited and described to Frankie what he was going to do with Alicia after the dance. He said to hell with Alicia's mother worrying, he was going to score for sure. Was he in for a letdown!

Frankie and I cracked right up. We knew Alicia's mother had had many nights to worry, but she didn't have to worry that night!

To My Beloved Teacher,
Mrs. Connors

We were pretty wild kids in the one-room schoolhouse (grades five through eight) in the middle of Chilson Hill. We had a sweet young teacher named Miss Clifton, and we liked her. She just couldn't cope with us. Willie Sears was the worst of the bunch. When he thought he needed the afternoon off, he'd go down to the basement and throw a big bunch of garlic in the furnace. In a few minutes, we'd be "garlic smoked-out" for the rest of the day. Even with all the windows open, it would be overnight before anyone could go back and stay in the classroom. Miss Clifton couldn't handle Willie. All she could do was go in the cloakroom and cry. Poor Miss Clifton.

If anyone wanted to throw spitballs or get up and wrestle around the room while a class was in session or have a water fight by the water fountain in the back of the room, they did it. Miss Clifton just could not control us. All she could do was go in the cloakroom and cry.

I felt sorry for her, but there was nothing I could do. Anyway, I liked being able to go out and swing on the swings whenever I felt like it, or take a nap on my desk. We heard rumors that the school board was mad. Things were coming to a head. We would have another teacher in the fall. But we didn't worry about that as we had a long summer vacation ahead.

Then it was the first week of September, and we were back in our seats. I was now in the eighth grade, one of the big shots. I had plans for sleeping and fooling away the year. It didn't matter. Nobody cared. But oh boy, there was a new teacher, all right! Mrs. Connors stood by her desk. She was a big, big woman. She had big strong hands and steel eyes. Suddenly, I decided I was going to behave myself, at least on the surface, at least enough to just pass and get through the year.

Things were pretty quiet for about a month. We were feeling Mrs. Connors out. Finally, Willie could stand it no longer. He sauntered out the classroom door and down into the basement to "garlic the furnace." He needed the afternoon off.

Mrs. Connors got up and went and stood by the basement door. In a minute, Willie came up the stairs and into the room. He was a big kid, but Mrs. Connors snatched him up, set him back into the cellar way, and locked the door. Then she said, "Eighth graders, open the windows." The smoke from the burning garlic seeped up out of the cellar and circled around us. Our eyes were stinging and our voices were hoarse, but we had class as usual, and no one dared act as if anything was amiss. At four o'clock, time to go home, Mrs. Connors opened up the basement door and called, "Wilfred, come up here!" He did, and I tell you, he was green around the gills. He staggered outdoors, and that little schoolhouse never smelled of garlic again.

After that, things were different. We knew our place with Mrs. Connors. Spitballs became much less common flying through the air. If Mrs. Connors caught you, you had to pick the spitball up, chew it, and swallow it down. She caught me once. I haven't thrown a spitball since.

Mrs. Connors was on a diet. She ate only bread and tea every noon at her desk. Sometimes she grabbed the edge of her desk and held on as if she were in pain. Sometimes she couldn't catch her breath and would stand with her back to us, gasping. Then she'd take a pill. Because she ignored these episodes, we kids did, too. No one would dare do anything else, but I knew she was sick.

I was not doing much schoolwork, and Mrs. Connors knew it. "Gloria, I want some good papers turned in." Since it was so much easier to coast along, I wanted to say I wouldn't do it, but I didn't dare. So I did a little better for a while. Then she called me up to her desk and told me she was sorry she had told me

I could do well. She said my papers hadn't improved much, and she realized she had made a mistake in thinking I was bright. I bristled. I wanted to tell her that I was smart and that I would show her so, only I didn't dare. But did I ever start to study. I studied every New York State Regents paper from way back. I went over and over Silent Reading, Spelling, Geography, History, English, and Arithmetic, all the eighth grade Regents back then.

I began to feel that maybe I could do it. I knew Mrs. Connors was watching me. I knew she was quietly pushing me. Suddenly, I not only wanted to prove to her that I could do it, but I wanted to please her as well. I wanted to tell her this, but of course, I didn't dare. Regents week came. Mrs. Connors called me up front and asked me what Regents I was ready to take, "One or two of them?" I said, "I'll take them all." She said, "All right. I know you can do it." I wanted to scream, "I only said that because I thought you'd say I couldn't take them all. I'm scared!" But I didn't dare.

For three days, I went on the bus down Chilson Hill to Ticonderoga High School. I looked around me. The town kids dressed differently, better, and some snickered at me. I was a "Chilson Hiller," a real hillbilly. I wanted to crawl back to Chilson and forget the exams, but I didn't dare. Mrs. Connors was there, waiting.

Well, I did pass those Regents, and with high marks. High nineties in all, with ninety-nine percent in Silent Reading. For the first time in my life, I was proud of me, but mostly, I was proud for Mrs. Connors. Some important people came to our schoolhouse and congratulated her on the good work she had done there and on producing an outstanding student. Then the important people came up to our farm with a prize check for me—$50, a fortune in those days. They looked around and I knew they couldn't believe their eyes. In our living room, there were no curtains and just an old blacked-up kerosene lamp on an orange crate, and no place to sit down as the two chairs were broken. So they just stood there and stared down at our old bare wooden floor. Mim watched them, and I knew she was embarrassed. She said we'd get a rug with the money. They handed her the check and left. We never got a rug, and I never saw the check again, but it didn't matter. Mrs. Connors had instilled in me a better gift—self-confidence.

At last, school was out for the summer. I wouldn't be back there the next fall. I was "going on" down to Ticonderoga High School. We kids were standing outside, waiting for the bus, and I felt very sad. I darted back up the steps and into the classroom. I had to say goodbye to Mrs. Connors. Because of her, I knew I could make it. She was standing, looking out the window, and I couldn't believe it, she was crying. She wiped her nose with her handkerchief, drew herself up to her five feet, eleven inches, and glared down at me. "Gloria, you'll miss the bus. Get out there with the other children." Boy, did I scoot out of there. I didn't even dare to say goodbye.

I heard Mrs. Connors died soon after that and was buried down in Putnam.

Well, it's been sixty-four years, Mrs. Connors, and what you did for me has helped me all my life. You cared, and now I finally dare to tell you. I love you and thank you. Thank you.

Carrie's Wintergreen Patch

When I knew Carrie, she was old, at least eighty-five, but she never seemed that old to me. She was always smiling though she had had a very hard life. No matter what happened, or no matter what anyone did, Carrie always told me, "Don't nobody give a damn, no way."

Carrie lived down off the Corduroy, through the woods, by the river. The ground was swampy there, and it was shady and damp. She lived in a little shack there. She kept repairing it with patches and mending broken boards until it looked like a patch-work quilt.

I liked to go over to Carrie's because she always was glad to see me. We used to go bullheading in her beat-up rowboat that she called Old Tub. She would crush some wintergreen leaves and add hot water and give me a cup of wintergreen tea before I started home. It was delicious with a little sugar in it.

Carrie told me she married a lumberjack named Brian when she was very young. He was awfully mean to her right from the start. She planned to run away as soon as she "got a few bucks together," but she got pregnant and had twins. She said that finished her dream of running away. Where could she take the kids? And she sure couldn't leave them with their mean, drunken father.

Carrie did all she could to keep the kids together. She fished the river and gathered berries and nuts for food. She had a little scrubby garden for potatoes and carrots. Sometimes she got a little money by going through her husband's pockets when he was sleeping drunk. She'd use the money to buy a small pig to raise.

Carrie said she loved kids and would have liked to have more, but the way things were, it was lucky she didn't. She said when the kids were born, she got "torn up inside, and couldn't have anymore." Brian took off when the twins were about four, and Carrie never heard from him again.

Across the water from Carrie's shack there was a little flat up above the water's edge that was covered with wintergreen plants. Carrie said she was going to move her house over there because the sun hit that flat from all sides and the wintergreen for her tea would be right outside her window.

Carrie asked me to help her move, and I said sure. We would do it when spring came. Even though I knew we could never do it by ourselves, saying sure made Carrie happy, and by spring she might change her mind. If not, maybe we could get some men to help us. I asked whose land the wintergreen patch was on. Carrie answered, "Don't matter. Don't nobody give a damn, no way."

Late in that summer, I noticed Carrie was looking thinner and didn't seem as busy as usual. She said she knew she had what her mother had died from, cancer, but she was going to beat it. She just had to move over on her wintergreen berry patch. All the sunshine there would make her better.

During the winter when I visited her, we decided that as soon as the snow melted, we'd get her "house" moved. We'd pull big parts of it through the water behind Old Tub. We could put the small parts in Old Tub. I could see Carrie was getting weaker and weaker. I said maybe her kids would come and help her. No, the kids had cut out when they were about 18 and never even said goodbye. Carrie thought her daughter had run off to Canada with someone and her son was "down Troy way," but she didn't know for sure. They had never contacted her after they left, and that was years ago. Carrie said, "Nope, don't nobody give a damn, no way, but I'll be okay, once I get over in the wintergreen patch."

Spring came. I visited Carrie on Tuesday. She said we'd start moving her shack on Saturday. She wouldn't let me skip any school to help. She was proud that I had started high school in Ti. She made me promise to finish school and then take off and do something. She said it was the only way I could make it because "Nobody don't give a damn, no way."

Carrie seemed awfully weak. I knew she could never help me move the shack. On Saturday, I was going to tell her that I was getting some men to help us, but they couldn't come for a while. Thursday came. I heard a fisherman had found Carrie dead on the ground by her shack.

I knew Carrie was gone, but that Saturday, I went over the Corduroy and down to her shack anyway. It was very quiet. A thunderstorm was slowly rumbling in from the west. Carrie's shack looked so lonesome, as if it were already sinking back into the earth.

I took Old Tub and rowed across to Carrie's wintergreen patch and sat there while the storm came. The lightning flashed and rain poured down. My tears mixed with the rain, and I kept thinking, "Carrie's okay now," but I missed her so much. The rain stopped, and a soft warm air settled over the wintergreen patch. I picked a few wintergreen leaves and chewed on them. They were so fresh, delicious, after being washed by the rain. Then I rowed Old Tub back and went over the Corduroy, home.

Carrie always said, "Don't nobody give a damn, no way." I felt maybe now she knew somebody did give a damn—me.

Crystal Summer

Very early in the summer of 1939, a big hurricane hit New England. It was worse in New Hampshire. Some forests were laid flat. The trees were all neatly fallen in one direction. They looked like boxes of toothpicks.

Bob, being a lumber contractor, got a big tract of trees to clear out and clean up by fall, so we packed up everything, left Chilson, and were off on a new adventure. Also, Mim was pregnant. She thought she might be, so she had a "rabbit test" done, and it came back positive. Mim and Bob weren't married yet, and Mim didn't want my father, who was in Florida, to find out. Believe me, we couldn't disappear out of Chilson fast enough for the summer. The hurricane had sure happened at the right time.

Somewhere I heard the word "crystal," and I thought it was beautiful. I decided I was going to have a crystal summer—everything was going to sparkle and shine.

When we got to our lumberjack quarters, it was in a beautiful, very old house way back on a dirt road up on a hill. I chalked up my crystal. The beautiful mornings, beautiful sunsets over the mountains, the delicious spring water, my little cousin, Johnny Baker, who was staying with us because his mother (Aunt Lil) was sick—all were crystal, and I again made up my mind I was going to have a beautiful crystal summer.

Now the lumberjacks weren't crystal. They worked like dogs during the week, drank weekends, and were dirty, sweaty and loud. They brought women up from Keene on the weekends and spent time up on a bluff of land above our house. Anyone who went up there, we knew what for. Mim and I wouldn't be caught dead up there.

However, the lumberjacks were kind to me. I liked them a lot, but they definitely weren't crystal. Except one—Freddie. He was only seventeen and hadn't taken up their ways yet. Freddie and I spent a lot of time together. He was awfully nice and treated me special. Secretly, to myself, I called him Crystal Freddie. Over the summer, he became known as my boyfriend by the lumberjacks, and they had a good time kidding us.

A woman came up the dirt road one day. She said she'd walked from Keene. (We heard later she'd been kicked out of there.) She looked so down and out and said she was looking for work. Mim asked her name, and she said, "Just call me Peanuts." That struck Mim and me as funny, but we didn't ask anymore. Peanuts stayed and helped us with the cooking, etc. I did ask her once where she came from, and she said, "Hell." I let it go at that.

Peanuts didn't pay any attention to the lumberjacks except one named Clarky. He was quiet and nice and never spoke unless someone spoke to him first. Peanuts and Clarky became a twosome.

We didn't have much time for play. We went swimming a lot down in the pond where the logs the men cut were piling up in the water. The logs were placed there, waiting until spring when flooding would carry them out of the pond and down the river.

Bubby, Freddie, Johnny, Peanuts, Clarky and I played Boss on the Log. It's a game like King of the Hill, only we played on the logs in the water.

Sometimes, Peanuts and Clarky would disappear into the grass on the bluff above us, and I swear, you could see the grass swinging and swaying around up there. Bubby saw it and always asked what they were doing. Freddie would grin and say they were playing Dog Chase the Rabbit. "Dog Chase the Rabbit?" Bubby wanted to go play too, but I'd grab him by the rear of his shorts as he started to rush away, and I'd say we had to get back to playing Boss on the Log.

It's a wonder we didn't get killed, jumping around on the logs, knocking or pushing each other off into the deep water between them. We'd sink down under the water and the logs would be grinding and crashing together above us. We never thought about the danger. We played Boss on the Log all summer, and nothing ever happened to anyone.

302

Johnny Baker and me.

Clarky and Peanuts were together every evening. The men picked on Clarky and said Peanuts was no good. They knew about her from Keene. He never said anything, but I knew it bothered him. No matter what anyone said, Peanuts was my crystal friend. We really liked each other.

Not having any radio or newspaper, we didn't have much contact with the outside world. When the lumberjacks came back from their weekends in Keene, they would tell us about the rumors they had heard.

They said something was awfully wrong in Europe. Then on September 1, in Germany, a man named Hitler sent his army into Poland and conquered it. It was many miles away, but those reports scared us and we felt threatened. What could be happening? The vague uneasy feelings about what Hitler was up to persisted. Definitely not crystal.

One morning, Clarky didn't come in to breakfast. Crystal Freddie told me he couldn't stand the teasing any longer, and he had taken off for parts unknown.

Peanuts was beside herself. For a couple of days, she moped around and kept running out to the road to see if Clarky was coming back. Finally, she convinced herself that he had just gone on ahead and was waiting for her in Keene.

That afternoon she packed her things in a duffel bag and said she was going to meet Clarky. He was waiting for her. She had an old pair of dress-up shoes with the high heels all worn over. She put them on. I said, "Wear your work shoes. It's a long way to Keene." Peanuts said, "No, I want to look my best when Clarky sees me."

No matter what I said, Peanuts was going. She hugged me goodbye and went down the road with her duffel bag over her shoulder. She looked bowlegged from the way she walked in those crooked-heeled shoes.

Our truck hauling logs to the pond. Freddie is driving.

The logs in the pond.

As she got to the bottom of the hill and started around the bend, I got this awful feeling that she was heading back into her hell. I hollered and hollered as loud as I could, "Peanuts, please come back, come back!" There wasn't any answer. Peanuts, my crystal friend, was gone.

Mim went to the hospital to have the baby early on the morning of September 15. Bob came home from Keene in the late afternoon and told us Mim and the baby girl were fine. Then he went back to Keene.

Knowing Mim and the baby were okay, I finished up the supper dishes and went to bed, tired but happy. About 3 a.m., something woke me up. Someone was standing by my bed, and he grabbed for me. I managed to get away by rolling over and jumping out the other side of the bed. It was Raymond H., a man Bob had brought in from Keene to take care of the horses and to keep the logging equipment in repair.

I ran upstairs to where the lumberjacks were sleeping. Knowing where Freddie slept, I shook him awake and he came down and stayed in my bedroom, sitting by the door until 5:30. It was almost light, and we figured it was safe for him to go back to his bed. We could get a catnap before getting up at six o'clock.

I had just closed my eyes and settled down when I realized someone was by my bed again—Raymond. I jumped up and said, "Get out of here, or I'll scream like crazy." Raymond said, "Okay, okay, but don't tell Mim about this." I stayed up and put the water on for coffee and got the men off for work.

Mim came home about one o'clock. Seeing my darling little sister for the first time was really crystal. Being so busy getting Mim settled and getting things ready for supper, I didn't have time to tell her about Raymond, but Freddie did.

Peanuts and Clarky.

Freddie told Mim out in the kitchen. She was so mad. She came flying into the dining room and told Raymond off. She told him in no uncertain terms to get.

The lumberjacks were glaring at Raymond. One said, "You bastard, you're dead if you don't get out of here," and the other lumberjacks were pushing their chairs back. Raymond took a flying leap for the door and slunk off down the road, running.

I was so embarrassed. In my hands was a big bowl of gravy that I was putting on the table, and half of it spilled. The men said, "Never mind, Yada, as long as you're okay," and they sopped up the gravy with their biscuits. I realized I was wrong. The lumberjacks were so crystal. Any doubt in my mind about that was gone.

And so my crystal summer was almost over. It was time to head back to Chilson to Grandma Granger's and school. Crystal Freddie was so nice. Maybe I'd just stay there—to heck with school. That's the way I was daydreaming as I hung up the wet dishtowels on the line to dry. This was my last evening before going home, or maybe it wasn't.

Just then, Crystal Freddie came around the corner of the house. He came over, took my hand, and said, "Let's go up on the bluff." Crystal Freddie shattered right before my eyes, and I ran in the house and started throwing my few clothes, and Bubby's, into a big box. Tomorrow morning, early, Bubby and I would be on the back of the old truck, squeezed in with the horses and stuff, headed back for Chilson. My crystal summer was definitely over.

Indoor Toilets vs. False Teeth

Chilson started going modern. Here and there, an indoor toilet was being installed. Grandma Granger was getting itchy to have one. The house had plenty of water from a large spring up on the side hill. She said it wouldn't be "nothing" to put one in.

Now Grandpa wasn't very keen on this idea. He wasn't much for change. He said for what time he had left on this earth, he needed the jolts of cold air up under him when he went to the toilet in the outdoor privy. He said it kept him aware of why he got up in the morning. Grandma said she didn't need no cold air shooting up under her to know why she got up in the morning, and she was going to have an indoor john, whether he liked it or not.

Grandpa got Uncle Amacy and George to do the work for us. They even got the toilet down in Ticonderoga and brought it right to the farm. They sweated and swore and bulled putting in a cesspool way out back. Grandpa ignored this and said he didn't want anything to do with such a stupid tarnation thing.

So that fall, after it was done, Grandpa still went out to the old three-holer. He said if anyone tried to tear it down, they'd answer to him. He said he wasn't giving up his familiar comforts of home.

I was staying with Grandma and Grandpa because Mim wanted me to go to Ticonderoga High School. She, Bob, Skishie (my baby sister) and Bub were away in Newcomb where Bob had a lumber job.

I noticed as the winter came on that the snow never had any tracks out the back door to the backhouse. Grandpa would rave if Grandma even asked him to get flour from the flour barrel,

308

which was still in the same room (pantry) with the new toilet. He said he would not go anywhere near where that newfangled thing was.

On Saturday, Grandma and I went down to Aunt Dot's to visit. Grandpa stayed home. I noticed he was hitting his hard cider pretty heavy that day. He said it was for his rheumatism, but Grandma said he just wanted to tie one on because he was mad at Tweedle because Tweedle wouldn't go ice fishing.

When we got home, Grandpa was pretty quiet. He looked different, and he sounded different when he talked. I kept looking at him closely, and finally, I realized he didn't have his false teeth in. After a while, Grandma noticed his teeth weren't in. She said, "Potty, go put your teeth in. You look like an old fool." Grandpa said he couldn't put them in because he couldn't find them. He didn't know where he'd lost them. He had to have soup for supper.

Grandma went upstairs, and I saw Gramp take a lantern and go and look in the new toilet. I said, "What are you doing?" He said, "Nothing," and went out to the privy.

Gram and I used the toilet. After a couple of times, it backed up all over the floor. We had to use the outdoor privy from then on until the next day when Uncle Amacy took the toilet up out of the floor, and there were Grandpa's teeth clogging up the pipe.

Grandpa's outhouse.

Grandpa was amazed. He said someone must have stolen his teeth and thrown them in the toilet. Grandma said, "You old fool. I know what happened. You drank too much cider. You were sick and vomited them down the toilet." Grandpa answered before he thought, "Yeah, the damn newfangled thing. I flushed and they were gone—not like a proper privy where you can fish them out from underneath."

Grandma said she knew he was using the new toilet. His teeth being in it proved it, and he might as well admit it. But Grandpa wouldn't admit it and never used the new toilet when anyone was around. He still made a big show of going out to the privy all summer and fall.

Halloween came, and Grandma Granger had a couple of the big boys pull the privy down and break it up. Grandpa couldn't say anything. He thought it was a Halloween prank. He talked big about getting a new privy put up. No one said anything, so he let it go, and go, until he thought we'd forgotten about it.

Now and then he said he was forced into using the new-fangled toilet as he couldn't get anyone to help him build a new privy, so Grandpa entered the modern age loving every minute of it but protesting to the end.

Who Lived Where
in Chilson—1930s

Going from Ticonderoga—starting at the bottom of Chilson Hill.

1. Brock (Mr. and Mrs., Blanche, Marie, 2 brothers—Frank and ?)
2. Old lady lived here—don't know her name
3. Hodgen (Mr. and Mrs., Cicilia, Pat, Betty)
4. Rafferty (Mr. and Mrs., Cleon, Jim, Anita, younger kids)
5. Bright (Gene, Gladys, Louise, Francis, Helen, Norman)
6. Craig (Mr. and Mrs., twins—George and Georgia, and younger kids)
7. Thompson (Mr. and Mrs., Nellie, two brothers)
8. Bright (Mr. and Mrs., Cecil)
9. Young couple with baby lived here—can't remember names
10. Rafferty (Chet, Silvia, Agnes)
11. Abare (Mr. and Mrs., Alva)
12. Sears (Mr. and Mrs., Clifford, Wiley, Tooty)
13. Wright (Archie, Mrs., Ernest, Joe, Clarence, Clayton)
14. Stubing (Mary, Gloria, Harland)
15. Litchfield (Elmer, Finn, Ernest)
16. Oscier (Joe, Effie, Junior)
17. Covell (George, Nellie, Marion, Carl, Dodger Wright)
18. Ostis (Dillon and Margery)
19. Blanche and Abby—forgot their last names
20. Latrell (Ed, Mother)

21. Huestis (Mr. and Mrs., Juanita, Grandfather Tefoe, brothers and sisters)

22. Hall (Mr. and Mrs., Melvin, younger brother—forgot name)

23. Treadway (Clara, Bill, Jimmy, John Hall)

24. Stovell (Frank, Mary, Angus)

25. Armstrong (George, Bette, Dick, Whitney)

26. Wissell (Summer, Dean, Jack, Maxine)

27. Putnam (Bell, Esther, George)

28. Fleming (Molly Fleming's grandmother)

29. Fleming (Molly and parents)

30. Moore (Lonson, Jenny—on Eagle Lake)

31. Moore (Herb, Ira, Helen—on Eagle Lake)

32. 2 or 3 rich people behind high fence along the road

33. Folded Wings (restaurant, camp—I think the Spauldings ran it)

This is what we considered to be the end of Chilson. You went on over the road to Paradox Lake, then Schroon Lake or North Hudson.

Side Roads off Chilson Road

Road to left just above 12—Palmer, Jonyea, Phillips

Road to left at Treadway's 23 Putts Pond Road—Stovell (Fred, Ida, Freda, Bertha). Hunsdon (Mr. and Lena). Goodrow (Emma, John, George, younger kids). Villmore (Fred, Kate, Marion, Anna, Bernard). Go left at Villmores—Hammond (Amory, Alice, Edna, Naomi Hall). Shepard (Mr. and Mrs., Hugh and brother). Go right at Villmores—Moore (Helen and Mother). Smith (Mr. and Mrs., Donald)

Road to right past Treadways—Hall Road—Vedeau (Paul, Dot, Connie, Bobbie). Armstrong (Tweedle). Granger (Rol, Etta, Leona). Flanigan (Mr. and Mrs., Ed, Owney). House of Ill Repute

Road to left at George Armstong's—Bear Pond Road—Bevins (Mr. and Mrs., Oscer, Clarence). Moore (Helen and Mother). Smith (Leon, Sue, Buck). Shirer (Mr. and Mrs., Irene, younger kids)

Road to right at George Armstong's—Corduroy Road—Hall (Mr. and Mrs., Frankie, Violet, Ana). Dougal (Mr. and Mrs., Mary, Stella, Frank, Helen, Mike)

Fires I Have Known

There was one thing in Chilson at that time no one caught on to—fires that were happening.

I listened to every word said around me. No one paid any attention to what they said in front of me. They figured I was just a kid and wouldn't understand what they were saying. Boy, were they wrong!

By listening, the first fire that I knew was going to happen was Barbara Moore's family home on Bear Pond Road. I knew they were only renting that house. I don't know who owned it. Barbara wasn't very well. I think she was diabetic. Her house sat down the field from Tweedle Armstrong's barn.

Anyway, when Barbara and family weren't home one evening, their house burned down. No one seemed to pay much attention.

Sue Cross Smith and her husband, Leon, lived farther on up Bear Pond Road. When Sue got mad, she would swear like a trooper, and she got mad often. I learned some great swear words from her.

Sue and Leon lived about three-quarters of a mile down Bear Pond Road from us. Their house burned down a while after Barbara's. I heard they had $50 of insurance on it. No one paid much attention.

Then at different times, places burned. I don't remember the order, but Flanagan's house on Hall Road burned. Up on Putts Pond Road a house around the corner from Villmore's house burned, and Top of the Hill dance hall burned.

I used to go with Edmond Palmer and his wife, Nellie, to Bovine's Tavern to square dance on Saturday nights. Nellie was my best friend. I remember Edmond had a heavy white sweater that I loved. Anyway, when I listened and heard that Bovine's Tavern was going soon, I prayed not.

Then that morning, when we went by on the school bus, only a little smoke was drifting up from the ground where Bovine's had been. No more fun Saturday night dancing there!

Our farm on Bear Pond Road burned after we moved to Newcomb from Chilson. Victor Hall was living there. I knew before we moved that it was going to be burned.

I knew of five other places that were burned. They were not in Chilson, but "thereabouts."

These fires were deliberately set, but there was never any suspicion about those fires that I know of.

When I look back I'm awfully glad no one ever got hurt or burned in these fires. Just luck!

The people who set these fires are long gone. I think I'm the only one left who knew what was going on and who did it—five of them. Being a kid, I was afraid of what might happen to me if I told.

How I Happened

(Mim Told Me This)

Mim and Dad got married in the fall of 1923. Mim was staying at home on the farm while Dad was back at Yale to finish his third year.

It was the first of July, and the Stubings (Dad's family) were up in their summer cottage on the back of Schroon Lake. Dad was with them, and every chance he got, with his parents thinking he was camping out with a friend, Dad would jump on the mail stage and come over and stay overnight with Mim. Dad hadn't told Gramma and Grandpa Stubing he was married, so he had to sneak his short visits to Chilson to see Mim.

Grandma Granger gave Mim and Dad the back bedroom. They took Dad's small bag of clothes up there. Dad showed Mim a "safe" (condom) he had, and he put it in the bedside table. They weren't going to take any chances of Mim "getting in the family way."

Aunt Leona was Mim's youngest sister. She was about twelve years old, the last of the family of twenty-one kids, very spoiled by everyone, a real rip.

When Mim and Dad went downstairs, Aunt Leona went into their bedroom. She looked through Dad's bundle of clothes and didn't find anything there to interest her. Then she looked in the bedside table and found the safe. She thought it was a balloon so she took it. She blew it up and tied a knot in the end of it while going downstairs.

My father and Mim on their wedding day.

When she walked into the parlor, everyone stared. She was throwing the "balloon" up and down in the air and telling everyone to look at how she could almost hit the ceiling with it.

Mim and Dad knew instantly where Aunt Leona got her "balloon," but they just stood there, speechless. Grandma Granger was mortified. She didn't want to admit that she knew what such a thing was, let alone know where it came from. So she pretended she didn't know what it was and said, "Poddy (my grandfather), get that old sausage casing away from her!"

When he started toward Aunt Leona, she screamed and kicked and screeched, "No one is getting my balloon!"

Gram snapped, "Get that away from her!"

Aunt Leona screamed and kicked all the harder while clutching her "balloon," so Grandpa rushed out the front door and retreated to the barn, his usual action when he didn't want to, or couldn't, cope with something.

Aunt Leona played with her "balloon" all evening, making squealing sounds with it by rubbing it between her hands and throwing it up in the air. Occasionally someone would try to catch it away from her, but she was too fast for them.

A few people stopped in to say hello to Mim's new husband, but no one stayed long. Everyone tried to pretend they didn't see what Aunt Leona was playing with, but with little success. Aunt Leona never let go of her "balloon" all evening, and when she went to bed, she deflated it and slept with it under her pillow so no one could get it.

When Mim and Dad went to bed, being young and newly married, they threw caution to the wind, and I happened. No one knew it yet, but I was on my way, and all because Aunt Leona stole Mim and Dad's "balloon."

P.S. Mim also told me she was awfully glad Aunt Leona did what she did because she got me.

Aunt Leona was very good to me as I grew up over the years in Chilson. She will always be my favorite aunt.

Mrs. Rite

The Rites lived at the very top of Chilson Hill in a big white house over the field from us.

Grace (Mrs. Rite's daughter) married Ben. Ben and Grace lived on the back dirt road down Chilson Hill in an old house. Ben and Grace had three kids fast. After the third one, Mrs. Rite got upset. She knew that Grace and Ben had no money. He didn't work much, so who was going to feed those kids? Joe, one of Mrs. Rite's sons, told Mim that Mrs. Rite had gone down and read the riot act to Grace. No more kids, and Grace had promised her mother she wouldn't have any more.

Soon after, one morning Mim, Bub and I were sitting in our front yard eating outdoors because it was such a beautiful day.

Joe took food down to Grace every morning. This morning we saw him come back, and he was grinning. He went quickly into the house. All was quiet.

Suddenly, the front door opened, and Mrs. Rite came running out. Her arms were flying in the air. She kicked the pillars on the porch. She kicked at the dog, who got out of the way in a hurry. She kicked the screen door. Then she ran back into the house.

It was quiet again. Then the back door flew open. Mrs. Rite kicked over some pots of plants. She pulled some clothes down off the clothesline. Then she ran back into the house, slamming the door behind her.

It was quiet for a minute. Then Mrs. Rite came slamming out the side door. She threw a lot of sticks off the woodpile in all directions and knocked over the bench where the men washed their faces and hands before going in to eat at meal time. Then she stormed back into the house. We waited, but she didn't come out again.

Mim said, "Well, that means Grace is going to have another baby." We resumed eating our cereal. Might as well. Nothing we could do about it.

Special Pal

Mim was gone again, and Bubby was staying over with Aunt Dean. It was lonely all by myself, so I walked down the road. I decided to go visit Marion, but she wasn't home. I skipped on over the road to Uncle Amacy's, but no one was there, either.

It was such a beautiful day that I didn't want to go back home. I continued up the hill until there, way up on the side of the mountain was the little farmhouse where the Peters family had lived for years. The mother and father had died, but the two sons, Olson and Hans, were still there. Only Olson was never home. He was always away somewhere.

The old farm was a lovely spot. Sheep were grazing on the hillsides, in fields of very green grass. I had seen pictures of Switzerland in school, and that's what it looked like, a little spot of Switzerland right in front of me.

I sat down by the side of the road to enjoy the beauty. Hans came up behind me from the back pasture. He was probably eighteen, very handsome and rugged. I looked at him and thought, "It would be nice to be your girl," but of course, I didn't say it.

Hans asked me what I was doing, and I said I was just taking a walk. He said he was looking for a new lamb that its mother had hidden somewhere. He asked me if I wanted to help him look. I jumped at the chance, and we went around the pastures looking behind big rocks and under bushes. No lamb, so we went up the side hill, and there, in a little ravine, was the lamb where her mother had hidden her. Hans picked her up, and we started down the hill. The lamb was adorable, and I asked to carry her. Hans put her in my arms. She was light as a feather and the sweetest little thing. She "baaaed" a few times. Her mother heard her and followed us to the barn. Hans put them inside where he said they'd stay until the lamb was a little older.

Hans invited me for supper. He had roast lamb in the oven and mint jelly to go with it. Talk about delicious! He showed me his herb garden by the back door. He said his great-grandmother had started it many years before. There were many herbs growing there—rosemary, dill, thyme and, of course, the mint.

After we did up the supper dishes, we played checkers. We were having so much fun making up new rules as we went along and trying to beat each other that it was getting dark before we knew it. Hans said it would be dangerous trying to get back home in the dark, and as long as Mim wasn't home to worry, I had better stay overnight.

Hans made up the front room couch and I slept there with lamb fleeces over me. I thought about Hans when he went in his bedroom and closed the door. It would be so nice to be his girl-friend, but without knowing why, I instinctively knew we would never be anything but the best of pals.

The next morning, after breakfast of cold lamb, new baked biscuits and hot tea, we walked out to the barn to check the baby lamb. She was fine. On the way back to the barn, we passed a small shed and I looked in the window. I could see paintings and asked, "What are those?" Hans, very reluctantly, said he'd painted them and he'd show me if I promised not to laugh. He opened the door, and we went in. There were paintings of sunsets, mountains and animals and portraits of people. I recognized his mother and father. The colors were gorgeous. Some pictures were bold with garish colors, and some were gentle pastels. He showed me how he mixed his paints, some he made himself.

Hans said he was going to burn the paintings. He didn't say why, and I didn't ask him, but I never saw the paintings again. He must have burned them.

However, Hans said he was going to paint a picture of me

first. He had me sit on the doorstep, and he painted for an hour. When I looked at the canvas, even though the picture wasn't done, I knew it was me. Hans had painted yellow all around me. It looked like sunshine. He said he'd finish the picture later. It was time for me to leave. He smiled and said, "Go with God." He always said that when we parted.

When I got home, Mim was busy putting Cloverine salve and a bandage on a deep burn she had gotten on her hand somehow. She asked where I'd been, and I told her that I had stayed overnight with Hans. I thought she'd have a fit when I said that, but she never looked up. She just said, "That's nice." I couldn't figure it out.

Hans never came to my house, but I went up to his farm often. He sold meat and fleeces from his sheep. A man in Ticonderoga came up to his farm every so often to pick them up. I helped Hans clean the fleeces, picked burrs and leaves out of them, and combed them. We worked together in silence, sometimes for a couple of hours, saying nothing. We didn't have to. We were good pals enjoying being together.

Some of Hans's sheep.

I realized Hans was different. He was a loner. The other boys never chummed around with him. I asked Clarence once about that. He looked at me quickly and said, "He's odd. Stay away from him."

I wanted to ask Hans why he never went anywhere and why he was always alone, but I didn't. I wanted to tell my best friends, Esther and Marie, about the time I spent with him, but I didn't. I didn't know why, but it seemed that it should be a secret. So Hans remained my special, secret pal.

We had many good times together on his farm, and I never left him but when he said, "Go with God."

The summer I was sixteen, Mim bought a hotel in Newcomb. She, Skishie and Bubby went up to stay there, but I was going to stay at Grandma Granger's and finish my senior year in Ticonderoga.

I felt lonesome, and I wanted to be with Mim and Bubby and Skishie, and I decided to finish high school in Newcomb. I wrote Mim a letter, and one came right back, saying Mim would pick me up Wednesday about 4 p.m.

It was Wednesday, so I had to hurry. I grabbed my cousin Jim's bike that was leaning against Gram's front gate, and I pedaled off to say goodbye to Esther and Marie and, of course, went up to Hans.

Hans was happy for me that I was going to Newcomb to be with my family. I didn't ask about his future plans. I thought he would always stay there on his farm with his sheep.

As I started to leave, Hans said, "If I could ever love a girl, you would be the one." I didn't understand what he was saying, and he knew it. So I only said, "Goodbye, pal." Hans whispered, "Go with God," and I was on the bike and down the road.

Suddenly I realized I was leaving my Chilson home, this time, forever. A sense of sadness came over me, but only for a minute because I was happy to be off for Newcomb and new adventures.

Songs

Too bad we don't have beautiful songs like this today—ha! We went around singing or whistling these songs as we walked around the road. We had no hand radios—never heard of such a thing.

Courting

Mr. Frog went a-courting—uhuh, uhuh Mr. Frog went a-courting and he did ride with a sword and a pistol by his side—uhuh, uhuh.

He rode up to Miss Mousey's door—uhuh, uhuh He rode up to Miss Mousey's door, a place that he'd never been before— uhuh, uhuh.

He said, "Miss Mouse, will you marry me?—uhuh, uhuh He said, "Miss Mouse, will you marry me? "Oh, not unless Uncle Rat will agree"—uhuh, uhuh.

Uncle Rat went a-running down to town—uhuh, uhuh Uncle Rat went a-running down to town to get his niece a wedding gown—uhuh, uhuh.

Oh, Mr. Frog would laugh and shake his sides—uhuh, uhuh Oh, Mr. Frog would laugh and shake his sides to think Miss

Mouse would be his bride—uhuh, uhuh. Then Mr. Frog fell in a well and ended up way down—uhuh, uhuh.

My Pony

I had a little pony. His name was Dabble Gray. I lent him to a lady to ride a mile away.

She kicked him, she lashed him, She drove him through the mire. I'd never loan my pony now for all that lady's hire.

Row, Row, Row

Row, row, row your boat, gently down the stream. Merrily, merrily, merrily, merrily life is but a dream. (Repeat, repeat)

Don't Leave

From the valley they say you are going Do not hasten to bid me adieu But remember the Red River Valley And the cowboy who loved you so true.

Round the Mountain

She'll be coming around the mountain when she comes. She'll be coming around the mountain when she comes. She'll be coming around the mountain when she comes.

Oh, we'll all go out to meet her when she comes. Oh, we'll all go out to meet her when she comes. Oh, we'll all go out to meet her when she comes.

She'll be riding six white horses when she comes. She'll be riding six white horses when she comes. She'll be riding six white horses when she comes. She'll be riding six white horses when she comes.

Down Mexico Way

South of the border, down Mexico way, That's where I fell in love, where stars above came out to play.

She sighed as she whispered, "Manana," never dreaming that we were parting,
And I lied as I whispered, "Manana," but tomorrow never came.

South of the border, I rode back one day.
There in a veil of white by candlelight, she knelt to pray.
And now as I wonder, my thoughts often stray—south of the border, down Mexico way.

Inky, Dinky, Parlez-vous

The dirty marines they ate the beans—parlez-vous The dirty marines they ate the beans—parlez-vous The dirty marines they ate the beans, They licked them up and lapped them down, Inky, dinky, parlez-vous.

Epilogue

To My Family

As I look through these stories, I realize that they are mostly about the people I knew during my early childhood. These people make that time among my favorite memories.

And because my stepfather had lumber jobs all over, we lived for a few months in many places, including Hague, Schroon Lake, Crown Point, Paradox Lake, Corinth, Palmyra, and Pitts-

Bub and me just before we left Chilson for good. August 1941.

field, Maine; Marlow, New Hampshire; and Bellows Falls, Vermont. So some of these stories didn't happen in Chilson, but "thereabouts."

No matter what happened where, there was always something going on that kept us laughing. Because of the people I knew and loved, I'm glad I lived when I did.

May you all have a long and happy life.

Love to you all,

Mom/Grandma/Great-grandma Rist

Adieu

Adieu, adieu, kind friends adieu, yes adieu. I can no longer stay with you. So hang your heart on the weeping willow tree And never, never think of me.
              Good-bye.

Bub and me in Newcomb, 1942.

1/14